To Ray
with appreciation for all
your help.
Best regards
Phil

CHRISTIAN SOCIALISM AND CO-OPERATION
IN VICTORIAN ENGLAND

CROOM HELM SOCIAL HISTORY SERIES

General Editors:
Professor J.F.C. Harrison and Stephen Yeo,
University of Sussex

CLASS AND RELIGION IN THE LATE VICTORIAN CITY
Hugh McLeod

THE INDUSTRIAL MUSE
Martha Vicinus

CHRISTIAN SOCIALISM AND CO-OPERATION IN VICTORIAN ENGLAND

Edward Vansittart Neale and the Co-operative Movement

Philip N. Backstrom

CROOM HELM LONDON

First published 1974
© 1974 by Philip N. Backstrom

Croom Helm Ltd
2–10 St. Johns Road, London SW11

ISBN 0–85664–156–1

Distributed in the United States of America
by Rowman and Littlefield
81 Adams Drive, Totowa, New Jersey, 07512

Printed by
Biddles of Guildford

CONTENTS

To my father,
a retired Baptist minister,
who, like Neale, has devoted his
life to the service of others.

ACKNOWLEDGEMENTS

Many individuals and institutions have assisted me in the research efforts leading to the publication of this work. Raymond Robinson, Chairman of the History Department, and other members of the faculty and administration of Northeastern University, have helped in providing necessary funds for travel and released time. Useful information and material were supplied by the following people: Margaret E. Dickinson (Neale's great granddaughter); Stephen Davis; Desmond Flanagan (formerly Librarian at the Co-operative Union, Ltd., now deceased) and his successor, R. Garratt; Walter Fogg; R. G. Garnett; Neville Masterman; the late David Owen; Noel Peyrouton; Morton Rothstein; Terry Williams; and Jack Haslam.

I relied heavily on the facilities of various institutions and would like to express gratitude to the librarians and staff of Cambridge University Library; Columbia University Library; Goldsmiths Library, University of London; New York Public Library; Wisconsin Historical Society Library; University of Wisconsin Library; and Widener Library, Harvard University. I am particularly grateful to the staff of the Co-operative Union Library, Manchester, who in addition to providing valuable assistance in research also arranged that my wife and I be given dinner each day as guests at the Co-operative Wholesale Society's dining room. The History Department at the University of Wisconsin permitted use of their facilities to duplicate microfilm.

Special mention should be reserved for J. F. C. Harrison of the University of Sussex and Peter Stansky, Stanford University, two extremely busy individuals who nevertheless took the time to read my manuscript, offer helpful criticism and encourage me in its final preparation. Their professional advice was invaluable.

I would like to thank my wife, Shirley, for her assistance in research, editing and proofreading with her usual efficiency and enthusiasm.

Lastly, Elizabeth Frances Paget, Neale's granddaughter, now deceased, gratiously invited me to her home at Bisham Grange and permitted the family papers to be reviewed and microfilmed. It was through her that I first learned about Neale's journal and manuscript autobiography.

INTRODUCTION

We often think that when we have completed our study of *one* we know all about *two*, because "two" is "one and one." We forget that we have still to make a study of "and."

A.S. Eddington*

The novelist Herman Hess once observed that 'the writing of history . . . however sincere the desire for objectivity – remains literature. History's third dimension is always fiction.' Although an exaggeration, this point of view touches a sensitive nerve as the problems, passions and prejudices of the historian's present time delimit the nature of his investigation and consequently colour his understanding of the past; what E. P. Thompson calls a ' "Pilgrim's Progress" orthodoxy' too often prevails, whereby research is squandered in ransacking a period for 'forerunners' of successful modern movements and ideas. Historical developments which appear lacking in immediate relevance are treated superficially and with condescension. The process of determining which books should be published is particularly subject to the whimsical interests of the moment: in assessing an earlier version of this study of E. V. Neale and the Co-operative Movement, for example, one reader commented that the manuscript was of 'distinct importance in a field of which the relative importance is debatable'; and an editor for an eminent publishing house observed that 'without going into detail, it always seemed to come back to the problem we started with, that Neale is an unknown name and his doings were unglamorous'. Like beauty, what is glamorous depends upon the eyes of the beholder, and unfortunately the glitter of aristocracy, the magnetism of unscrupulous men, the vicarious excitement of wars and other bloody encounters, sometimes blinds scholars to other realities which may in the long run be more significant.

While the relative importance of Co-operation in today's world may be a point of debate, this surely was not the case in the 19th century. The hopes and aspirations of thousands of common people in England and Europe were then reflected in the building of the Co-operative Movement, which the late G. D. H. Cole described as unique for having within itself 'the social force that could make it a powerful instrument of economic transformation'. However unsuccessful it might have been

*As quoted by James Blish, *Cities in Flight* (Garden City, New York, 1970), p. 47.

1

in fulfilling its promise as an instrument for the realisation of socialism, the Movement nevertheless went on to become one of the century's most prominent institutional symbols of 'self-help', that most all-pervading of the Victorian panaceas. In 1866, when William Gladstone and·John Bright were arguing for an extension of the franchise, they both appealed to the practice of Co-operation as evidence that great numbers of working men had become responsible citizens with an economic stake in the country's interests and should in consequence be allowed to vote.

Neale's personal contribution certainly merits attention; his name is well known to the labour historian, and many of the more important studies of Britain in the 19th century make favourable reference to him. Beatrice Webb wrote of Neale: 'I believe that in all the annals of British philanthropy no more honourable example can be found of a life devoted from first to last to the disinterested and self-denying service of the wage-earning class.' And G. D. H. Cole, after commenting on the beneficial results of the Christian Socialist Movement, also used superlatives: 'And the greatest of all was Neale, who, having sacrificed most of his fortune . . . gave the rest of his life to the [Co-operative] Movement . . . . ' But both Cole and Webb, while extolling Neale's virtues as a Christian Socialist and philanthropist, tended to undervalue his more practical contributions, particularly his pioneering work as a co-operator. Indeed, ironically, Beatrice Webb was partly to blame for the fact that posterity has all but overlooked him. Mrs Webb's deftly written but distorted short history of the Co-operative Movement published in 1891 presented Neale and his friends, the insistent proponents of Producers Co-operation, as narrowmindedly impractical idealists whose efforts not only had little to do with the Movement's success, but may even have inhibited it. Unfortunately, this book had great influence and set a precedent for later historians.

Research reveals that Co-operation owes a great debt to E. V. Neale, who more then any other single individual contributed to its successful development during the middle and later 19th century. His was the constructive genius most responsible for drafting the necessary Acts of Parliament and designing the administrative apparatus, federal in form, by which a myriad of autonomous co-operative undertakings could be legally bound together into a powerful national and, ultimately, international movement. Driven by an unrelenting compulsion to reconstruct society (born out of a study of Hegelian philosophy and Utopian Socialism), he spent his lifetime trying to make Co-operation an effective force in combatting Capitalism.

By the early 1850s, when Neale was emerging as the most important figure within the Christian Socialist Movement, the messianic ideals preached by Robert Owen had already generated a considerable amount of activity in the North of England. While Neale and his friends struggled against overwhelming odds to establish self-governing workshops in London, co-operative stores were almost effortlessly multiplying within the industrial areas of Lancashire and the West Riding of Yorkshire. Northern co-operators followed the lucrative example of the Equitable Pioneers, who had founded a retail store at Rochdale in 1844 which successfully attracted member/customers by providing them with periodical dividends proportionate to purchases. Neale was almost alone among the Christian Socialists in appreciating the economic and social significance of this development. He imaginatively conceived that co-operative stores, acting collectively, could serve as practical foundation stones upon which to build a movement capable of changing the mode of production. If the stores continued to multiply, formed wholesale centres, and synchronized their individual efforts by joining together in a broadly based co-operative union, they would, in effect, be creating a great new market of their own while accumulating enormous profits. The implications were obvious: given possession of both the necessary capital and a controlled, reliable market, they could launch producers' co-operatives with full assurance of success. Private enterprises, lacking those advantages, would be gradually squeezed out of existence, unable to compete. This was Neale's vision, but he knew that it could never materialise in the absence of central co-ordinating institutions serving practical functions, and thus he came to play a most prominent part in building the major federal organs which together constitute the administrative heart of the modern Co-operative Movement: the Co-operative Wholesale Society (or CWS), the Insurance Society, the *Co-operative News*, and, above all, the Co-operative Union.

In E. V. Neale's case, the achievement of a lifetime may be summed up by the single word 'unification'. Before the termination of the Christian Socialist Movement he had already begun to work systematically towards that end, mailing questionnaires to all kinds of working men's associations with a mind to determining the exact nature and extent of Co-operation in Britain. On the basis of the data gathered during these years he wrote several widely circulated pamphlets specifically designed to introduce uniformity by bringing the many separate co-operative associations together under common operating procedures and constitutional rules. And this was only a beginning.

Throughout his life he continued to prepare informational handbooks as well as prospectuses, passbooks and model rules for new societies.

Neale was rewarded for his outstanding contributions when, in 1873, he was elected General Secretary of the Co-operative Union, thereby becoming the Movement's foremost public representative. After his appointment to this office even those men who vehemently opposed his utopian socialist ideals were usually forthright in acknowledging his importance: Dr John Watts typically wrote that 'Co-operation owes more to Mr Neale than to any other dozen – he thought he might say any other twenty men, unless it were the original [Rochdale] pioneers.' Watts was not exaggerating, as General Secretary Neale was indefatig-able. A listing of his activities, above and beyond his formal duties as chief executive, would fill several pages to the point of overflowing; suffice it to say that the calculation of the evidence strongly suggests that for many years the progress of the Movement was largely dependent upon the services of Edward Vansittart Neale. Why then has he remained a relatively little known leader? Beatrice Webb's short history of Co-operation was instrumental in placing him in the second rank, but this must not be overstressed. In a real sense Neale consigned himself to historical oblivion. He was compulsively altruistic and made little attempt to establish a personal reputation on the basis of his achievements, indeed preferring instead to manipulate behind the scenes, allowing other men to take the bows and gather the applause. He staked no strong claims even to those organisations which he directly established, to say nothing about the many others which he either inspired or helped along the pathway to success.

Though several eminent historians have intimated that Neale was an important force within the Labour Movement, no one to date has sought the proof. This is quite understandable, for only after sifting through a great mass of trivia in the countless pages of the dull, colourless *Co-operative News* could anyone find the valuable nuggets of source material that would, when collected together, tell the full story of Neale's significance. And this is not an attractive prospect, particularly for those who may have read Beatrice Webb's comments about that periodical in *My Apprenticeship*: 'A grind and no mistake! Six hours a day reading and note-taking from those endless volumes of the *Co-operative News*. A treadmill of disjointed facts, in themselves utterly uninteresting and appallingly dry, and not complete enough to be satisfactory.' She goes on to speak of 'aching eyes', 'dreary sense of time and effort wasted', and the fact that the whole experience made her feel 'sick and irritable, and in . . . off times . . . desperately cross'.

Moreover, the perusal of any one annual volume of the *News*, with Neale as the subject of investigation, is quite sufficient in itself to dampen enthusiasm. He was an unbelievably prolific journalist, writing anything running from a sentence or two up to a full scale article (more often than not about some lustreless legal technicality) in practically every weekly issue. Were it not for the fortuitous discovery that Neale had written a most interesting Journal, begun during his student years at Oxford and kept more or less faithfully for twenty years, the temptation to abandon the project of writing his biography would have proven irresistible. Reading the Journal, however, provided the needed incentive: fascinated by this shy, introspective nephew of William Wilberforce, whose overly-tender Evangelical conscience led him to become a socialist, it was impossible to stop short of tracing his unusual career through to its ending in 1892. The undertaking proved rewarding indeed. The research, however tedious at times, uncovered a most intriguing personality – I grew ever more impressed with the merit of the man, his integrity, his humanity, and above all his importance as an inspirational leader. No area of co-operative endeavour, when explored in depth, appeared to be unmarked by Neale's genius. The conclusion seemed inescapable: in the same sense that Robert Owen may be referred to as the father of co-operative ideology in Britain, so Edward Vansittart Neale should take his rightful place beside him as the father of Co-operation, in its modern form, as an organised movement.

One byproduct of this biographical study came as something of a surprise. With little expectation of finding information which might detract from the popular view of British Co-operation (as being an exemplary Victorian working class movement which 'has always been unquestionably democratic')*, it proved at the last necessary to take a very contrary, if not thoroughly revisionist position. Few of the traditional notions about the subject withstood the test of investigation completely unscathed; and it was perplexing to discover that the familiar models used by historians when formulating concepts about 'working class' men and movements could not be readily applied to Co-operation. With consternating regularity, analysis transformed axioms into enigmas. Aside from the fact that working men were the primary patrons and dividend-receiving members of the co-operative stores, it is questionable whether the overall efforts of the co-operative

*Sidney Pollard, 'Nineteenth-Century Co-operation: from Community Building to Shopkeeping', *Essays in Labour History*, Asa Briggs and John Saville, eds. (London, 1967), p.111.

consumers actually add up to a 'working class movement' in any literal sense. Although all store members had the basic right to democratic participation, the nature and extent of their direct involvement varied from locality to locality and the available evidence scarcely makes allowance for confident generalisations. Did working men usually take advantage of their right to determine policy even at the local level? Was the average co-operative store, in fact as well as theory, a successful example of working class democracy?

Given Neale's importance as a builder of the Movement, it is noteworthy that when an octogenarian, shortly prior to his death, he realised that Co-operation's central organisations, painstakingly devised and perfected for the purpose of bringing about social change, were unsuited to the task, and he was preparing to break connnections with them. For it was then evident that Neale had miscalculated from the beginning by placing undue faith in the theories of the co-operative consumers. The stores which multiplied in the North of England had followed the exemplary leadership of Rochdale's Equitable Pioneers, who, inspired by Owenism, had at first hoped to accumulate capital for use in advancing the cause of Socialism, the objective being the establishment of utopian communities. But burgeoning wealth generated indifference and their original ideal was soon reduced to rhetorical cant, while reality came to be enumerated more crudely in terms of pounds, shillings and pence: it is common knowledge that Co-operation was so successful as a consumers' movement that most of its leaders abandoned their community building socialism to become shopkeeping capitalists. Neale, as General Secretary of the Co-operative Union, unremittingly strove to resuscitate their old commitment to emancipate the labouring classes by revolutionising the means of production, but in vain.

The English Wholesale Society served as the major catalytic agent in bringing about the change in ideals. The CWS ultimately came to corner the co-operative market, and its directors (led by J. T. W. Mitchell) used the Society's vast economic power to impose their own policies on the Movement. The CWS is usually touted as an example of successful democratic action by working class consumers, but this contention is certainly misleading. At best the workingman's influence had to be second hand, for individuals could not act directly in choosing the Wholesale's policymakers – it was a federal body, the membership of which was limited to societies, chiefly stores. And in actual practice the involvement of the individual societies, when calculated in terms of their participation in the electoral processes, was more characterised by apathy than enthusiasm: a great number of stores did not bother even to exercise their franchise, with the result that the ambitions of the Wholesale's managerial elite remained largely unchecked. Soon after its establishment, the CWS became a self-perpetuating bureaucratic machine which was economically conservative and ideologically inflex-ible, and within the shadow of its narrowly materialistic influence the entire Co-operative Movement was gradually transformed into a great impersonal business enterprise.

Neale had always believed that wholesale societies should initiate the work of co-operative production; therefore he was pleased when the English CWS concluded a decade of phenomenal growth by establishing several workshops in 1873. His pleasure, however, was short lived. Within two years it became apparent that the CWS intended to manage these workshops for its own monetary advantage, with a strict mind to making profits, in exactly the same exploitative fashion as a private capitalistic industry. This was the final straw bringing about the raw conflict of ideals which plagued Neale for the remainder of his lifetime and shook the Movement to its very foundations.

Perhaps this outcome was inevitable. However humble the beginnings, could any movement of consumers ever become an effective instrument for the achievement of socialism — or even be expected to retain for long a legitimate claim to the loyalty of the working class? Within the context of socialism's economic model a working man is unique only in his productive functions; as a consumer he loses his special class identity and his objectives are almost certain to reflect the prevailing mode of production in society. Unfortunately, under capitalism the interests of producer and consumer are likely to be in conflict. The Christian Socialist, John Ludlow, had been quick to recognise this, and as early as 1851 had warned Neale that it was dangerous to place too much emphasis on the co-operative store, predicting that when the middle man had finally been eliminated, as desired by the northern co-operators, 'the opposition of interest between producer and consumer would be exhibited in its nakedest form.' Let the old co-operative spirit be once lost, he insisted, the only motivation of 'selfish consumption' would be to obtain merchandise as cheaply as possible. Ludlow's warning involved no overstatement: by the late 1870s most of the important co-operative committeemen in the Northwest were thoroughly indoctrinated with the ideas of the bourgeoisie, some going so far as to use very derogatory terminology when speaking about working men. 'All profits to the consumer' became their sole gospel, and Neale was chagrined as strikes broke out in so-called co-operative mills. If the workers themselves spoke in any measurable way about the Co-operative Movement, it was by establishing a labour union for the Movement's employees and by repeatedly striking.

It is difficult to find any evidence that the Wholesale's committeemen (or for that matter the majority of co-operative administrators) represented either the wishes or the economic interests of labouringmen identifiable as such. Beatrice Webb referred to them as being working-class capitalists and it is surprising that no one appears to have questioned the credibility of such a paradoxical definition, which seems to be derived merely from the fact that most co-operators began their lives as working men. Many of England's great industrialists were born in a cottage (a fact not overlooked by Samuel Smiles) retaining in their revealing accents of speech the lingering traces of humble origins; yet no one called them, then or afterwards, working-class capitalists. Surely the economic status and managerial occupation of the eminent directors of the Co-operative Movement place them within the ranks of the middle class, as would any conceivable cultural model which might be devised to investigate, define or delimit class structure. What cultural milieu had absorbed the lives of men who could insist, when speaking of employees, that it was 'a bad idea to pander to, pet, and spoil servants', or who could write articles condemning demands for higher wages under such titles as 'The Working Man: A Problem'!

If, on the basis of present evidence, it is difficult to establish the degree to which the working masses themselves were speaking through the medium of the Co-operative Movement, it is certainly much easier to determine who among the Movement's middle and upper class leaders were speaking for them. In the Annual Congress (the Movement's most representative body) and elsewhere, Neale and his idealistic friends repeatedly fought Co-operation's bureaucratic managers to a standstill; and an analysis of the issues involved clearly demonstrates that it was the former who upheld the cause of the common labouring man. Therefore, if there is a single theme to this biography, it consists in the declaration that those who were pejoratively called 'individualists', described as hopelessly anachronistic and utopian, and most often written off as being of little account, were, in reality, the authentic heroes of the working class, and that their failure within the Co-operative Movement, though perhaps predictable from the beginning, should be calculated as a great loss rather than a gain which contributed to progress.

PART ONE

THE FORMULATION OF THE IDEAL

I

GENTLEMAN TURNED SOCIALIST
1810–1849

> What fact more conspicuous in modern history, than the
> creation of the gentleman? Chivalry is that, and loyalty
> is that, and, in English literature, half the drama, and all
> the novels, from Sir Philip Sidney to Sir Walter Scott,
> paint this figure.
>
> Ralph Waldo Emerson, *Manners*, 1844

The Royal Crescent in Bath still attracts tourists and recalls to their
minds the classical proclivities of the eighteenth century leisure class; a
great residential structure comprising thirty individual dwellings, it
overwhelms viewers with more than one hundred massive Ionic columns
supporting a cornice which extends unbroken in a magnificent
semi-ellipse over 600 feet in length. Here it was, on 2 April 1810 that
Edward Vansittart Neale was born, in the home of his maternal
grandfather, Isaac Spooner, at once inheriting the style of life
symbolised by the magnificent ellipse: an independent income, comparative ease, an education which provided all the cultural benefits
implied by the great Ionic columns, and all the munificence of the
privileges which went along with being a gentleman. Edward could
hardly have been born under the protecting shadow of a heritage less
likely to lead to a long, hard-working career in the service of labouring
men, yet his peculiar destiny was to become the man who was, above
all others, responsible for designing and subsequently building the
organisational and administrative structure for the modern British
Co-operative Movement.

Both sides of his family provided Edward with examples of success
and occasionally greatness. Oliver Cromwell was numbered among his
ancestors and living relatives included William Wilberforce and Nicholas
Vansittart, who was Chancellor of the Exchequer (1812–24) in the
Liverpool administration. His father was the Reverend Edward Neale,
L.L.B., an Evangelical rector of Taplow, Buckinghamshire, and the
second son of George Vansittart of Bisham Abbey (1745–1825), who
was an M.P. for Berkshire during Pitt's administration. The Reverend
Neale, thus born a Vansittart, had adopted a new surname in 1805
upon inheriting the Neale family's property in Allesley near Coventry;
it was through this latter line of progenitors that Edward could boast of

the connection with Oliver Cromwell.[1]

The Vansittarts were of Dutch extraction, their name deriving from the old town of Sittart in Limburg. They had been established in London late in the seventeenth century by a merchant adventurer, Peter van Sittart (1651–1705), who had amassed a large fortune trading in the South Seas, the East Indies, and the Baltic, gaining distinction both as a Governor of the Russia Company and a Director of the East India Company. In 1780, George Vansittart purchased the historic manor of Bisham with its picturesque Abbey by the side of the Thames – a residence rich with memories from the past. The great fighters and crafty politicians of the Neville family had lived there: Salisbury, who died like a hero at the siege of Orléans, and Warwick, whose daring exploits brought about the rise and fall of kings. Later the building fell into the hands of some Benedictine monks from whom Henry VIII wrested it for use as a hunting lodge; and his daughter, the virgin queen Elizabeth, stayed there with friends for several years prior to her accession. Ultimately Edward Vansittart Neale was destined to inherit the Abbey which, like the Royal Crescent, reflected both his heritage and the way of living which moulded his character.[2]

G. M. Young once observed that 'a boy born in 1810' would find himself 'at every turn controlled, and animated, by the imponderable pressure of the Evangelical discipline',[3] and Young's generalisation has an especially poignant meaning for Neale. The most significant personage on the maternal side of the family was William Wilberforce, his uncle, who, with the possible exception of John Wesley, was the most well-known representative of the 'Evangelical discipline' that ever drew breath. In 1797 Wilberforce had married Barbara Spooner, the daughter of Isaac Spooner of Elmdon in Warwickshire: Barbara's sister Anne was Edward's mother. It would be difficult indeed to exaggerate the impact of Evangelicalism on Edward Vansittart Neale: it penetrated every facet of his life during the formative years, overriding every other influence.

At age 21, Edward wrote an autobiographical sketch and began a Journal, which he kept more or less faithfully for almost twenty years.[4] While these documents are rich with information about his experiences at Oxford and afterwards, they are somewhat less illuminating as regards his childhood. In the beginning he was educated solely by his father, a stern disciplinarian, but ultimately was sent to reside at Hitcham where a tutor named Joyce maintained a small private school.[5] Edward makes little more than a passing reference to the fact that he began Latin at seven, remembered 'the joy . . . felt on conquering the first difficulties in Phadrus's fables',[6] and that 'numbers' was the particular specialty of his tutor at Hitcham. By far the most important aspect of his early education was its influence on him socially; in recalling the time, at age fifteen, when he went to reside at Hitcham, he wrote: 'The alteration was to me very important. I was thrown among the society of others.'[7] The fact that previously Edward had lived only among sisters while being tutored by his father undoubtedly delayed his social development, and from his stay at Hitcham to the termination of his studies at Oxford he was plagued by a shyness very difficult to overcome. In consequence he tended to isolate himself and indulge in daydreams.

There is thus little in the tradition-bound youth of Edward Vansittart Neale to anticipate his future career. It seemed likely that he would take some place, either great or small, within the English oligarchy. In glancing over Edward's ancestors and living relatives, the names Cromwell and Wilberforce stand out — both men were great reformers. Yet in the reactionary atmosphere of Edward's youth the traditions these men represented, the Puritan and the Evangelical, had gone sour: their advocates were not greatly concerned for the physical welfare of the lower classes and, although often demonstrating a sentimental touch of much resented paternalism for the 'deserving' poor, stood stolidly behind established privilege.[8] While Edward's wealth and position proved exceedingly valuable when placed in the service of the working classes, they seriously impaired his social perception; until early middle age, he conceived of personal success only within the context of his own class and for many more years cleaved to paternalistic notions that markedly warped his understanding of the trend toward political democracy.[9]

I resolve . . .
To watch particularly over Impurity, Ambition, Pride and Discontent, my four great enemies at present.

Neale's Journal, Sunday, 2 January 1831

Edward was seventeen when he entered Oriel College, Oxford. 'From being rather boyish in my ideas,' he recalled, 'I was suddenly to be transported among men . . . I was now to be brought into an unlimited competition with those of my own age.'[10] He had set high goals for himself, aspiring to the fluent wit and elegant graces of a 'Sheridan in society' and of a 'Canning in oratory'; he would be 'one to whom fortune always granted a merited success'.[11] Edward, beginning too confidently, was due for the customary surprise. It was not so much

that he had overrated his own ability as that he was quite unprepared
for the way of life at Oxford. From the strictness and rigidity of his
schoolwork at Hitcham he was thrown into Oxford's free-wheeling way
where he was pretty much left to his own designs. Lacking in
self-discipline, irregular and desultory reading was the bane of his
college years which, with the best will in the world, he was never quite
able to effectively combat.[12] Moreover, the excitement of Oxford's
academic and social activity exaggerated some of Edward's childhood
weaknesses; his impatience, for example, the desire to discover all about
everything at once, was turned into nervousness, a tendency to
interrupt in conversation and what he described as 'terrible stam-
mering'. Much of his initial enthusiasm was quickly dissipated. His
natural shyness reinforced, Edward continued to build his castles in the
air: being slight of stature he day-dreamed of a visit from the
mythological King Oberon, 'myself turned in and out comes a strapping
six foot genius'.[13]

He had started out at Oriel without the customary public school
background, and its absence presented him with additional problems.
Some lessons learned in a public school could be taught nowhere else,
one such being how to get along among a group of boys and make close
friendships.[14] As a result Edward often found himself alone and
frustrated, his fertile imagination playing havoc with his delicate
Evangelical conscience. Daydreams about girls, leading as they usually
did to 'liscentious thoughts' and 'impurity' (Edward's euphemism for
masturbation) caused a debilitating accumulation of guilt feelings. In
the first place the practice was considered sinful; Christians arduously
pointed out that in the Old Testament God had stricken Onan dead
for 'spilling his seed'. Indeed, at Oriel, Provost Hawkins preached at
least one sermon to the students on the subject. And if sin was not
worry enough for a boy who believed in a literal hell, there was the
added fear that health might be damaged by such a practice. Edward
ultimately found it necessary to at least partially reassure himself by
consulting a medical text, and he concluded:

> 'I find no particular disease mentioned as springing from self-
> pollution, only general bad effect on constitution, but it is a vile
> practice and utterly repugnant to Christian and even *natural* feelings
> of purity and duty, and with its great parent indolence must be
> overcome as I trust by God's grace it will.'[15]

Reference to love, licentious thoughts and impurity were so frequently
recorded in his Journal that upon re-reading it over the Christmas

vacation of 1835 he added a clarifying notation to the top of the very first page: 'If any persons besides myself should ever open this volume let them know that by liscentiousness or impurity is not meant intercourse with women a sin of which up to this date I cannot accuse myself thank God.'

It should not be assumed, however, on the basis of Edward's immature ramblings in his autobiographical sketch and college journal that he was uniquely ill-adjusted or unhappy, for like most young people he had a strong tendency to over-dramatise himself. Guilty feelings notwithstanding, Edward was no ascetic. He sailed and played tennis, was ashamed neither of his rowing nor his cricket, rode well but not exceptionally and shot rabbits; he seems to have adjusted easily to wine parties which he frequently attended without becoming drunk enough to express any worry in his Journal. On at least two occasions, Provost Hawkins threatened to rusticate him if he were not more regular in chapel attendance. Furthermore, like a typical young aristocrat, he ran himself deeply into debt and had great difficulty with the necessary but unpleasant task of so informing his father. For all his pious sincerity and religious resolution, there were undertones in Edward's Journal which suggest the words later penned by James Anthony Froude about his own Oxford days: 'The men I lived with were gentlemanlike, many of them clever and well informed, but they neither intended nor tried to do more than pass without discredit.'[16]

Despite the traces of superficiality, however, Edward's first few years in college were characterised by a serious change in his mental attitude generated by an exposure to religious doctrines which conflicted harshly with his own narrow, evangelically-orientated beliefs. During this period the Tractarian movement was in its incipiency, its ideals rooted in the humble ministrations of the Rev. John Keble whose views were then being widely popularised by three young Fellows of Oriel: John Henry Newman, Hurrell Froude, and Edward's cousin, Robert Wilberforce. Following Keble's example, they rejected both the emotionalism of the evangelical and the rationalism of the Broad Churchman, emphasising instead the Christian life, a simple unostentatious devotion to pastoral duties, the strict observance of the Sacraments, and a total abandonment of self to God. It is of great significance that Edward Vansittart Neale was numbered among the very last of those students to be personally tutored by J. H. Newman, and the warm friendship of their relationship went beyond usual academic arrangements: when Edward was reading for his final examinations Newman worked steadily with him, even during the long vacation.[17] Sunday after Sunday in the silence of his rooms at Oriel, Edward recorded synopses of his tutor's sermons at St Mary's, filling the pages of his Journal with the mixed emotions they stimulated.[18] As Newman himself had only recently rejected a position of fervent Evangelicalism to accept the tenets of the High Church School, his Sunday missles at St Mary's were well calculated to challenge all of Edward's basic assumptions.[19]

By the summer of 1830 numerous entries in Edward's Journal displayed growing intellectual discontent, especially with the stark Evangelical dogma of the exclusiveness of salvation.[20] In the fall he attended missionary meetings with his aging Uncle Wilberforce and was repelled by the misplaced zeal and 'party spirit' which dominated this gathering of the 'converted'. 'Almost incredible', he commented afterwards, 'would that our people could abstain from sending all the heathen to Hell. It is an idea by no means needed as a spur to exertion — perfectly gratuitous and unspeakably horrible.'[21] The restless, inquisitive mind revealed in the Journal was deeply marked by John Henry Newman's ideals; indeed, when the great tractarian and future Cardinal taught that the study of history would provide a key to the riddles of theology, and that true happiness could be found only in the sublimation of one's own interests to the needs of others, he furnished a major foundation for Edward's philosophy of life.

The year 1830 was a crucial one for Edward. Not only did he come to doubt the truth of evangelical religion, but he revised his political views as well: 'My . . . opinions have this year undergone a considerable change,' he confided to his Journal, 'I am become a Tory . . . and I trust I shall ever remain so.'[22] The theological problem had caused considerable mental anguish, while the political transition had been accomplished with relative ease. Though his immediate family circle appears to have been mildly Whig, there were other outstanding family examples on the Tory side, such as Lord Bexley of Kent, Liverpool's old inept Chancellor of the Exchequer, and Uncle Wilberforce. Moreover, Edward had come to his first understanding of politics during the Canning period and even as he entered Oxford was a great admirer of the late Prime Minister.

In the months that followed his political change of heart, up to the final passage of the Reform Bill over two struggling years later, Edward's entries in his Journal express only the standard arguments offered by the opponents of reform. Although he was in advance of some Tories in feeling that a little constitutional reform might be excusable, he was willing to make only those changes which would terminate the most glaring abuses, and these merely because he feared that otherwise the party in favour of reform would continue to gain strength and possibly in an 'unguarded moment' pass a democratic measure, in which case all would be over. To the '*mob*' Edward would 'never *concede* a step,' he would allow them only the right to justice and the protection of their private property.[23] Actually, little space in Edward's Journal was devoted to the matter of national politics though on occasion he showed considerable enthusiasm about the subject. After hearing Gladstone, then a fellow-student at Oxford, deliver an extremely effective anti-reform speech during a debate at the Union (17 May 1831),[24] Edward ecstatically day-dreamed about a political career replete with great oratorical moments of his own in the House of Commons.[25]

Edward's romantic imagination was indefatigable, and productive of indolence. His attitude towards reading for honours was negative, if not completely indifferent; and he would not apply himself to study systematically even in the face of his final public examinations during the closing months of 1831.[26] Throughout this period there is an excess of elaborate, meandering theological argument in the Journal, which implies that Newman must bear some responsibility for Edward's apparent lack of initiative. Surely Newman's persistent preaching on the subject of humility and perpetual denigration of pride and ambition tended, at least in Edward's case, to directly counteract the desire for academic excellence. Almost paraphrasing a page from his mentor's sermons, Edward whimsically reflected: 'Is it not the desire of distinction in however small a degree that is wrong as soon as it becomes a motive to action, and how wretched a one it is.'[27] He read widely and thoughtfully but selected material which was for the most part quite unrelated to the demands of the impending oral examinations. Nevertheless, the results when published in the honours list surprised Edward and appear to have dealt a heavy blow to his pride: in the Classics he received a third class, an 'unexpected degradation' only slightly mitigated by his achievement of a second in Mathematics.[28]

Edward returned home in December of 1831 chastened, worried that he might be a subject for condolence and carrying the added burden of having to oppose his father in his choice of a career: he planned to study law in preference to becoming a clergyman.[29]

'I feel driven to come out in my true colours coûte que coûte. The Gospel word is very true, he who loves father or mother, wife or child, more than truth is not worthy of it.'

Neale's Journal, Sunday, 20 August 1848

Edward entered Lincoln's Inn on 16 January 1832, and for the next eighteen years, up to his active involvement with the Christian Socialists in 1850, his mind was troubled by a compulsion to find a substitute for his dwindling Evangelical faith. The process of Edward's intellectual development involved the slow agonizing transformation of Christianity as submission to formula, into Christianity as service to mankind. Although scarcely any of his contemporaries carried their convictions so far as to become avowed socialists, Edward's religious experience was characteristic of the times; indeed, the black delirium of religious doubt, often resulting in loss of faith, alienation from loved ones, and the desperate search for a secular chiliasm to substitute for scepticism, was one of the most common themes in Victorian writing from *Sartor Resartus* to *Robert Elsmere* and beyond.

Few of those fortunate enough to escape the negative rigours of an Evangelical background fully appreciate the power which it can exercise over every part of life. There is no question but that Edward found it difficult to slough off the habits of mind developed in his youth. He never went to such 'worldly' entertainments as the theatre or to a ball without feeling qualms; while he rejected with his mind the idea that they were sinful, he remained apprehensive enough to vent elaborate apologetics in his Journal: 'In amusements I see no other line than to abstain from those whose immediate tendency is injurious to the public, as bad plays, etc., or which I find to injure my own mind making me vain, proud, dissatisfied with simpler pleasures, etc.' He questioned the deleterious effect which large parties might have on servants, particularly if one had 'difficulty in knowing when to stop', and on one occasion even felt guilty for strolling on a Sunday in London's Zoological Gardens.[30]

Edward's attitude towards women especially continued to be influenced by his lingering Evangelical morality, and he was inclined to be priggish and hypocritical. While his own thoughts still led to 'impurity', he delved into the psyche of each one of his loves to discover whether or not she might be deficient in some Christian virtue. Edward demanded that a woman be simple, serious and submissive, and her attitude towards the Church as well as such questionable delights as dancing was all important. She might dance a little, but was it proper for her to find the practice too enjoyable? Love must be a perfect blending of physical attraction and moral virtue. In a poem to the last of his loves before marriage, Edward wrote:

'Anna, 'tis not alone thy silken hair
Nor graceful form nor mild yet thoughtful eye
Nor many gifts I love. I prize the union rare
Affection, talent and simplicity.'[31]

Thus Edward remained bound by the social and moral conventions of the evangelical persuasion; and in all probability he would have ultimately returned to the orthodox fold with doubts suppressed and faith renewed, had it not been for the untimely death of his sister Caroline in May of 1836. Her loss came as a profound shock. She was the sister nearest his own age, a close companion as well as a confiding friend. Being overly zealous evangelicals, the first concern of Edward's parents was to convince themselves that their daughter had been saved from hell, her 'habits of prayer and reading the Bible' being taken as reassuring evidence.[32] Their attitude thoroughly repelled Edward, shattering his last remaining illusions about evangelical Christianity. It was an absurd faith which taught a literal hell and could take such tokens as prayer and Bible reading as confirmation of salvation. He found it increasingly difficult to communicate with his father on the subject: 'How can I tell him,' he sadly wrote, 'that my heaven and salvation and happiness and hell are all internal.' Far from looking forward to life after death, Edward trusted it 'to be the intention of God to bring all his creatures' to the point of finding 'a heaven on Earth'.[33] Without being entirely aware of it he had passed a milestone on the road towards socialism: if heaven was to be sought on earth then the broad moral implications of Christianity took on far greater importance than the narrow details of theology — works of charity became more important than belief.

Called to the Bar on 4 May 1837, Edward became a Chancery Barrister and a month later, on 14 June, he married Frances Sarah Farrer. The union certainly promised to expedite his social advancement to say nothing of his legal career. Frances was the daughter of Sir J. W. Farrer, a Baronet of Ingleborough, Yorkshire, one of the Masters of the High Court of Chancery; moreover, as a result of her mother's first marriage, her half-brother was John Scott, soon to be second Earl of Eldon. Edward's wedding was a practical matter and despite attempts at rationalisation in his Journal, it is clear that he was neither physically nor romantically attracted to Frances; indeed, he had undertaken the task of wooing her with the callous determination of an accomplished fortune-hunter. 'What I have most important to record is a new love,' he coldly noted, 'and one which began in reason and judgment much more than imagination, and which offers a fair prospect

of marriage in a not very remote distance.'[34] There is pathos in
Edward's calculating if not mercenary entry into a union designed to
bring to both parties a lifelong sense of frustration and intellectual
incompatibility. It was Tennyson who in *Locksley Hall* wrote of such
marriages, 'Cursed be the social wants that sin against the strength of
youth!' Edward treated Frances as though she were merely a reflection
of himself, vainly trying to share with her the frequently impious
ramblings of his restless mind without understanding that she was
neither intellectually interested nor emotionally equipped to cope with
them. As husband and wife they both lived under the shadow of the
Farrer-Scott connection, and Edward could not have chosen in-laws less
sympathetic to his developing ideas. Frances' family traditions were
Tory to the extreme: it may be recalled that John Scott, the first Earl
of Eldon (Lord Chancellor, 1801–27) was responsible for many of the
reactionary policies so frequently attributed to Castlereagh. The future
would have been very different for Edward had he found a more
compatible wife; but lacking the fulfilling spiritual and physical
intimacy of a happy marriage he was left with the lonely freedom to
devote himself totally to the work of implementing his social ideals.

Frustrated by his emotionally starved relationship with Frances, still
bothered by 'impure' thoughts and strongly drawn to other women,[35]
Edward found a way of sublimation as well as consolation in the study
of theology. Prior to Caroline's death and his subsequent marriage to
Frances he had come to have doubts about orthodox Christianity and
in consequence had chosen the Law for a career; yet the overall effect
of these early doubts was superficial as he had complacently continued
to conform to the old Evangelical patterns. But now, with this period
of relative apathy terminated by grief as well as depressing family
problems, he seriously searched for a religious foundation upon which
he could reconstruct a new life, and in the process make some practical
contribution to society. Edward felt called to follow the example of his
uncle Wilberforce's well known works of charity but no longer had even
a whit of toleration for the latter's theology.[36]

Mid-summer, 1838, while the printer's ink was still fresh, he
purchased the Rev. F. D. Maurice's *Kingdom of Christ*, a book destined
to become an inspiration for those who sought a progressive social
message in the Christian gospel. Edward entirely concurred with
Maurice's interpretation of the Incarnation as the prime evidence of
God's love, not being merely a way to save man from hell but the
positive symbol of His adoption of all mankind: thereby all men were
simultaneously children of God and brothers in Christ, divinely

enjoined to live for one another with the charity and willingness to sacrifice self so perfectly exemplified by Christ's death on the cross. This was a motive to charitable undertakings which was dynamically affirmative, contrasting starkly with the bleak spirit of guilt, fear and exclusiveness which characterised William Wilberforce, who could only bequeath to his nephew a posthumous theological warning: 'Remember that we are all fallen creatures, born in sin, and naturally depraved. Christianity recognizes no *innocence* or *goodness of heart*.'[37] Edward, however, was not to rest for long on this theological plateau. Maurice's Anglican orthodoxy, however progressive, represented only the beginning of a climb towards the more cosmopolitan plains of Continental Idealism and, ultimately, French Socialism.

An avid reader, Edward soon went on to master the German works of scholarship which proved that the Bible was a typically human document, abundant with inaccuracies and major contradictions.[38] German higher criticism thus ravaged the body of traditional Christian belief, dependent as it was on the facile assumption that the Holy Scriptures constituted an accurate, divinely-inspired, historical account which, for the most part (excepting the obvious parables and poetry), must be taken literally. Yet, despite the new evidence from abroad, Edward still refused to exchange his Christian faith for complete scepticism. What did it matter that the Bible was filled with human error when its teachings of brotherly love and sacrifice were capable of inspiring the lives of men such as Newman, Wilberforce and Maurice? Would not the universal practice of these virtues be productive of heaven on earth? In the last analysis, then, the insistence on Biblical infallibility appeared to be clearly irrelevant, in no way necessary to justify or validate Christ's teachings. Johann Gottfried von Herder's writings were the first to furnish Edward with a logical basis, other than intuition, for escaping the traditional belief that Christian truth must be based on the literal interpretation of a single book. Divine purpose, Herder insisted, was realised in the course of history through the finite medium of ordinary human relationships, and not handed down, free from error, from on high. Divine will was written in the mind of the folk to be articulated in saga and myth; though both distort facts and revel in fantasy, they may still remain vehicles for the conveyance of divine truth. By reasonable analogy this argument was applicable to the Bible. Ironically, Newman had helped to prepare Edward to accept Herder's views when he preached that church tradition was on a par with the Bible as a part of God's revelation. Because it was impossible to vest church tradition with a life of its own, independent from other human events, it followed that history itself (as the record of all the religious, cultural, social and political achievements of mankind) must evidence the working out of God's will among men, and thereby constitute the basic substance of divine revelation. Indeed, with variation in emphasis and terminology, this was the generally accepted premise of the philosophical idealists. Edward read widely from Kant, Fichte, Schelling and Hegel and was gratified to find that their views ran parallel to his own. Like himself, though deprived of their dependence upon an infallible Bible, they did not falter in their defence of Christian principles. At the very least, it seemed apparent to them that the moral teachings of Christ were divinely inspired; even Hegel felt that beneath Christianity's poetic language and not infrequently erroneous doctrines, lay buried the same philosophical truth which he proclaimed.

Thoughtful Christians should not have regretted the growing disbelief in Biblical infallibility (though many did and some, like Newman, turned their backs on the entire question of higher criticism). As for Edward, he was numbered among those students of the Scriptures who inwardly rejoiced: it was now possible to condemn such deleterious dogmas as original sin and eternal damnation, both so opposed to any enlightened notion of human decency, while continuing to stress that the fundamental New Testament message of love and sacrifice was, unquestionably, divinely inspired.

As a barrister, Edward Vansittart Neale was painstaking and conscientious but only moderately successful: the work was a source of little satisfaction. Despite his wife's connections he neither wanted nor achieved distinction, and his leisure hours were devoured by the search for a more meaningful occupation. It was not to be easily found: he remained uncertain about his basic principles, disposed towards reading, thinking and writing rather than practical action. Nevertheless, the radical direction of his intellectual growth was evident from the beginning, determining his behaviour and complicating his family relations. As the decade of the 1840s opened he started a study of Utopian Socialism and talked about the feasibility of a great social transformation. He had become interested in the working classes, met occasionally with the Odd Fellows, and frequently visited the penitentiary for which in the spring of 1842 he idled away some time in devising a ventilation system which was never implemented.[39] Soon thereafter, Edward acquainted himself with the activities of Jeremy Bentham and Lord Brougham with the result that he joined forces with the Law Amendment Society and ultimately published two books in support of radical land reforms designed to break down the aristocratic barriers to freedom of ownership and facilitate the conveyance of real property.[40]

Edward's restless mind had brought him to the place where he was willing to accompany the German philosophers in their abandonment of orthodox belief, even in holding the 'religion of man' to be the end towards which Christianity was meant to lead. But he could proceed no further with their ideas as they remained confined to the cloudy realm of metaphysics and theology, constructing, with no empirical evidence, elaborate schemes to explain all of reality.[41] It was important for Edward to find an answer that would speak to more than just the intellect, one that would give expression to his newfound convictions and release all of his pent up emotional energies in some practical way. Men should be brothers, but the present role of society was one of competition, animosity and class division which left the lower orders starving while the privileged few kept the earth's bounty to themselves. Philosophy might aid in the diagnosis but Edward sought a remedy and ultimately found it in the doctrines of Utopian Socialism.[42]

It was only a short ideological jump over the Rhineland from German Idealism to French Socialism: both were in their inspiration religious, seeking to establish a Kingdom of God on earth – but the French socialists, particularly Fourier, had the necessary advantage of possessing some practical plans for this accomplishment. Fourier especially appealed to Edward because, unlike England's Robert Owen. he did not view man materialistically as simply a creature of circumstances, to be passively molded by a properly paternalistic environment into a superior social being. Fourier believed that men were spiritual creatures with calculable, innately existing wants and needs, and as such should never be treated like manipulable clay: man's environment should be shaped to fit man's nature – not the reverse. The great French Utopian envisioned a new social system founded upon self-sustaining communities called phalanstères which were specifically designed to satisfy basic human passions rather than to subject people to any external standard of what was good. Because Edward felt that human nature reflected the will of God, he was naturally inclined towards Fourier's variety of Socialism which sought to amplify rather than to change human nature.[43]

Edward was driven by a compulsion to reorder the social environment to meet his own psychological needs, and his conversion to utopian socialist doctrines was a product of this compulsion. Unity – harmony – love – these came to be the ingredients of his prescription for humanity's ills precisely because he felt the lack of their healing

qualities in his own life. His relationship with a stern, inflexible father
had left much to be desired: it was archtypically Evangelical and
therefore maximised moral confrontations while minimising personal
communication. His marriage was similarly defective.[44] Edward knew
first hand that differences of opinion, particularly on religion, produced
alienation and its concomitant, loneliness. Evangelical Christianity,
however, did for a time satisfy a need in his life, and the drive to
replace it with something equally fulfilling was of the utmost
importance. There was a socially dynamic side of Evangelicalism that
Edward was unwilling to abandon, a side that has been often
overlooked. Its cold, stern, puritanical asceticism was balanced by a
pietistic fervour of the kind that had 'strangely warmed' John Wesley
and which produced a sense of oneness with God, an inner harmony,
and a deep belief in the Messianic promise of a new millennium wherein
the lion would be made to lie down with the lamb. For his entire life
Edward clung to this warmer pietistic influence, to the chiliastic vision
of ultimate harmony. In this sense he always remained a 'true believer'.
His attraction to the utopian socialists was all but inevitable, for they
were driven by the same concern with harmony, both inner and
outer – for the individual and for society – which compelled him.
Indeed, the model communities, designed to implement their ideals,
were too close to the 'New Jerusalem' for coincidence; behind their
teachings, from their Calvinistic denunciation of the present 'sinful' or
abnormal state of society to their glorious hope of dotting the
countryside with harmonious communities, lies the same old Christian
Messianism. In the doctrines of Utopian Socialism, Edward had
discovered his mission in life: he must work to end the injustice of
divisive individualism in favour of communitarianism. All the newly
created dischords of capitalistic society must be ultimately resolved
into God's pre-ordained harmony.

On 15 November 1849, Edward made a last entry in the Journal of
close to twenty years which, after following him from his restless
college days to maturity, still left him unfulfilled. This last note,
however, has a deeply penetrating sound, of summary as well as of
promise, for his historic relation with John Ludlow, F. D. Maurice,
Thomas Hughes, Charles Kingsley and the other Christian Socialists is
here only months away:

'To many persons I may . . . appear an object of envy, a wife of an
affectionate disposition, a family arising healthily and not unattractive, a fortune placing me above want if it is prudently

managed, family connexions placing me among the classes who are most regarded in my own country, and yet if they could look within, could see how isolated, disappointed, hampered, I feel, how aimless my life, how little hope I see of ever finding myself in a position more satisfactory, they might lay aside their envy. I long to be actively engaged in advancing that great cause of social regeneration to which I look forward with so much hope. But how to gain this object, I see not the way. I cannot feel that confidence in my own powers which would make me sanguine of success in the difficult attempt to realize the beginnings of such an undertaking, and then my family ties clip away the resources which as a single man, or one married to a person who shared my views, I might have had. At present I have made a beginning of collecting materials to frame a work on the subject, at least thus to try to promote it.'[45]

Edward seemed to hear the same cadence as his future colleagues and with his final words began to move in step with them. He lamented the recent cholera epidemic and cried for remedial action just as John Ludlow and his friends, already active in sanitary reform work, were trying to initiate a plan for a National Health League.

'A day of so-called thanksgiving for the cessation of cholera, not in itself objectionable, had not the thanks proceeded on the sup-position that the cholera ceased in answer to our prayers, and had not our superstition precluded all expressions of joyousness. We may well thank God that the powers by which we are surrounded are so balanced as to make the Earth a healthful and pleasant dwelling for us. We may chuse [sic] the cessation of a great sickness as a fit time to call men's attention to this admirable order. But to turn the cholera into a "judgment," to maintain that God, for something which we as a nation have done to offend him, has found this summer a special pleasure in killing *poor* people who lived in ill-drained and watery situations until on being begged not to go on that way he gradually left off . . . is a poor means of bringing men to feel confidence in, or reverence for, the great being in whom we live and have our being. And yet into what does the theory that the cholera is a "judgment" removed in answer to our prayers resolve itself but into such a supposition as this. I am confident that addresses far more calculated to go home to men's hearts and lead them to do good might be delivered on the hypothesis which . . . points to the localities where disease manifests itself as the warning voice of God to us not to let such things continue.'[46]

Notes

1. The title to the surname Neale may be illustrated as follows:

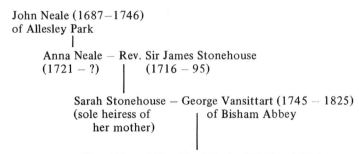

John Neale (1687–1746)
of Allesley Park

Anna Neale — Rev. Sir James Stonehouse
(1721 – ?)   (1716 – 95)

Sarah Stonehouse — George Vansittart (1745 – 1825)
(sole heiress of   of Bisham Abbey
her mother)

Rev. Edward Vansittart Neale (1769 – 1850)
of Allesley Park and Rector of Taplow
(assumed surname Neale in 1805)

The family papers (hereafter referred to as the Neale Papers) at Bisham Grange, Marlow, Bucks., were of primary value when compiling information about the family, especially an untitled manuscript account of Bisham Abbey by Florence Vansittart Neale, Edward's daughter-in-law, and his own brief auto-biographical work, written when he was 21, 'A Sketch of My Past Life'. The *D.N.B.* and *Burke's Landed Gentry* were also useful, as was Henry Pitman, ed., *Memorial of Edward Vansittart Neale*, (Manchester, 1894).

2. For information on Bisham Abbey and its history, Pitman's *Memorial* and Florence Vansittart Neale's manuscript account (as cited above) are invaluable.

3. G. M. Young, *Victorian England; Portrait of an Age*, (London, 1960), p.1.

4. 'A Sketch of My Past Life' and the Journal, located among the Neale Papers, will be hereafter referred to as 'A Sketch' and the Journal.

5. 'A Sketch', p.2.

6. *Ibid*. Phaedrus misspelled by Neale.

7. *Ibid*., p.6.

8. Indeed, Cobbett once described Wilberforce as 'the worst enemy of the people then living'. See Charles E. Raven, *Christian Socialism, 1848–1854*, (London, 1920), p.12.

9. See e.g., E. V. Neale, *Labour and Capital*, (London, 1852), p.31.

10. 'A Sketch', p.7.

11. *Ibid*.

12. He was not untypical in this respect. See: A Graduate of Oxford, *The Students Guide to a Course of Reading Necessary for Obtaining Honours*, (Oxford, 1837), p.4.

13. Journal, p.43; 53–54.

14. Thomas Mozley, *Reminiscences Chiefly of Oriel College and the Oxford Movement*, (London, 1882), I, 130. Mozley recalled that Henry Wilberforce, Edward's cousin, who was also a student at Oriel during these years, lacked a public school background and consequently had some amusing difficulties.
15. Journal, p.116.
16. Waldo Hilary Dunn, *James Anthony Froude, A Biography*, (Oxford, 1961), I, 47.
17. Journal, p.29.
18. See e.g., *Ibid.*, pp.58, 59.
19. *Ibid.*, p.84.
20. *Ibid.*, p.44.
21. *Ibid.*, p.45.
22. *Ibid.*, p.63.
23. *Ibid.*, pp.115–116. See also pp.57–58, 73, 75, 82–83, 117, 119.
24. See John Morley, *The Life of William Ewart Gladstone*, (New York, 1903), I, 72.
25. Journal, pp.85, 105.
26. *Ibid.*, pp.46, 115, 117.
27. *Ibid.*, p.54.
28. *Ibid.*, pp.122–123.
29. *Ibid.*, pp.126–127, 129.
30. *Ibid.*, pp.129, 167.
31. *Ibid.*, p.155.
32. *Ibid.*, pp.149, 155.
33. *Ibid.*, pp.152–154.
34. *Ibid.*, pp.162–163.
35. *Ibid.*, pp.172–178.
36. *Ibid.*, pp.167–168.
37. From Wilberforce's *A Practical View of Christianity*, as quoted by E. P. Thompson, *The Making of the English Working Class*, (New York, 1966), p.374.
38. Journal, pp.170–171.
39. *Ibid.*, p.177.
40. *The Real Property Acts of 1845, Being the Acts to Render the Assignment of Satisfied Terms Unnecessary; To Amend the Law of Real Property; to Facilitate the Conveyance of Real Property; and to Facilitate the Granting of Certain Leases. With Introductory Observations and Notes.* (London, 1845). *Thoughts on the Registration of the Title to Land: Its Advantages and the Means of Effecting it with Observations upon the Bill to Facilitate the Transfer of Real Property, Brought in by Mr. Henry Drummond and Mr. Wood* (London, 1849). He also drafted a Parliamentary Bill to reform the law of conveyance, see Richard Cobden to Edward Vansittart Neale, November 28 1849. Neale Papers.
41. Journal, p.171.
42. The first direct references to Socialism appeared in Edward's Journal, August 29 and 30 1841, where he spoke of writing a

review of Fourier's system for inclusion in a book. Journal, pp.172–174.

43. E. V. Neale, *The Characteristic Features of Some of the Principle Systems of Socialism*, (London, 1851), passim. See also E. V. Neale, *Associated Homes: A Lecture . . . with Three Engravings of the Familistère at Guise, and a Biographical Notice of M. Godin, its Founder*, (London, 1880), p.vi.

44. Journal, p.173.

45. *Ibid*, p.180.

46. *Ibid.*, pp.180–181.

II

THEORY AND PRACTICE;
CHRISTIAN SOCIALISM AND CO-OPERATION
1849—1854

> We have used the Bible as if it was a mere special
> constable's handbook — an opium-dose for keeping
> beasts of burden patient while they were being over-
> loaded — a mere book to keep the poor in order . . . We
> have told you that the Bible preached the rights of
> property and the duties of labour, when (God knows!)
> for once that it does that, it preaches ten times over the
> *duties of property* and the *rights of labour*.
>
> Charles Kingsley, *Letters to the Chartists*, 1848

In 1849 it appeared that the *Communist Manifesto* was justified in denouncing Christian Socialism as 'but the holy water with which the priest consecrates the heartburnings of the aristocrat'. Feeling guilty about the miserable condition of the lower classes, the original Christian Socialists, like Neale, acknowledged that their religion enjoined them to serve society, but found it painfully difficult to translate this idea into action. The great Chartist demonstration of 1848 had impressed F. D. Maurice, John Ludlow and Charles Kingsley with a common desire to somehow Christianise socialism and to socialise Christianity, but from the outset differences in temperament and personal belief hampered their attempts to work together in a practical way.[1]

Ludlow was intellectually a product of the socialist tradition: raised and educated as a Frenchman, he had been strongly impressed by the work of Lamennais and the liberal Catholics, as well as by Fourier and Proudhon.[2] Kingsley and Maurice, however, were conservatives after the fashion of Coleridge and Carlyle; though their Christianity was forward looking, they were socialists in only a very vague way, if at all.[3] Indeed, Maurice felt that the status quo constituted a divine order which man might greatly modify but should not basically alter. Not unlike Coleridge he would teach men to recognise the basically good purpose which lay at the heart of all *existing* institutions and would argue that this purpose had been frustrated by economic competition and the philosophy of rampant and unchecked individualism. Only to combat these negative forces did he make allowance for change. Paradoxically, while his progressive theological views incited others to

29

action, Maurice himself neurotically shyed away from all really
practical work. He had even forced his colleagues to abandon their
plans for creating a National Health League, despite the horrors of the
cholera epidemics in London.

For months the Christian Socialists had floundered without a
distinct purpose or direction while futilely looking to Maurice for
leadership; finally in the autumn of 1849, Ludlow took control of the
situation, transforming the impatient little group of well-intentioned
Christians into a practical movement dedicated to the principles of
Co-operation. Inspired by the success of the self-governing workshops
(*les associations ouvriers*) in Paris, Ludlow convinced his colleagues of
the need for constructing similar organisations in England.[4] On 11
February 1850, they began by launching an association of tailors in
London and before their co-operative efforts were brought to an end,
the small band of enthusiasts were able (thanks largely to Neale's
money) to launch no less than twelve such undertakings. The Christian
Socialist Movement did not fail for want of either effort or enthusiasm.
Only Maurice continued to be reluctant; as a matter of fact, it was
surprising that he had supported such schemes in the first place. And
from the beginning, Ludlow blinded himself to the fact that Maurice
saw these new associations of workingmen as instruments of protest
rather than of change and would be, in consequence, unwilling
permanently to identify with them.

In June 1850, the Christian Socialists officially constituted themselves
as the 'Society for Promoting Working Men's Associations'.[5] Hoping to
overcome Maurice's almost morbid doubts about such co-operative
ventures, he was named President of the Society and given full power to
choose the members of its governing 'Council of Promoters'. One of
those chosen by him was Edward Vansittart Neale.

Although Neale was first drawn to the Christian Socialists through
reading an advertisement for the Working Tailors Association, Maurice's
affiliation with the group doubtlessly rendered the attraction irresistible. Neale had known Maurice as a casual acquaintance at Oxford, and
afterwards, as we have seen, had been deeply influenced by the latter's
progressive theological views. Here were men like himself who sought to
bring human society into conformity with religious principles, and who
appeared to have found in the Working Tailors Association a practical
means of doing so. As a Christian Socialist Neale moved within an aura
of eager impatience which led him, as Ludlow later noted, into
'over-hasty judgment'.[6] Though already middle aged, he retained the

vigour of his youth; he still walked at a rapid pace, uttered sentences at a speed which was conducive to stuttering, and had a tendency to jangle the nerves of those whose enthusiasm was less easily roused. Neale added a touch of frenzy to the work of the brotherhood as he bent himself to the task of Association giving both his time and money with abandon. His life to this point had been a matter of the expedient – he had merely been acting out the expected role for a man of his wealth and social position – but now the substance of his daydreams seemed about to materialise; his 'over-fertile brain' (again to borrow Ludlow's words)[7] appeared to have found its appointed task. Neale had done his preliminary work well, his knowledge of socialist theory being as broad as his pocketbook, and it is clear that this infinitely impressed his colleagues. Thomas Hughes, for example, remembered Neale as the man who had put him in touch not only with the French socialists but with Karl Marx and Ferdinand Lassalle as well, and in addition had taught him something of 'the enormous importance of the social question for all nations'.[8]

Yet, despite the ease with which Neale was assimilated into the Christian Socialist Movement, Ludlow, being frankly suspicious of the new recruit, was quite surprised when Maurice appointed this wealthy barrister of Lincoln's Inn to membership in the Council of Promoters. Ludlow construed the religious teachings of Maurice as Christian Socialism's energising force and he had not been long in discovering that Neale's theology was 'vague and lax' – that Neale was no Maurician.[9] Certainly, as a fervent Christian believer, Ludlow could not help but find fault in a man whose socialist quest for a heaven on earth had brought him to the point of abandoning even the doctrine of individual immortality.[10] Moreover, it was clear that Neale, unlike Maurice and his disciples, was not trying to 'Christianise' Socialism, for to him Socialism was the fulfillment of Christianity – its desired end. The social gospel of love, brotherhood, and the essential divinity of man, had been clothed in the symbolic myths of Christian theology merely because of the primitiveness of popular understanding at the time the Bible was written. But since then, under God's guidance, man's knowledge had been developing through history, and Neale felt that it had now come to the point where one could separate the truth from its theological trappings. Years later he stated that the Christian part of the Christian Socialist Movement was 'rather a something floating over it than definitely embodied in it'.[11] Whether or not this was actually the case, it is clear that Neale himself always tried to avoid mixing any specific references to Christianity with the practical work of Co-operation and as a result his views conflicted bitterly with Ludlow's.

Neale's wealth also aroused Ludlow's suspicion, and with greater justification. Without much effort Neale became the most eminent of the Promoters – 'ten times as important as the council at large' was Ludlow's opinion.[12] If the Council gave £50 out of its funds, he maintained, and Neale £500, it was bound to appear to the workingmen of the associations that the Council was Neale's debtor. On at least one occasion Neale even threatened to withdraw his money (upon which, unfortunately, the Society soon grew dependent) if his colleagues took a line of action with which he disagreed.[13] At this stage in his life there was little evidence of the humble, self-effacing yet subtly effective leader that later co-operators so respected and admired. During the Christian Socialist period Neale's conduct too often tended to conflict with his principles, his background of wealth and privilege leaving sharp angularities in his character. While bewailing the unequal distribution of wealth, he almost invariably, if unconsciously, accepted those who possessed it as the best elements in society. Conservative in his political and social thinking, he was less interested in deranging the existing class structure than in introducing a new society where the rich could, through the practice of Co-operation, utilise their wealth for the good of all. Though he would have acknowledged the ultimate desirability of a classless society, he was not so eager to see it established overnight. His conservative beliefs, however, were not necessarily inconsistent with the doctrines of socialism then being preached. The early socialist thinkers were often politically reactionary and could by no means be counted upon as supporters of working class democracy – indeed the opposite was more frequently the case. For instance, Robert Owen's *New View* encompassed much that was old: it was surprisingly topheavy with paternalism, being dedicated to Neale's Uncle Wilberforce and the future George IV; as one recent authority maintains, where most men have political responses, Owen had only a blank.[14] The same criticism could be justifiably levelled at Edward Vansittart Neale.

Among the most decisive happenings in the brief history of the Christian Socialist Movement was Neale's introduction to the northern co-operative stores and consequent conversion to a belief in the primacy of Consumers Co-operation.

Had the modern Co-operative Movement come to centre around self-governing workshops, it might be said to have begun with the establishment of the Working Tailors Association in 1850, but

Co-operation is a consumers movement (its basic components being retail stores rather than factories) and as such looks back to Rochdale for its beginnings. In that city in 1844 a small group of labourers, who soon came to be known as the Equitable Pioneers, established a co-operative store in Toad Lane. They intended to supply themselves with dry goods and groceries of good quality free from adulteration and at a reasonable price, but from the outset were more than simply workingmen with aspirations to carry on business for themselves. Followers of Robert Owen, they planned to use the money saved by eliminating the services of the middle men (wholesalers and retailers) for the establishment of home colonies.

As businessmen they were uniquely successful, but this had little to do with their idealism; it was a result of the fact that unlike most Owenites they refused to fling themselves into the teeth of the capitalistic system. The majority of the previous ventures in co-operative shopkeeping had attempted to eliminate profits, root and branch, by selling merchandise at cost, and all too frequently failed because in drastically lowering prices they incurred the wrath of private tradesmen who would band together to force them out of business. In contrast, the Pioneers determined to turn capitalism to their own ends: they sold at the usual prices thus making rather than eliminating profits and, after deductions for running expenses and education, distributed them to their own members in the form of a periodic dividend proportionate to purchases. This was a tidy way to encourage customers without lowering prices – the more one bought the higher one's dividend. By this method they hoped that it would be possible gradually to accumulate enough capital to build Owenite home colonies. In time, however (as not a few contemporaries dolefully predicted), the 'divi' became an end in itself and the old communitarian inspiration was reduced to mere cant gravely enunciated only at annual Co-operative Congresses. It was here that Neale was to find his mission: ultimately his most important goal would be to win a new reprieve for the old idealism.

Even as the Christian Socialist Movement was getting underway, the North of England, especially around Manchester and in the West Riding of Yorkshire, had already come to be freely peppered with co-operative stores patterned after the Rochdale example. Curiously enough, Maurice and his friends were only dimly aware of their existence.[15]

It was Lloyd Jones, an erstwhile Owenite turned Christian Socialist, who initially provided Neale with first hand information about the burgeoning development of Consumers Co-operation, and the latter, always mercurial in making decisions, became at once an enthusiastic champion of the co-operative store.[16] It was not that he lost faith in the workshops; to the contrary, he still felt them to be necessary to resolve the antagonism between capital and labour. Neale merely extended his philosophy to include stores where the 'opposition of interest' existing between the buyer and the seller could also be resolved into harmony. He had, however, come to believe that the establishment of stores was the best *first step* to take on the pathway toward the Co-operative Commonwealth; thus, in October 1850, he opened an experimental co-operative store in London at 76 Charlotte Street, Fitzroy Square, a propitious location indeed, for it was the site of the old Owenite center. By the following spring the enterprise had expanded into the Central Co-operative Agency, Neale's *cheval de bataille*, optimistically projected as a major wholesaling centre for all of England.[17]

The new organisation was broadly designed: while wholesaling for the consumers, it could also function as an exchange agency for goods made by societies of producers, thus serving both sides of the Co-operative Movement. Thomas Hughes enthusiastically joined the venture along with Jules Lechevalier and Lloyd Jones – all three were then prominent Christian Socialists. Neale also enlisted the aid of Joseph Woodin, an expert in the grocery business who would do the purchasing and settle matters of quality and price.

Though Neale's wealth made him the most powerful of the Christian Socialists, he still remained one of the least well known; indeed only Maurice and Kingsley enjoyed reputations that extended much beyond the London area. But the founding of the Central Co-operative Agency marked the start of a critical change in Neale's fortunes; it was chiefly through his position as the director of this new venture that he came to achieve prominence within the wider arena of the national labour movement, and simultaneously began to acquire both the popularity and the attributes of leadership so necessary for his future career. He travelled extensively to promote the Agency's interests, making many valuable contacts throughout England, particularly in the North. He frequently visited the Labour Redemption Societies at Bury and Leeds, coming to be so popular among the workers at Bury that they considered him as a possible political candidate.[18] Month by month Neale made new acquaintances, not a few of whom were well known national leaders such as James Hole, one of the founders of the Leeds Redemption Society; G. A. Fleming, Owenite District Missionary for Leeds, erstwhile editor of the *New Moral World* and affiliate of the

National Association of United Trades; James Rigby, who had preceded
Fleming as District Missionary; and Thornton Hunt, the editor of the
Leader then living in London.

It was evident that labouring men's interest in Co-operation had
undergone a revival: the collapse of Chartism had turned many away
from politics, leaving them especially receptive to co-operative doctrine
with its unique social and economic emphasis. Feargus O'Connor's old
paper, the *Northern Star* (once Chartism's most influential journal but
afterwards grown cautious with age), had followed closely the
achievements of the Central Agency enthusiastically reporting Neale's
plans for 'improving the condition of producers'.[19] At the time of its
creation that most powerful of mid-century trade unions, the Amalgamated Society of Engineers, had come under the spell cast by the
Christian Socialists; the summer of 1851 found Neale lecturing to the
Union of Working Smiths on 'the moral and Christian basis upon which
Association was founded'.[20]

Trade unions were particularly tempting targets for propaganda.
They were well organised bodies in possession of capital and Neale felt
that if provided with correct information they were ready to begin
immediately the job of establishing stores and workshops. Consequently, unwilling to miss any opportunities, he expanded the work
of the Central Agency to include the full scale promotion of
Co-operation, even in the sphere of production (thereby seriously
encroaching on the official function of the Society for Promoting
Working Men's Associations). As a first step Neale had established a
'committee of consultation' which included in its membership a
number of prominent labour leaders and radical journalists; and
subsequently, on the committee's authority Jules Lechevalier drafted
an elaborate circular letter to be sent out to trade unions, expounding
the general principles of Association while particularly emphasising the
benefits newly available through affiliation with the Co-operative
Agency.[21] The circular proved very successful in attracting the
attention of trade unionists but generated much ill will among the
Christian Socialists. It made only a passing, almost snide reference to
the existing work of the Society for Promoting Working Men's
Associations, and therefore in effect proffered the services of Neale's
Agency as a preferable alternative.[22]

The record of Ludlow's unfolding conflict with Neale evokes pathos: as
lawyers the two men shared chambers at Lincoln's Inn stubbornly
retaining their friendship in the face of bitter, nerve-racking disagree-

ments; both were utopians, equally compulsive in their insistence that harmony must be the guiding principle of human relationships. There was literally an element of desperation in their fruitless search for common ground. At every major crossroad in the brief history of the Christian Socialist Movement they turned to face in opposite directions, until finally it was the issue of the Central Co-operative Agency which brought their battles to a climax.

No sooner had the Agency gotten underway than Ludlow expressed his strong doubts about the consumer's theory, warning Neale that the co-operative retail stores would become dangerous if allowed to challenge the primacy of co-operative production – that is, the primacy of the workshops. If for a moment the consumers lost sight of their idealistic goals, they might find it to their advantage to exploit workingmen: let the co-operative spirit be once lost and the only motivation of 'selfish consumption' would be to obtain merchandise as cheaply as possible. With uncanny accuracy Ludlow predicted that when the middle man had finally been eliminated, as desired by the northern co-operators, 'the opposition of interests between producer and consumer would be exhibited in its nakedest form'.[23] Actually, the argument which developed from Neale's primary dedication to Consumers Co-operation was only one manifestation of a more fundamental disagreement. Soon after the establishment of the Agency the emphasis of Neale's socialist beliefs had notably shifted: influenced by his new acquaintances, he had become more Owenite than Christian Socialist.

Had the Co-operative Agency remained in its place as a wholesaling centre for the stores, Ludlow might have confined his objections to the realm of words alone. But the day that Neale mailed the circular letter to trade unions, Ludlow dug in his heels and brought an end to compromise. The Agency was clearly becoming a rival organisation which challenged all of his most cherished beliefs: Neale had deliberately avoided all reference to Christianity in the Agency's Constitution, he treated his employees autocratically and refused to share profits with them, he emphasised consumption over production, and as evidenced in the circular to trade unions, was intent upon duplicating the practical activities of the Society for Promoting Working Men's Associations. Feeling that there was no longer any place for indecision, Ludlow demanded (30 October 1851) that the Council of Promoters expel the officers of the Central Co-operative Agency. Failing in this he resigned from the Council in anguish, surrendering his position of leadership.[24]

Neale had won but there were no laurels given out. He wished the Movement to be inclusive and non-sectarian and consequently still sought support from all quarters; then Charles Kingsley suddenly came forward to present new obstacles to his plans. Kingsley was not at all opposed to expanding the practical activities of the Central Co-operative Agency but petulantly complained about some of Neale's new allies, particularly the journalists, Thornton Hunt, G. J. Holyoake, and G. A. Fleming. In a long consternating letter he denigrated these men as 'nomadic and irresponsible', and advised Neale to avoid their company. There was no mincing of words: Hunt was described as 'a narrow and ignorant twaddler', and Holyoake simply

> 'a blackguard. He glories in calling himself an atheist; and any man who does that must be either fool, knave, or both. His writings and manner are narrow, conceited, ignorant, currish and insolent. He has been imprisoned (wisely or not, no matter to us) for blasphemy under circumstances, which if you will read his own account of the case, were most disgraceful to him.'

'Our great desire,' Kingsley insisted, 'has been, to enlist men of landed property, capitalists, gentlemen of every sort, to help us with money, land, learning, and parliamentary influence.' Any alternate route, he warned, 'must end, not in comprehension but in division and anarchy'.[25]

Neale had become friendly with Thornton Hunt, the son of Leigh Hunt, whose politically radical newspaper, the *Leader*, was giving the Agency very favourable notice. The trouble began, however, when Hunt attempted to similarly accommodate Charles Kingsley, commending his example and quoting from his writings. Kingsley did not appreciate such attention. Other prominent contributors to the *Leader* included G. J. Holyoake, the Secularist, and George Henry Lewes; the latter, along with Thornton Hunt, was coming to be identified in London's inner circles as notoriously libertine.[26] 'Respectable people,' Kingsley complained to Neale, 'were naturally beginning to åsk how far I favoured bigamy and atheism,' and the upshot was that Kingsley exchanged hard words with Hunt whom he accused of 'insolent and ungentlemanlike effusion'.[27] It became apparent to Neale that with men of Kingsley's ilk for colleagues the Christian Socialist Movement was destined to remain very provincial indeed.

Ultimately, it was Holyoake who was the most seriously offended. Like Hunt, he had initially extended a hand of fellowship. Writing for the *Leader*, he repeatedly championed the Central Agency and in the fall of 1851 had expressed his enthusiasm even more actively by volunteering to act as the representative of the Agency on a tour of Scotland and the North of England. Neale accepted his offer but the connection was destined to end as abruptly as it had begun,[28] the fierce antagonism generated by Holyoake's well known opposition to Christianity being the main reason for the breach.[29] Oil and water would not mix, and Holyoake became the recipient of a spiteful letter (signed by Neale as well as by his colleagues) notifying him that it was felt 'desirable' to terminate his affiliation with the Agency due to the 'strong objection which many of our best friends and persons with whom we are publicly connected, feel to the opinions identified in popular apprehension with your name'.[30] Neale's signature on the letter doubtlessly delayed for years what ultimately became a close friendship between Holyoake and himself.

Charles Kingsley was not alone in his concern about the new friends Neale was collecting among labour journalists and unionists. Many of the Chartists still remained unconvinced that the only hope for labour's emancipation lay in the old paternalistic nostrums of the utopian socialists. They were alarmed by the evident attraction of the new labour unions to Co-operation, which they viewed as a major detraction from political action; and furthermore, Co-operation was now often preached in conjunction with Christianity, that most notorious of stumbling blocks in the path of labour's progress.[31] It was only fitting that Ernest Jones, the driving force of old-line Chartism in its declining years after 1848, should take up arms against this new threat. Jones was a deservedly popular leader: like Neale he was of upper class birth but had completely torn out his social roots to resettle them among the labouring classes, and had recently served a term in prison for political agitation on their behalf. The Christian Socialists were singled out by Jones as major opponents and it was Neale who first went out to meet him. A debate was carried on in the pages of Jones' own *Notes to the People* which revealed very serious differences of opinion.[32] It is of some historical significance that Karl Marx later claimed to have been the shadow force behind Jones as he pressed his literary attack against the panacea of Co-operation.[33]

Neale wrote to refute Jones with the calmly measured, temperate and paternalistic phrases which, when combined with a certain messianic flair, constitute the classical utopian socialists' position: he referred to the primary importance of social and economic as opposed to political reform, stressed voluntaryism ('the whole value of this principle depends upon its being *willingly* accepted'), and sang the old song about harmony between classes and the basically, good will of many rich and noble born. He even named philanthropic noblemen and cited charitable undertakings as evidence of this good will. Communism, he argued, involved a great principle, but inasmuch as it substituted *Law* for the voluntary 'utterance of *Love*', it was destined to produce in the end only 'a mass of atoms mechanically held together, by pressure from without – for conscience, the will of the majority – for the sense of duty, pains and penalties'.[34]

Cobbett had devastatingly denounced 'Villages of Co-operation' as 'parallelograms of paupers' and T. Sherwin spoke of them as communities of vassals, both cutting deeply into the heart of Owen's basically paternalistic, autocratically conservative views.[35] With no little justification, Ernest Jones similarly dissected Neale:

> 'I do not degrade the working-man to a mere pensioner of the rich and labour to a thing allowed to live on sufferance by the toleration of "noble-born" philanthropy . . . .Aye! Sir! despite your "philanthropic list of noblemen," – and your demoralizing charities.'[36]

Above everything else, Neale wished to unite all of the diverse men and movements seeking social reforms. Yet the Christian Socialists as a group had not only antagonised Chartists but had also earned the enmity of many like Holyoake and Hunt who had, at first, extended an ernest hand of fellowship. Neale's compulsions were such that he could not long tolerate such a condition. He soon determined to create a new organisation which would at once accommodate his own social ideals and those of his fellow Christian Socialists, while being catholic enough to include Owenites, secularists, and anyone else who cared to participate. He envisioned something on the order of a secularised version of the Society for Promoting Working Men's Associations; and the vision took a substantial form when in the spring of 1852 Neale founded the Co-operative League. The purpose of the body was largely educational, its activities centring about evening lecture-discussion sessions where papers could be read by members as well as other prominent co-operators and social theorists.[37]

The first evening meeting was held on 30 March, with Neale reading an address on the League's objectives. His search for that 'state of superior social arrangements under which it would be possible to feel to other men as to our brethren' had led him to the Christian Socialists. Now, under the spell of Owenite thought, he spoke of his quest for these arrangements as a search for the 'science of society' Obviously disillusioned with the sectarianism of his Christian Socialist coadjutors,

Neale explained to those present that the main purpose was to get men of *different* schools of co-operative doctrine to exchange their thoughts and feelings. This was why, the word 'League' had been selected for a title; he wanted it clearly understood that the organisation would in no way inhibit any individual's opinions. Those who participated would be united only by their common belief 'in the possibility of discovering a science of society'.[38]

Owenites were the League's most conspicuous supporters from the outset expressing enthusiasm for Neale's designs: Dr Henry Travis was present at the first meeting and favourably summarized the proceedings n a letter to Robert Owen.[39] During a later session Owen himself was to participate[40] and the roll call of his disciples frequently included such names as James E. 'Shepherd' Smith, James Rigby, G. A. Fleming, Henry A. Ivory and James Corse. In addition, there were in active attendance those former Owenites who were now prominent in the Christian Socialist Movement.[41] Many of the Christian Socialists, however, refused to affiliate themselves with the League; Ludlow would have nothing to do with it, and with Thornton Hunt listed as the League's Librarian, it was not hard to predict Kingsley's negative reaction. Years later Ludlow noted bluntly that 'although Neale did not see it the "Co-operative League" was simply the setting up of non-Christian as against Christian Socialism. It never did anything substantial, and vanished as soon as we were out of the way.'[42] But this judgment is too harsh: though the League was created in reaction to the exclusiveness of the Christian Socialists, Neale wanted the two organisations to work together and even suggested that the League and the Society should meet jointly.

Neale published a digest of the League's proceedings (the *Transactions of the Co-operative League . . .*)[43], established a library of useful reading material, and finally, as one of the organisation's most important functions, maintained direct communication with as many existing co-operative societies as possible. By 24 April, he had directed questionnaires to societies throughout England requesting detailed information on their membership, financial condition and educational activities.[44] In this effort Neale had an ulterior motive: he wanted information which would enable the League to evaluate accurately the nature and extent of practical co-operative enterprise in England. Data was scarce – much more had to be accumulated before Neale could make any sensible prescriptions for Co-operation's future.

To say that Co-operation in England in the 1850s lacked definition is to understate the situation. While it is true that the work of the

Equitable Pioneers had gained considerable attention, Rochdale was not viewed as the centre of a Co-operative Movement – indeed, no such centre existed, nor for that matter was there much of anything to be called a Movement. There was little concurrence on the vital question of what constituted 'true Co-operation': was it a matter solely of establishing home colonies? Would it include a manufacturing establishment owned by a small minority of its labourers and registered as a joint-stock company? Could the word Co-operation be applied to a store which looked no further than the accumulation of dividends for its members? Furthermore few men had any very accurate notion of the extent of Co-operation because spontaneity was at once its benefit and its bane. Local societies could germinate, flower temporarily, then wither and die in almost complete isolation with little more than a whisper of local publicity. Anyone could begin a co-operative venture but binding all of the separate efforts into a Movement was both the most important and most difficult undertaking. It was this latter objective which was the great underpinning purpose behind Neale's Co-operative League, indeed behind all of his endeavours.

He had begun the work of both the League and the Agency by mailing questionnaires to all kinds of associations of labourers; on the basis of the returns he was able with reasonable accuracy to assess the nature and extent of the Movement's progress. As his knowledge grew, his first step towards introducing uniformity was an extraordinarily successful effort to marshall all of the independent co-operative activities together under common operating procedures and constitutional rules, publishing under the auspices of the Co-operative Agency, 'Suggestions to Aid in the Formation of a Legal Constitution for Working Men's Associations', 'Rules for the Formation and Management of Co-operative Stores' and 'A Model Plan for a Set of Account Books'.[45] These publications were soon in great demand all over England, being read and used by trade unionists as well as co-operators.

At first it had looked as though the League was destined for success,[46] but like the Christian Socialist Movement it soon expired. Perhaps W. Henry Brown was correct in declaring that 'it fizzled out for lack of practical application', but whatever the reason for failure, the League, like so very many similar organisations, was less important in its own right than in its function as a stimulant.[47] Surely its effect on Neale was invaluable: it brought him into a close working contact with some of the most charismatic leaders involved in the origin and spread of both French and English Socialism,[48] and the topics discussed at meetings and dutifully reported by Neale as editor of the *Transactions* served to enhance his understanding of the matters then closest to the minds of labouring men and which would remain popular in the Mechanics Institutes throughout England for some time afterwards. In his work with the League Neale took a last refreshing drink from the fountain of utopian idealism characterising an era which had almost slipped by; he carried this draught of idealism to a generation of co-operators who, because of their smug Victorian self-satisfaction and social indifference, sorely needed it.

If the League died from having little practical application this was surely not the case with the Society for Promoting Working Men's Associations which took on too much work, losing its balance through overactivity. In January 1852, the great Engineer's lockout began and maximised the zealous efforts of Neale and the Christian Socialists to convert trade unionists.[49] From its outset the most fascinating aspect of the conflict turned about the working engineers' enthusiasm for co-operative production, which they attempted to transform into a weapon against their employers – if the latter wouldn't negotiate, they threatened to set up workshops of their own; the Amalgamated Society's Executive Committee voting to put aside £10,000 for this purpose.[50] This decision and its subsequent ratification by an overwhelming majority of the Society's branches was a lure which irresistibly attracted Neale: he rushed to defend the engineers in a public lecture, its title restating the question asked by Sidney Smith and the Central Association of Employers, 'May I Not Do What I Will With My Own?'

Supporting the working engineers without equivocation, Neale's answer to Smith's well-publicised query was an emphatic 'no'; but nevertheless it was evident that he was less interested in popularising the Amalgamated Society's cause than in reinforcing its recent decision to establish self-governing workshops. Declaring Co-operation to be the 'true solution' to the crisis, he reminded labourers that trade unionism, in itself, involved no socially regenerative ideal and advised them to preserve it only for the purpose of promoting co-operative associations and for securing the social benefits of insurance against sickness and death. This was small fare indeed to offer a labour union in the midst of a strike, fighting desperately for its life. But Neale was very concerned that the unions represented only a narrow aristocracy among labouring men, feeling strongly that their restrictive practices tended to lower the status of the working population as a whole by keeping the unskilled from bettering their position.[51] Like Marx, he condemned the labour unions for conforming to 'individualist' principles and wanted, above all, to encourage their leaders to mould them anew into engines of social transformation.[52]

Neale's hope that the workers would turn toward Co-operation was temporarily realised, and he could credit himself in having abetted their turning. But the final result was disappointing for labour union resolutions and the personal involvement of labour's leaders did not make up for the lack of funds. The new enthusiasm for Co-operation was quickly disspelled. Unfortunately Neale had built castles in the air on the basis of trade unionism's periodically recurring and always temporary flirtation with co-operative production, and it was in so doing that he took his most severe financial losses.

He was now a man of action as well as words, even as he enjoined meeting after meeting of workingmen to establish self-governing shops, he lavishly invested his personal fortune in such undertakings. They all failed disastrously. Neale's greatest single loss came about as the result of his purchase of the Atlas Works for use by the Amalgamated Society of Engineers: the skilled labouring men soon proved their inability to operate it economically, but he refused to abandon faith in them, with dogged determination maintaining the factory as it went steadily deeper into debt until finally the sale of everything – factory, tools and stock – was not sufficient to discharge the association's financial obligations.[53]

At the peak of the enthusiasm for converting trade unionists, anything had seemed possible. Anticipating a substantial increase in the demand for co-operative products once the unions were sponsoring a myriad of workshops and stores, Neale had greatly expanded the facilities of the Central Co-operative Agency. But the failures like those of the iron works soon testified to the incompatibility of the marriage of trade unionism and Co-operation. The Agency, over-extended and running ever more deeply in the red, was finally forced to close its doors in 1857. Neale had had reservations about labour unions *per se*, even as he drew them toward his co-operative schemes in 1852; by the decade's end, in disillusionment, he was ready to forget them entirely.

'If the faith was all that we held it to be,' Thomas Hughes distressingly wrote to Lord Goderich in October 1855, 'not even our clumsy proclaiming of it and our astonishing differences in general beliefs could have made such a hash as we did of a good deal of our work.'[54] The collapse of the Atlas Works had been symptomatic. One by one the workshops established by the Society for Promoting Working Men's Associations had flickered out of existence – each failure cutting away at the optimism of the Christian Socialists while taking an additional portion of Neale's dwindling wealth. A few associations, most notably the original Working Tailors, were to linger on for a few more years but the spirit of the Christian Socialist Movement was dead. The failure of the workshops should not be overstressed, however, as the most important single reason for the Movement's dissolution stemmed from the perpetual disagreement between the promoters themselves. Ludlow and Neale were unable to agree on basic principles while Maurice and Kingsley had hesitated at every step taken to the cadence of practical co-operative work. Indeed, as regards the great questions then agitating the Labour Movement, it appeared that each of the Christian Socialists sought after a different end. Finally Maurice was able to sidetrack his colleagues into education with the creation of the Working Men's College of London in 1854, which undertaking was destined to be the most lasting of their practical efforts.[55]

> It is the special characteristic of what we call co-operation to make of the principle of union in itself the motive for uniting — to unite, not for the sake of carrying out some particular work, but from the belief that the evils of society generally spring from disunion, and that the only means of effecting a radical cure of them is to substitute universally the unity and concord of reasonable action for the antagonism of competitive struggles.
>
> E. V. Neale, 1878[56]

Neale had come to believe that unity, harmony and love were the principles that must determine man's social relationships. During the Christian Socialist period, despite many shortcomings and failures, he worked out a practical mechanics for implementing these principles and in so doing laid the foundation for the modern Co-operative Movement. Even when Neale created controversial and very divisive bodies such as the Agency and the League, his underlying purpose was to counteract, and thereby resolve, the disharmony occasioned by the exclusiveness of his colleagues, especially their narrow emphasis on co-operative production and Christian sectarianism. Above all else he devoted himself to the cause of co-operative union.

The wholesaling agency in London represented Neale's most conspicuous achievement during these years and consequently has been emphasised by historians to the point of obscuring the fact that most of his energies were directed towards a much higher end. Neale had quickly come to believe that the Movement could never be effective

without having some sort of strong federal organisation at its head
providing unity and a clear sense of direction for the individual
associations. As early as September 1850, a trip to Paris to visit the
associations ouvriers had confirmed his suspicions that socialist ideals
could not long survive the continued multiplication of isolated
self-governing workshops; he found that several of the Parisian
associations were actually competing with one another.[57] Upon
returning to London, Neale unsuccessfully tried to convince the
Christian Socialists of the need to centralise more effectively their own
efforts, submitting plans for the establishment of a powerful organ
which he proposed to call the Co-operative Labour Union; significantly,
it was in delimiting the functions of this body that he first speculatively
anticipated the future extension of Co-operation into the areas of
retailing, wholesaling, banking and insurance.[58]

Though temporarily put off by his friends, Neale did not abandon
his designs for a central union; having awaited only the proper
opportunity, he revivified the idea after the Christian Socialists
launched the first in a series of national conferences in the summer of
1852. He eagerly concluded that the conference, meeting annually,
could serve as an effective nucleus for a national federation of
co-operative societies and created the necessary apparatus to accomplish this end in the form of a new body to be known as the Industrial
and Provident Societies Union.[59] It was a broadly extended version of
the old Co-operative Labour Union, yet this time his colleagues proved
receptive: the passage of Ludlow's Industrial and Provident Societies
Act (which finally legalised co-operatives) had made it necessary
thoroughly to overhaul the constitutional machinery of the Christian
Socialist Movement, with the result that the Society for Promoting
Working Men's Associations was abandoned in March 1853, its place
being taken by two completely separate organisations, the Association
for Promoting Industrial and Provident Societies, and Neale's new
Union.[60]

This development represented the ultimate victory for Neale. The
Union assumed responsibility for all practical co-operative work,
becoming, in effect, the new focal point of administrative power within
the Christian Socialist Movement. His plans had been carefully made in
the hope that the future would indeed see the organisation become a
federal centre for all the associations in England. The Union was
burdened with no limiting references to religion and the constitution
specifically provided that it was to be governed by the National
Conference and its democratically appointed Executive.[61]

Neale's 'genius of constructiveness' was never more in evidence than in the period immediately following the passage of the Industrial and Provident Societies Act of 1852. His directives were making an impact in every area of co-operative endeavour; and in contrast to the confusion prevailing in the Movement as a whole, most of Neale's efforts could with facility be woven into one consistent pattern for national co-operative unity. He had a roadmap for the Movement which he followed with dogged consistency despite a few necessary detours: what is most intriguing is the extent to which Co-operation, in evolving its modern federal administrative structure, utilised the routes which he prescribed. At the peak of his power when the second Conference opened in Manchester in 1853, Neale was appointed Chairman and delivered an opening address described by one historian as Neale's 'Manifesto'.[62] Speaking optimistically, if prematurely, as though the conference delegates did indeed already constitute the executive organ of a thriving Industrial and Provident Societies Union, for the first time in a major public address Neale mapped the trail he expected them to blaze on their way towards the co-operative millenium. As previously mentioned, since 1850 Neale had thought the co-operative store to be the easiest first step along the way. The next step, he explained, was to combine the stores into centres of supply, that is, wholesale centres such as the Central Co-operative Agency. The preceding steps having assured a stable market, co-operative workshops would follow and lastly, the fourth step would be to 'institute among these productive institutions a system of exchange of labour, founded upon principles of strict justice'.[63] Although Neale did not on this occasion elaborate upon it, the productive institutions constituted in his opinion the ante-chamber to the ultimate in socialist theory, the utopian community.

The fundamental contribution made by the short series of Christian Socialist conferences has been singularly neglected. Working through these national meetings, Neale for the first time furnished English co-operators with all of the basic administrative and functional components necessary for the creation of a powerful movement: he directly inspired Rochdale's Pioneers to establish a Wholesale Department; initiated a banking society (the Co-operative Freehold Land, Building and Investment Society); began publication of a newspaper (the *Co-operative Commercial Circular*); and in the Industrial and Provident Societies Union, with the Conference itself at its head, provided a central headquarters.[64] Co-operators had only to take these tools in hand and the modern Co-operative Movement could have been launched by the mid-1850s. But Neale's efforts, however prescient, were premature – the times were not yet right.

In the summer of 1854 Neale was President of the Conference when it met in Leeds. It was the undisputed central co-operative organisation, with the field cleared of rivals, meeting in a town exceedingly well located to draw support – yet it was poorly attended and significantly the largest block of those present was from London. Most discouraging, some time prior to the Session, Neale's scheme for the Industrial and Provident Societies Union had been scuttled. Abandoning their resolute design to unify all practical co-operative work by creating one common administrative centre, the delegates at Leeds settled instead for a union based on the mere affirmation of a set of moral platitudes accompanied by a pledge to carry them forward by the method of lectures and publication.[65] Indeed, even this watered down version of central union was too strong medicine for some co-operators: the Conference Executive found themselves forced to plead that in proposing unity they had no intention of fettering either the 'individual liberty' of the societies or subordinating their individual interests 'to those of a majority'; nor did they 'wish to see a mere pretence of union when the spirit of union is not present'.[66]

Thus Neale's hopes were dashed to pieces on the rocks of self-interest. Most of his other efforts proved equally abortive: the Investment Society was strangled for lack of financial support, and the *Co-operative Commercial Circular* was also short-lived; though the latter remains an exceedingly rare and valuable publication as Co-operation's only organ from 1853–55, its demise leaving a vacuum which was not filled until 1860 when the *Co-operator* was born.[67] The lucrative work of wholesaling, however, proved an exception to the rule of failure. Neale successfully prodded Rochdale's Pioneers into functioning as wholesale agents for the North of England; and as a result the Pioneers' Society opened the special Wholesale Department which ultimately proved to be the direct forerunner of the modern Co-operative Wholesale Society, the great CWS.[68]

Had Neale given up the work in 1854, his contributions should still have been of sufficient importance to merit his inclusion among the founders of the British Co-operative Movement.

Notes

1. The best general account of the Christian Socialist Movement is Torben Christensen's *Origin and History of Christian Socialism*

1848–54 (Aarhus, 1962); but C. E. Raven's *Christian Socialism, 1848–1854* (London, 1920) is still indispensable.

2. See N. C. Masterman, *John Malcolm Ludlow; The Builder of Christian Socialism* (Cambridge, 1963).

3. For an excellent short account of the complex relationship between Maurice and Ludlow, see Peter R. Allen, 'F. D. Maurice and J. M. Ludlow: A Reassessment of the Leaders of Christian Socialism,' *Victorian Studies*, XI (1968), 461–482.

4. Contrary to common belief, Ludlow never envisioned the self-governing workshop as an end in itself. Like Neale, he was more influenced by Fourier than by Benjamin Buchez or Louis Blanc. See Ludlow's Autobiography, Ch. XXII, pp.425–426; XXIII, p.444. Ludlow MSS, University Library, Cambridge, MS Add. 7348, Box 1. Page numbers in the Autobiography are approximate due to confusion in pagination.

5. The entire Constitution is conveniently reprinted in G. D. H. Cole and A. W. Filson, *British Working Class Movements, Select Documents, 1789–1875* (London, 1951), pp.434–443.

6. John Malcolm Ludlow, 'Some of the Christian Socialists of 1848 and the Following Years,' *The Economic Review*, IV (1894), 34.

7. *Ibid.*

8. Pitman, *op.cit.*, p.6.

9. Masterman, *op.cit.*, p.114.

10. Journal, p.174.

11. E. V. Neale to Richard T. Ely, 29 November 1882. Richard T. Ely Papers, Wisconsin Historical Society, Madison.

12. Ludlow, Autobiography, XXVIII, pp.511–512.

13. See Ludlow to Neale, 10 December 1851. Neale Papers.

14. E. P. Thompson, *op.cit.*, p.783.

15. Neale to Ely, *op.cit.*

16. Ludlow to Neale, 23 July 1850. Neale Papers. Ludlow, Autobiography, Ch. XXI, p.421.

17. The best single source for information and documents relating to the Central Co-operative Agency is Jules Lechevalier St. André, *Five Years in the Land of Refuge; a Letter on the Prospects of Co-operative Associations in England; Addressed to the Members of Council of the Late Society for Promoting Working Men's Associations, Now Re-Constituted Under the Title the 'Association for Promoting Industrial Provident Societies'*, (London, 1854). See esp. pp.19–21 and Appendix, pp.57–59. Many of the documents in this volume, separately published, are available at Goldsmith's Library, University of London.

18. *The Christian Socialist*, II (1851), 325. *The Leader*, II (1851), 158.

19. *The Northern Star and National Trades' Journal*, XIV (1851), 4.

20. Christensen, *op.cit.*, p.250.

21. 'Address and Proposals of the Central Co-operative Agency to the Trade Societies in London and the United Kingdom,' *Christian Socialist*, II (1851), 310–312.

22. *Ibid.*, p.312.

23. John Ludlow, 'Working Associations and Co-operative Stores,' *Christian Socialist*, I (1851), 241–242. Neale responded to Ludlow and a controversy ensued, see pp.261–263; 265–266; 273–275.

24. See Ludlow to Neale, 10 December 1851. Neale Papers. This lengthy letter is extremely valuable as it candidly discusses the conflict between the two men and reveals the depth of Ludlow's bitterness. Relating to the controversy, Neale also received letters from Charles Kingsley (15 November 1851) and Charles B. Mansfield (5 November 1851). Neale Papers. Mansfield agreed with Ludlow while Kingsley supported Neale.

25. Kingsley to Neale, 25 October 1851. Neale Papers.

26. Lewes later became the common law husband of George Eliot. For background material consult Joan Bennett, *George Eliot, Her Mind and Her Art*, (Cambridge, 1962); also Gordon S. Haight, *George Eliot and John Chapman* (New Haven, 1940).

27. Kingsley to Neale, 15 November 1851. Neale Papers.

28. The most important communications related to the incident are as follows: Lechevalier to Holyoake, 5 September 1851. Letter introducing Holyoake as the agent of the Central Co-operative Agency, 5 September 1851. Holyoake, 'Report . . . to Messrs Lechevalier, Woodin, Jones', 9 December 1851. Lechevalier, Woodin, Neale, Hughes to Holyoake, 10 December 1851. These letters are from the George Jacob Holyoake Papers, Library of the Co-operative Union Limited, Manchester, Lancs.

29. Though Holyoake supported the Agency, he disliked Christian Socialism and hated Lloyd Jones. See e.g. *The Reasoner and Theological Examiner*, X (1851), 265–266; 331–332.

30. Lechevalier, Woodin, Neale, Hughes to Holyoake, 10 December 1851. Holyoake Papers.

31. For example, in May 1851, the *Leader* published with apparent approval 'a note by Walter Cooper (a Chartist turned Christian Socialist) which was very unsettling in its implications: 'Frederick Maurice and Robert Owen have shaken hands, the *Christian Socialist*, the *Edinburgh Review*, and the *Leader* have all joined in the discussion; the Chartists have become Socialists, and Poor-law guardians throughout the country are groping their way to the divine principle of concert – which shall make the rich and poor partners without violence or spoilation.' The *Leader*, II (1851), 465.

32. See especially *Notes to the People*, I (1851), 27–31; 407–411; 470–476; 543–546; 561–566; 588; 606–609.

33. John Saville, *Ernest Jones: Chartist* (London, 1952), p.42.

34. *Notes to the People*, I, 562–564.

35. E. P. Thompson, *op.cit.*, pp.782–783.

36. *Notes to the People*, I, 588. See also, John Ludlow, 'Mr Ernest Jones and Co-operation', *Christian Socialist*, II (1851), 339–340, 354–356, 401–403; 'The Padiham Discussion on Co-operation', *Christian Socialist*, II (1851), 385–393. Ironically, in later years Jones advocated Co-operation, see e.g., *The Co-operator*, IX

(1869), 50, and *The Social Economist*, III (1869), 1–3.

37. Raven, *op.cit.*, pp.273–274.

38. 'Preface' to the *Transactions of the Co-operative League, formed March 1852, to Promote the Scientific Investigation of the Principles of Co-operative Action, With a View to their Application to Practice*, (1852), Pt. I, pp.5–9. The quotation is from p.6. See also p.16.

39. Henry Travis to Robert Owen, April 1852. Bundle 29, #2028, Owen Collection, Library of the Co-operative Union Limited, Manchester, Lancs.

40. *Transactions* (1852), Pt. III, pp.76–87.

41. Namely, Lloyd Jones, Walter Cooper, Cuthbert Ellison, Thomas Shorter and Lord Goderich.

42. Ludlow to E. R. A. Seligman, 24 July 1886. Seligman Collection, Columbia University Library. Ludlow maintained that most of the Christian Socialist Promoters viewed the League as a rival organization, see his Autobiography, Appendix to Ch. XXXVII, 'The Co-operative League'.

43. The *Transactions* was published in 1852 in three Parts: Pt. I in May; Pt. II in July; Pt. III in October.

44. *Transactions* (1852), Pt. I, pp.14–15.

45. Christensen, *op.cit.*, p.284.

46. *Transactions* (1852), Pt. II, pp.44–45. In the summer of 1852 a plan was submitted for the establishment of new branches.

47. W. Henry Brown, *A Century of London Co-operation* (London, 1928), p.81.

48. Men such as Louis Blanc, Etienne Cabet and Pierre Leroux. See *Transactions* (1852), Pt. I, Appendix, p.57. The format of the *Transactions* included an elaborate appendix devoted to foreign co-operation. See also Louis Blanc to Neale, 17 May 1852, and two other undated letters from Blanc, in the Neale Papers. The above citations specifically refer to plans by French socialists to publish two periodicals to support themselves while in exile.

49. One of the most interesting contemporary accounts of this famous lock-out is John Ludlow's *The Master Engineers and Their Workmen. Three Lectures on the Relations of Capital and Labour, Delivered by Request of The Society for Promoting Working Men's Associations* (London, 1852).

50. E. V. Neale, *May I Not Do What I Will With My Own? Considerations on the Present Contest Between the Operative Engineers and Their Employers* (London, 1852), p.53. The Engineers' enthusiasm for Co-operation grew even stronger as they failed in the struggle against their employers; see *Journal of Association*, No. 20 (10 May 1852), 153. In June 1852, the ASE officially became 'a society for the promotion of co-operation in the iron trades', Christensen, *op.cit.*, p.268.

51. Neale, *May I Not Do What I Will With My Own?*, See esp., pp.14, 35, 46–48, 51, 53.

52. However, unlike Marx, he opposed political action. *Ibid.*, p.28. See

also *Journal of Association*, No.20 (10 May 1852), 159.

53. Raven, *op.cit.*, pp.252–255, 309–310; Thomas Hughes, 'Edward Vansittart Neale as a Christian Socialist', *The Economic Review*, III (1893), 47–48. For Neale's view of the failure of the iron works, see Benjamin Jones, *Co-operative Production* (Oxford, 1894), pp.134–135. As late as 1856, Neale was still working with the ASE promoting co-operative workshops, but at this time even the idealists scoffed. James Rigby wrote to Robert Owen, 7 April 1856: 'The Amalgamated Engineers are going to try their hands at "Saving the World" by making Capital and Labour *unite* in an Engineering Establishment. I expect they will gain some experience at the loss of a few *thousands* of "*Yellow Canary Birds.*" Well! it is after all the *least injurious* way of spending the "Tin". The name of the firm is "Phoenix Iron Works Company" – Neale is preparing the rules and as soon as they are printed I will send you a copy.' Owen Collection, #2741.

54. Edward C. Mack and W. H. G. Armytage, *Thomas Hughes; The Life of the Author of Tom Brown's Schooldays* (London, 1952), p.72.

55. See J. F. C. Harrison, *A History of the Working Men's College, 1854–1954* (London, 1954), passim.

56. E. V. Neale, *The 'Co-operative News' and Why Co-operators Should Support It* (Manchester, 1878), p.4.

57. Raven, *op.cit.*, p.260.

58. E. V. Neale, *Memoir Relating to the Position and Prospects of the Associations* (London, 1850), 11 pp.; reprinted in Lechevalier St. André, *op.cit.*, Appendix, pp.59–66. See also, *Scheme for Formation of the Working Associations into a General Union* (London, n.d.), 15 pp. The latter appears to have been published in 1851.

59. *The First Report of the Society for Promoting Working Men's Associations – To Which is Added a Report of the Co-operative Conference, held in London, at the Society's Hall . . . on the 26th and 27th of July 1852* (London, 1852), Appendix, pp.72ff. Christensen, *op.cit.*, pp.329–330.

60. Christensen, *op.cit.*, p. 326ff.

61. See esp. 'Plan for an Industrial and Provident Societies Union', *Report of the [2nd] Co-operative Conference Held at Manchester . . . 1853* (London, 1853), pp.52–62. The Constitutions for both the Association for Promoting Industrial and Provident Societies and The Industrial and Provident Societies Union are reprinted in Lechevalier St. André, *op.cit.*, Appendix, pp.67–82.

62. Christensen, *op.cit.*, p.335. 'Prefatory Address of the Executive Committee Appointed by the Conference', *Report of the [2nd] Co-operative Conference Held at Manchester . . . 1853*, pp.3–7.

63. *Ibid.*, p.6.

64. For information on origin and development of the Co-operative Freehold Land, Building and Investment Society consult: *Christian Socialist*, I (1851), 77; *The Operative*, No.72 (15 May, 1852), 438–439; *Journal of Association*, No.27 (28 June, 1852),

215–216; *Report of the [2nd] Co-operative Conference . . . 1853*, pp.63–67; *Co-operative Commercial Circular*, No.11 (1 Sept., 1854), 73, 80.

65. *Co-operative Commercial Circular*, No.10 (1 August 1854), 65–66; No.11 (1 September 1854), 79–80.
66. *Ibid.*, No.11 (1 September 1854), 78.
67. The *Circular* is available at University of London as well as at the Co-operative College in Loughborough, Leics.
68. In 1851, Neale's Agency made the initial contacts which led the Pioneers into the field of wholesaling. See e.g., G. D. H. Cole, *A Century of Co-operation* (London, 1944), p.129ff.; Lloyd Jones, 'Who Suggested the Plan of the Wholesale?', *Co-operative News*, VIII (1877), 297. See also *Co-operative Commercial Circular*, No.6 (1 April 1854), 36–37; No.11 (1 September 1854), 78; No.12 (1 October 1854), 84–85; No.16 (1 February 1855), 113–114; No.17 (11 March 1855), 125–126.

III

REFLECTION AND RENEWAL

> The men of sentiment are the architects; the practical
> men are the masons, and brick-layers, and hodmen. Who
> is the world indebted to for its noble structure of society
> but the 'theorists'? The man who first proposed to lift
> man out of his primitive condition was a theorist,
> because he proposed something different from the then
> condition of man and his surroundings.
>
> Abraham Greenwood, 1887

The years following the collapse of the Christian Socialist Movement
were most certainly hard ones. Frances Neale had never been very
understanding about the calling of her husband's social conscience; now
he had become improvident with money, spending it recklessly in
co-operative ventures. By itself, the lack of communication between
them was a bearable burden, but to see the heritage of generations
incautiously wasted must have been a hard trial for a proper
gentlewoman and Victorian wife. After losing their large house in the
West End the Neales were forced to move to a more modest residence;[1]
finally Allesley itself, the old family estate in Warwickshire, had to be
sold to meet the hunger of creditors. Of this necessity, years later,
Neale's daughter-in-law Florence wrote:

> ' . . . he, with his son's consent (as it was entailed) sold Allesley near
> Coventry. The only things that he brought from Allesley were the
> portrait of Oliver Cromwell . . . now hanging in the dining room and
> some lace.'[2]

Perhaps it will never be known exactly how much money Neale
expended in these early co-operative efforts. Thomas Hughes once
informed Edward Owen Greening that the loss must be somewhere in
the vicinity of £60,000 and Greening was importune enough actually to
publish this figure in the *Agricultural Economist*. But Neale was quick
to deny it in a subsequent issue of the same periodical, and continued
to do so when the subject arose, in much the same words, for the rest
of his days:

> 'I am ashamed to own that I have no accurate record of the loss, but
> I do not estimate it at more than £40,000 [not gifts, Neale pointed

out, but investments at 5%] . . . I crippled myself without doing permanent good to anyone. But this I cannot regard as commendable. The only praiseworthy part in the transaction, in my judgment, is: (1) That I was willing to incur the risk of loss from the desire to promote a great cause; (2) That the success of these trials did not discourage me from continuing to work for that cause.'[3]

This unconscionable extravagance, more than his social radicalism, strongly alienated him from his family, for a certain amount of paternalistic eccentricity might be expected from a gentleman, especially a nephew of William Wilberforce – even Lord Shaftesbury had for a time worked with the Christian Socialists to establish an association of needlewomen. Until Neale's great losses became evident, he had managed to bring his friend and cousin, A. A. Vansittart, to support Co-operation, and as for the Wilberforce connection, cousin Samuel, the future Bishop of Oxford (singularly known for his ludicrous arguments against Darwinism) went so far as to buy himself a suit of clothes from the Working Tailors Association.[4]

Neale's own special pleading for £40,000 rather than £60,000 as the total cost of his failures bears some analysis; friends in the Co-operative Movement pointed to his losses with pride; his family thought them to represent the height of imbecility – he must have sided with the latter as it is not hard to find undertones of self-contempt in his statements on the question.[5] Moreover, the family tradition hints that Neale's method of obtaining the necessary money was much less than judicious. 'I always understood,' one of his great-granddaughters wrote, 'he used some of his clients' cash with which he was entrusted, and to pay *that* back was why he went to live in a small house at Hampstead and West Wickham.'[6] If this was true, it might explain Neale's refusal to take pride in the great sacrifice which more than anything else gained him fame as a philanthropist, as well as shed some light on the willingness of his son to alienate Allesley.

It is certainly paradoxical to discover in this lonely enigmatic man so gifted with organisational genius and analytical intelligence an exceptional inability either to judge other men's characters or to deal wisely with his own money. He had a complete faith in mankind and trusted individuals to a degree which particularly alarmed his family. On at least one occasion his trust was rewarded by fraud and theft, and generally his greatest and most spectacular failures can be related in one way or another to a misplaced faith in someone else's intelligence or good intentions. He sincerely attempted to follow the Biblical injunction (which he perpetually quoted in his published works) to become 'as little children' full of faithful trust, hope and love.

On 2 April 1860, Edward Vansittart Neale was fifty years old, not as sure of himself as a leader of men or as a manipulator of money, and about to enter an intensely introspective and intellectually active period of his life, characterised by renewed attention to religion and philosophy. The 'naturally impatient, self-relying, rather scornful worker of 1849, fond of short cuts, and subtle ways of baffling difficulties and defeating opponents',[7] had mellowed as had his native land – he into the philosophical reflections and re-evaluations of late middle age, England into the comparative ease of mid-century. Many Englishmen now smugly affirmed their belief in the dogmas of capitalism, individualism and self-help, which they credited with having turned their small island into the world's workshop and richest nation. Prosperity in the 1850s appeared to validate the negative rigours of classical economy, generating social indifference: perhaps those who remained in squalor were indeed inferior human beings; if so, men who sought to relieve their suffering were running a fool's errand indeed. The failure of the Christian Socialist workshops had lent credence to the arguments of those who labelled all such efforts utopian and unrealistic.

In such an atmosphere, if only to reassure himself, Neale felt compelled to systematise thoroughly his basic beliefs; above all, it was necessary to convince the new complacently sceptical generation that the organisation of society under capitalism was immoral, and thus vindicate the old yet valid prescription for a thoroughgoing social transformation.

Neale still sought to build the foundation for his socialist beliefs out of the substance of philosophy and religion. In 1863 he published a lengthy treatise entitled *The Analogy of Thought and Nature*, which stands as the most ambitious declaration of his Christian Socialist views. Underlying the effort was Neale's basic determination to demonstrate the universal relevance of the practical work of Association; and when finally completed, the book constituted an elaborate metaphysical exposition in support of Co-operation. The *Analogy* was manifestly Hegelian: 'There is a law of thought,' Neale wrote, 'a law brought to light by Hegel; and by means of this law it seems possible to penetrate into the mysteries of existence, to an extent quite impractical without its aid.'[8] He followed the German philosopher in describing thought as a dialectical process whereby the logical subject progressively unfolds itself into its own objects.[9] The action was constructive, he stated, and

involved the continued evolution of unity out of combinations of
opposites; it was a process whereby the internally contradictory
potentialities of all things resolve themselves into higher unities.

Neale wrote his philosophical treatise to explicate the relationship
between human thought (which he investigated chiefly by means of
introspection and a study of history) and the universe, or 'Nature'. He
interpreted Hegel as asserting that a single law applied to both – that
there was no essential distinction between human thought and the
ultimate thought, or force, out of which the universe itself had arisen.
Neale took issue with this insofar as he himself believed that the
relationship between man's thought and Nature could only be
understood as an analogy: he felt that the laws of thought were to
human understanding what the order of the universe was to God's
understanding. 'From our own faculty of thought and the properties
involved in its exercise,' he explained, 'we may be legitimately entitled
to infer the character of the power whose action we perceive in the
universe.'[10]

If the law of thought could be validated by personal introspection
and a study of history, Neale looked to the natural sciences to support
his contention that there was an analogous principle operative in the
physical universe and, perhaps begging the question, found precisely
what he was searching for – a universal tendency in nature for unities
to emerge out of myriads of warring forces: 'All science, points to the
thought that *bodies are produced by the realisation of ideal judgments*,
that is, by the combination of opposite movements or directions of
force into indivisible unities.'[11]

Working from this premise Neale sought to explain the ultimate
meaning behind all of reality, from 'warring atoms' to the social
institutions which he wished to construct 'in accordance with the
Divine law – the law of Love'.[12] It was this divine law of love that
became the central theme of his metaphysics:

> 'According to the definition of the nature of thought . . . it is a will
> whose essential character is, to pass out of itself in order to realise its
> own energies; transforming itself into its object, and identifying
> itself with its work. Now, what is this definition but a metaphysical
> description of love? The law of thought then, is one with the
> manifestation of unselfish action . . . . Now, if the *essence* of
> *thought* be a principle of *love*, its *opposite* must be a principle of
> *selfishness*.'[13]

The material world could be understood in terms of the same force. 'In the elemental atom,' Neale explained, 'the selfish principle is at its maximum. Each atom exists by asserting its individual nature against all others, with which it is brought into accordance only through the adjustment of conflicting forces, produced by a wisdom external to itself.'[14] What was this external wisdom that Neale would introduce, almost as a kind of *deus ex machina*, to explain the workings of the universe? A divine being whose essence was Loving Will, the 'Logos' of the Christian Scriptures.

Although Neale's writing style is almost absurdly complicated, the meaning of his philosophical construction makes its way gradually into the reader's understanding. He indicates the way toward ultimate harmony throughout the entire universe by a process of perpetual self-transcendence: individual atoms, competing elements, opposing energies brought first into being and then into harmony by the ideal judgments of a divine will; human history with its competing cultures full of divergent social streams each making its individual and distinctive yet divinely calculated contribution to future unity; the whole creation, from the physical architecture of the natural elements to the social architecture of human events, bonded into one great unity by God's love.

Perhaps *The Analogy of Thought and Nature* is more important as an aid to understanding the theoretical basis of Neale's unique variety of Christian or (to use a better term) theistic socialism, than as a contribution to scholarship in its own right. It underlines Neale's primary dependence upon Hegelian thought, while affording added insight into his obsessive belief in co-operative union. But this should not deter us from concluding that he was an able student in his day of both science and logic. If the work was abstruse and sometimes mystifying, this merely reflects those same characteristics in Hegel himself. Even Karl Marx's early explications of Hegelian philosophy in the working out of dialectical materialism are exceptionally difficult to read and subject to differing interpretations.

The *Analogy* failed to stimulate Neale's contemporaries in the way he intended because he was a generation too late: the Englishmen he wished to persuade no longer had the inclination to deal in metaphysics. One of those who reviewed the book well summarised the popular attitude of the times by restating the pungent lines from Mr Punch's metaphysical catechism as a part of his critique:

'What is Mind? No matter.
What is Matter? Never mind.'[15]

It remains one of Neale's failures that he never wrote the major works in explanation of his socialist views which should have logically followed *The Analogy of Thought and Nature*.[16] Yet, to one familiar with his life's work as an organiser and propagandist it is clear that he did indeed pioneer unique routes for social advance, through trial and error gradually extricating those portions of other men's philosophies which had proven successful in practise, and welding them into new ideological formulae for achieving socialism through the medium of the Co-operative Movement.

In the Central Agency and Co-operative League Neale developed a close working relationship with Owenites and was strongly influenced by their opinions; however, after the collapse of the Christian Socialist Movement, he had become disillusioned with their spirit of benevolent but often heavy handed paternalism. His own behaviour as a Christian Socialist, motivated by a similar spirit, had generated much antagonism: though sincerely charitable by intention he severely undercut John Ludlow's self-confidence, permanently impairing the latter's capability as a leader; stubbornly uncompromising and sometimes scornful he had occasionally used his money to manipulate his colleagues. When, in later years, Neale wrote critically about Robert Owen it is very probable that he was painfully aware of the authoritarian angularities in his own personality and was indirectly seeking to chasten himself:

> 'I do not question the benevolence of Robert Owen, who deserves unfeigned respect for the purity of his motives, and the fearlessness of his honesty. But there are no worse law makers than men of uncompromising benevolence, except men of uncompromising piety. Law rests on justice . . . .
>
> Mount your benevolent man on the high horse of law, and he will complacently trample on other men's wishes, "all for their good." Mr. Robert Owen was one of the most benevolent of men; but a more unmitigated *tyranny* can scarcely be conceived than his "New Moral World" would have been if it could have been realised. Benevolence is the salt of society; without the salt society loses its savour: but it does not follow that men could live on salt only.'[17]

Evidencing much the same spirit, in the spring of 1860 Neale wrote to Stephen Hawkey (the mentor of St. Mark's, an innovating parochial school in Windsor to which he had recently contributed some money) and warned him against trying to awaken students simply by giving commands.

'Man can be truly educated only by *simultaneously* awakening his intellect *and* his affections: and each of these processes must be conducted according to *its own law*. You cannot awaken the intellect by cramming it; to awaken it you must make men *think for themselves*: they must go through the tough work of overcoming difficulties and understanding (*standing under and dissecting*) their own thoughts. You cannot awaken their affections by commanding them, to awaken them you must exhibit *love in action*: you must make men feel that you love them, by *sympathising* with them . . . taking an interest in their wishes; not *requiring* that they should take an interest in yours.'[18]

These lines reflect Fourier's concept of human nature. In Neale's hagiography of socialist saints, the Frenchman had once again taken precedence over England's Robert Owen — while the latter had sought to impose the authority of a strictly controlled environment to mould man into a new being, the former wanted to stimulate and awaken man as he was. During the Christian Socialist period Neale's plans for unifying the Co-operative Movement implied a high degree of central control; but now a new and ever-growing libertarian emphasis (approaching anarchism) began to modify his efforts. This development became especially pronounced during his later career as General Secretary of the Co-operative Union when he implacably opposed the trend towards bureaucratism.

In the future, Fourier's concept of 'Association' would figure prominently in almost all of Neale's socialist propaganda and towards the end of his life he referred to the French utopian as 'the man who has probed the evils of our present society more thoroughly, and traced out the conditions of effective reform more scientifically, than any other writer who has handled this all important topic.'[19] Fourier (the most patient and long-suffering of the socialist pioneers) more than any other man, fired Neale's enthusiasm, providing him with new inspiration and challenge especially during times when his spirit was depressed by misfortune. Yet Neale was not dependent upon Fourier in formulating his own theories, for he went well beyond the eminent Frenchman in devising schemes that were considerably more sophisticated and practical. Into his unique ideology of co-operative socialism he blended elements from almost all of the differing schools of communitarian thought and even borrowed ingredients from capitalism to serve as catalytic agents.

It has become common to interpret socialism's key principle, the public ownership of the means of production and distribution, as commanding the policy of nationalisation – public ownership being identified with state ownership. There is a tendency to forget that a substantial number of 19th century socialists were opposed to utilising political power, even transitionally, as an aid in achieving their ends, and would utterly reject the notion of state ownership. Indeed, Marx himself felt that after the workers had captured the state, using it to complete the process of revolution, it must ultimately wither away, giving place to the anarchy of the classless society. It should be stressed at the outset that despite Neale's emphasis on voluntaryism and self-help, as an alternative to political action, he was nevertheless a thoroughgoing socialist in fundamental agreement with the idealistic objectives sought by all the major socialist theoreticians: where differences arose they were more concerned with means than with ends.[20] Clearly delimitating Co-operation within the socialist stream of influence, Neale even believed himself to be standing on the same platform as Karl Marx and Ferdinand Lassalle, though he was vigorous in protesting the medicine these men prescribed for purging capitalism, particularly the fast-acting variety which Marx dispensed.[21]

Certainly there was more than a little self-interest reflected in Neale's condemnation of the methodology of Marxism. He never completely escaped the logic of the social class to which he belonged: while willing to see his own property ultimately filled with home colonies – the end result of a gradual process of co-operative reform – he could not bring himself to approve any direct action involving violence, confiscation, or even heavy taxation, all of which would have precipitously reduced his status and standard of living and perhaps endangered his life. Yet Neale's negative reaction was not altogether a personal matter, and he was always careful to couch his arguments against sudden or violent revolution within the realm of morality and practicality. 'Assuredly,' he wrote, 'to think that the victory of reason is to be earned by the exercise of force, and the reign of love to be the natural fruit of a reign of terror, must be the maddest of mad delusions.'[22] Neale insisted that the issue of great social change did not depend merely upon numbers, maintaining that when August Bebel, the German Marxist, recommended the revolution of the masses, he forgot to bring Krupp's guns into consideration.[23]

While rejecting Marxism, Neale agreed with Lassalle that not only the transition to collectivism should be a gradual one, but that the process must ultimately involve the establishment of co-operative producers' associations: on the other hand, Lassalle also theorized that the *state* should be required to provide the credit for establishing these associations, an idea which Neale decried as 'gliding into a better condition, without the trouble of self-sacrifice, by the magic of credit voted by universal suffrage.'[24] Lassalle had asked of the state 'not so much help as a whole hand, but only that of a little finger'; even a little finger was too much for Neale, who retorted that 'experience has abundantly shown, that no application of money is more liable to abuse than that of grants out of the public purse for private purposes, which are almost certain to get into the hands of precisely those persons who are the least likely to make a good use of them.'[25]

Very early in the course of his study of socialism, Neale had been alarmed by what he considered a characteristic German tendency to place too great faith in the power of government as a means of bringing about change; however, there was one German, Dr Schulze-Delitzsch, a forthright critic of Lassalle, who appeared to be on the right track. Schulze-Delitzsch had introduced (first into Germany, but soon spreading into Austria, Italy and Belgium) a system of 'people's banks'. These organisations, like the co-operative stores in England, were originally designed to enable the working classes to accumulate their own capital for use in the establishment of self-governing workshops and other co-operative associations. They were initially appealing to Neale because they introduced no new revolutionary mechanisms that might jar people into reaction; pragmatically utilising the capitalistic tools at hand, 'the approved methods by which individuals have created wealth for themselves', they could extort 'from competition itself the weapons by which it may be conquered'.[26]

Lassalle maintained (in words reminiscent of Ernest Jones' sharp criticism of British co-operatives) that people's banks were pathetically defective as instruments of radical reform. Neale agreed: he always recognised that people's banks, and for that matter co-operative stores as well, would prove inadequate if taken as ends in themselves – if labourers should fail to use them as a means to implement larger ideals. Their importance lay in the fact that they taught, by living example, a vital first principle, voluntary union for self-help. It was Neale's view that, when universally applied, this principle was capable of bringing about permanent social reform. Moreover, banks and stores served a valuable intermediate function by facilitating the accumulation of a 'collective fund', that could 'convert capital from the master of labour into its servant'.[27] Thus Neale continued to sing the optimistic song of the old Rochdale Pioneers: but at this point his vocalising was an exercise in nostalgia, for most of the men who originally composed the score had long since forgotten the lyrics. The actions of the co-operators whom Neale so ardently supported, the followers of Schulze-Delitzsch in Germany as well as the consumers of the North country in Britain, proved the validity of Lassalle's criticisms. They had forgotten their former plans to emancipate the *producer* and, using their growing capital in the customary way, themselves became masters of labour.

Neale's approach to the major systems of economic thought was both eclectic and pragmatic, and, as his more doctrinaire socialist critics had prophesied, this led him to place undue emphasis upon inadequate instruments of change: co-operators did in fact abandon community-building for shopkeeping, wholesaling and banking. Impatient with the slow movement towards some future utopia, they settled comfortably for present gain. The critics themselves were not without blemish, for they also were hesitant to follow plans that involved moving gradually towards a far distant goal. Surely this weakness in many socialists constituted a grave danger, for their willingness to entertain violence and/or add to the power of the state was hardly less calculated to corrupt human society than a little capital in the hands of a few thousand comfortable co-operators. To single out the Marxists, it could be argued that their most important contributions do not in fact revolve about their theory of revolution or their concept of the dictatorship of the proletariat, that most powerful of all forms of state power, but rather turn about their having taught people to see society within the framework of history and, most important of all, to recognise the inherent oppression in the system of capitalism – its waste of men and materials, its alienation of the working classes and their depersonalisation.

Possibly the major defect of the Marxists, if not of Marx himself, was their single-minded preoccupation with the question of violently overthrowing capitalism and the grasping of political power. Other factors contributing to exploitation and alienation, such as the nature of the work process itself or the way in which factory labour was organised, were comparatively neglected. It was especially in these latter areas that Neale's willingness to learn a little from every system of thought had great importance. He refused to abandon either the heritage of the utopians or his Christian morality and was in consequence interested not only in the easily abstracted and dehuman-ised questions of supply and demand, ownership and control, but in improving the quality of the product, the pleasantness of the work, and adding to the dignity of the individual worker. Neale was most insistent that socialism accommodate man's spiritual as well as physical needs and in this area he felt the ideas of the old utopians to be especially valid:

> 'Fourier, for instance, unfolded, with all the anticipating minuteness of genius, the principles by which manual labour may be made attractive, instead of being so wearisome as it now usually is. Robert Owen has dwelt upon the vast influence of the surroundings of men (or circumstances as he said) on their characters. It is open to the Co-operator to study the teachings of both these eminent thinkers; to adopt the suggested means of rendering labour attractive; [and] to study carefully the influence of men's surroundings on their characters.'[28]

Neale described the co-operative method to consist 'in using the resources put into our hands by the present system, in order gradually to replace it by another'[29] – this illustrates the extent of Neale's pragmatism. Co-operators should not, at the first, depart at all from the economic arrangements peculiar to the world of competition. They should adhere to the prices fixed in the open market and adopt the most common modes of conducting exchanges; stores and people's banks would accumulate capital even as did the private concerns. But once the co-operative sector of the economy had expanded to the point where it equalled or overbalanced the private sector, the great social transformation that Neale anticipated would get underway in earnest. Although the method was pragmatic, the ultimate revolution would be no less comprehensive than that dictated by the Marxist syllabus, for both involved the extirpation of the ideology of competition as well as its physical embodiment, the capitalistic state. Neale would 'transform the whole machinery of production and distribution into public functions'.[30]

> 'Co-operation then is called on to create a new social state, which, growing over against the present state as the Church did of old, only now under its shelter instead of in conflict with it, may, like its precursor, ultimately absorb the law-making power within its own circle, and can then complete what may be requisite for its perfect consolidation, by the same sort of authority, as that whereby, in all ages and countries, the minority have been required to give up for a reasonable compensation, rights of which the majority feel that the cession is necessary for the general welfare.'[31]

Neale took more time devising means for ending the domination of capitalism than in explaining precisely what he would put in its place;

nevertheless, the nature of the 'new social state' he sought to create is manifested throughout his writings and in his practical work. Like the anarchists and many of the utopians, Neale wished to replace the existing centralised 'political' state, where authority came from above, with a new 'social' state where ultimate power rested with the people associated together in locally autonomous 'natural' units such as co-operatives. Embodying the essential principle of self-help through association, such organisations were the key to Neale's plans for social reconstruction. Yet it was clear that in a modern industrial society they could not survive in isolation but must be unified in some way for purposes of overall co-ordination and mutual advantage. In the light of this necessity Neale concluded that the system of federalism, where authority came from below, would provide the only logical framework for uniting these bodies without destroying their essential character.

The anarchists, Proudhon and Bakunin, were especially strong in their emphasis on the federal system, prophesying a future world harmoniously united by voluntary federations of workers co-operatives and communes. Neale similarly envisioned the development of a great system of interdependent and interlocking federations, as self-governing associations of men came to form themselves into countless varieties of federal organisations for practical purposes such as production, distribution, mutual insurance and education. Ultimately each community could be reorganised as a federal body representative of its constituent associations. Indeed, as Neale projected it, every conceivable social function from entertainment in workingmen's clubs to medical care in hospitals could be carried out by associations either acting on their own or in federation with one another. At the top the Co-operative Union would become the overall co-ordinating body, its membership including all other federations as well as the individual associations. Such was Neale's dream when he called upon English co-operators to create 'a new social state'.

> 'But "E.V.N." is, and always was, a Conservative. What think your readers of that? Don't they wish all Conservatives were like him? Did they ever meet his equal under such a name?'[32]
>
> William Nuttall, 1882

The great irony of Neale's life was that he ultimately became the leader of a powerful movement which benefitted from the organisations he designed, while rejecting the purpose behind them. It was especially evident after the passage of the Reform Bill of 1867 that the majority of co-operators were comparatively satisfied with England's economic system and had become thoroughly politicised supporters of the Liberal Party. In consequence they were somewhat bewildered by Neale's doctrines which stood in stark contrast: his socialism seemed anti-quarian as well as unrealistic; and, in addition to taking such a dubious position, Neale insistently called himself a Conservative. To many leaders in the Co-operative Movement this combination of beliefs appeared confusing and contradictory.

Though Neale's juxtaposition of conservativism and socialism was often misunderstood, it involved no basic contradiction. At least part of the confusion stemmed from changing times; old words took on new meanings when passed from one generation to another. Neale matured during a period when it was possible to define conservativism and socialism without specific reference to political systems or parties, with the result that he formulated views in both areas that were, for the most part, unpolitical, even anti-political. Neale's conservativism (in the tradition of Coleridge, Maurice and Carlyle) was nine-tenths philosophy and mixed easily with his socialism. In fact, the two ideologies rested on common fundamentals: both insisted that human society be seen as an organic whole, not as a collection of competing individuals (or 'warring atoms' as Neale would put it), and that an individual could realise his fullest potentialities only through a course of service to the community and not by pursuing selfish ends.

When presenting his views Neale could be aggressively insensitive to the party bias of his co-workers, as he chose to refer even to Liberalism in a basically philosophical rather than political context. He declared his opposition to the Liberal Party, as such, because it sought merely to improve 'the institutions belonging to competitive society' and thereby detracted from the basic necessity of constructing 'the better order of Co-operative society'. But if Liberalism was taken to mean 'freedom from old prejudices, habits, or attachments, which stand in the way of human progress,' Neale concluded, then 'the true Co-operator is at once a thorough Liberal and a thorough Conservative'![33] This rhetoric seemed perverse to a generation awakened by the political theatrics of Gladstone and Disraeli, and accustomed to reflecting more party than principle in their use of the terms Conservative and Liberal. William Nuttall (a prominent co-operator from Oldham) refused to take such statements seriously, especially Neale's claim to be a Conservative:

'What would he conserve? Certainly not the monarchy, for its members are neither "producers" nor "distributors". He would not conserve the landlords as a class, I am sure, for his only care for the

Irish Land Bill was that he should make it more "radical" than it
is . . . . He cares no more for the modern aristocracy – the manu-
facturer, the banker, the merchant, or shipper – than for the
landowner . . . . When the land and all the property is transferred to
the "producers", what is there left for Conservatives to conserve?'[34]

Over-zealous in his desire to implement reform, the anarchist
Pierre-Joseph Proudhon once seriously compromised his principles by
standing (successfully) for election to the French Assembly. Following
an analogous pattern, Neale frequently found it expedient to support
Liberal political policies publicly; for outside the realm of philosophy,
the backward-looking Conservatives had no acceptable programme for
the future. Neale's faith in progress, his belief in the necessity of radical
change, was too firmly implanted for him to have found much
sympathy in traditional Conservative circles. As a socialist he looked to
that future time when England would be dotted with communes; but as
he had selected an evolutionary route towards this destination, he
found himself (like the Labour Party of England's future) being forced
into an often frustrating collaboration with Liberals: it was the old
pitfall for radicals; if one could not arrive at perfection all at once, then
one was obliged to support those measures, however piecemeal and
inadequate in themselves, which appeared to be leading in the right
direction. Several of Neale's closest friends – Thomas Hughes, Walter
Morrison, and Lord Goderich – sat as Liberals in Parliament, and like it
or not the party affiliation of these men reflected that of the majority
of co-operators.

It is of no little significance that John Bright in arguing for the
extension of the franchise had appealed to the progressive example of
the Equitable Pioneers; and William Gladstone, as the question was
introduced to the House of Commons, proclaimed that the town of
Rochdale 'probably has done more than any other town in making
good to practical minds a case for some enfranchisement of the working
classes.'[35] To Edward Vansittart Neale such logic was irresistible and
his old hostility to political reform weakened perceptibly (though never
totally). By 1867 he was not only willing to extend the franchise, but
even drew up plans for this purpose, sending them to Sir Stafford
Northcote (Conservative Cabinet member and close confidante of
Disraeli) as well as to Gladstone himself.[36] For similar reasons in the
1880s Neale supported Henry Fawcett's campaign for proportional
representation as well as Gladstone's Irish Land Bill, the provisions of
which he unsuccessfully sought to *extend* to include government grants
for co-operatives, with the idea of stimulating a revival of ventures such

as E. T. Craig's old Ralahine Community of the early 1830s.[37] In the final analysis, Neale was nothing if not a pragmatist.

By the late 1850s Neale had relinquished his position of leadership in the drive to cement English co-operators into a powerful federal union, and even ceased to attend conferences on anything like a regular basis.[38] In regard to 'unofficial' involvement, however, he was far from an inactive co-operator. He remained very hard at work, but his contribution consisted largely in written propaganda and legal services. It was in the latter area that his labours were most conspicuous — he would one day be referred to as 'Co-operation's Barrister'. Even as he had maintained a column called 'Legal Questions Answered' in his own publication, the old *Co-operative Commercial Circular*, so he continued to give legal advice to his working class friends both in the pages of the *Co-operator* (a newspaper edited by Henry Pitman in the 1860s)[39] and through extensive personal correspondence. A goodly number of the periodic reports sent to the *Co-operator* by the various societies, mentioned legal snarls which Neale had untangled.[40] Indeed, letters from West Wickham, Kent, reached into all of the major co-operative centres in England, and some, like those sent to the Equitable Pioneers of Rochdale and the CWS, influenced decisions on matters of business which involved thousands of pounds. Most of the Co-operative Movement's significant steps forward raised complex legal problems which Neale painstakingly worked out, largely without compensation.

He also continued to be moderately active in London, meeting on occasion with a group of idealists who began again to resuscitate his yearnings for co-operative union. In 1862 Holyoake with the aid of William Edger had formed the London Association for the Promotion of Co-operation (an organisation similar to the old Christian Socialist Society) and Neale became an honorary member along with such other notables as Francis W. Newman, Thomas Hughes, and John Stuart Mill.[41] Mill appeared with Neale at a soirée held by the Association in 1864, the latter taking the chair and both men giving speeches.[42] The evening's gathering had been called to celebrate the success of the Metropolitan and Home Counties Purchasing Association, a new federation of stores united to buy groceries and other provisions in bulk so as to reduce prices, a step into wholesaling activities reminiscent of Neale's old Co-operative Agency.

But only in the North were there advances made in the field of wholesaling which were destined to be of lasting significance. If Neale's grandiose plans for an all-comprehensive union began to falter before the more pedestrian aspirations of the northern consumers' societies, at least the impulse to wholesaling remained very much alive. This was to be expected. The union promised to make co-operators no richer, whereas with a wholesale society it was quite the reverse, and consequently Neale's efforts in this sphere were rewarded; a few years earlier, as we have seen, the Pioneers Society had responded to his proddings by establishing a special Wholesale Department. But success had by no means been assured by the mere act of the Equitable Pioneers taking the helm. Again, the Movement's essential lack of unity blocked progress, for Rochdale could lay no claim whatsoever to the loyalty of other co-operators. Moreover, the business of wholesaling involved great risks, as the Industrial and Provident Societies Act of 1852 made no legal provision for it; indeed, Tidd Pratt, the Registrar of Friendly Societies (who Thomas Hughes once described as 'an aggravated and imbecile ass')[43], at first refused to accept and register the Rules for the new Department. Even its strongest defenders, Abraham Greenwood, William Cooper and Samuel Stott, spoke of the undertaking as only a temporary expedient, an interim arrangement that would be terminated once co-operators could finally establish an autonomous, federally organised wholesale society. For the time being, however, any such separate federal organ was legally impossible because only individuals, not societies, could hold shares in co-operative organisations registered under the already outdated Act of 1852. So once again, as the decade drew to its close, co-operators braced themselves to storm the legal barriers. It was Abraham Greenwood and J. T. W. Mitchell of the Rochdale Pioneers who first determined to take action and in 1859 Neale was called in for consultation with the result that, a year later, he was assigned a committee to help him draft the necessary Parliamentary Bill.[44]

Neale's new Industrial and Provident Societies Bill successfully concluded its parliamentary journey in 1862. During the entire period of its passage he had kept himself busy introducing deputations, interviewing and persuading political leaders to lend their support; seldom had an Act of Parliament owed so much to the efforts of a single individual.[45] But when he finally wrote to Rochdale to request his lawyer's fee, the sum was negligible.

'I have had so much trouble about the bill, that I must ask you for a fee of seven guineas, but of this I wish £5.5.0 to be paid as a subscription to the Cotton Famine Relief Fund. For the remaining £2.2.0 you may send me a Post Office order payable at Charing

Cross with an acknowledgement of the payment, for the subscription. I will then send you a receipt for the £7.7.0.'[46]

He had requested the money as gravely as though it had been hundreds
of pounds; the Pioneers were greatly amused, and never forgot the
incident. Years later they were still fond of making references to their
'expensive' lawyer.

In addition to the very small committee that aided Neale in drawing
up the Parliamentary Bill, a larger one had also been chosen, being
delegated with the responsibility of drafting a Constitution for the
prospective federal wholesale society. The two committees were not
mutually exclusive and Abraham Greenwood, the most important
member of both, was ultimately to put forward the plan which was
accepted as a basis for action. He called for an organisation which was
patterned after Neale's old Central Co-operative Agency; this was not
surprising as Greenwood had been closely involved with the Agency
when, as a buyer for the Pioneers of Rochdale, he had transacted much
of his business through its Swan Street, Manchester, branch. At that
time he had done all in his power to insure the Agency's success.[47]
After undergoing some modifications, Greenwood's design was passed
on to Neale, who drafted the final Rules for the new body which was
duly registered with Tidd Pratt in 1863 as the North of England
Co-operative Wholesale Agency and Depot, Ltd. – a title soon changed
to read simply the Co-operative Wholesale Society.

Now Neale knew the sweet taste of success. Yet he and Greenwood
had had a few misgivings, for they were thwarted at the outset in their
attempt to keep the Wholesale's sphere of activity limited: they wished
it to serve merely as an agency of the societies to facilitate buying and
distributing. Their misgivings were justified as the term 'depot' had
been added to the title in signification of the victory of those
who wished the Wholesale to be comparatively free to lay up supplies
and sell on its own behalf. Although it was the unique creation of the
stores and remained their agent for supplies, it was given by its creators
great latitude for independent action, with the result that it soon
became, for all practical purposes, almost totally autonomous. Indeed,
the CWS was destined to achieve inordinate strength and develop gross
appetites, the great Gargantua of the Co-operative Movement spreading
into every area of business endeavour, its membership by the decade's
end approaching a quarter of a million, its trade rising to nearly two
million pounds. Idealists gradually disappeared from the organisation.
Some went the natural way of mortality: William Cooper died in

October 1868, followed seven months later by James Smithies.[48] Others appeared to harden their hearts. Abraham Greenwood remained a leader until 1898 but kept his old fire hidden in a well of silence which he appears to have dug deeper year by year. A new breed of men climbed to power, typified by J. T. W. Mitchell, who thought in terms of self-interest and were either dead or dying to the utopianism which had motivated so many of the founders.[49]

During the Christian Socialist period, as previously mentioned, Neale established a co-operative union, a newspaper, a scheme for banking and a wholesale. All were important as prototypes for permanent organs of the modern Co-operative Movement. He was similarly influential in the establishment of the Co-operative Insurance Company.

The Insurance Company came in on the same crest of enthusiasm that carried the Co-operative Wholesale Society to success; indeed, it is most significant that the very same men were involved in originating and subsequently managing both organisations – men susceptible to the dialectics of utopian idealism and frequently paying that idealism lip-service, yet pragmatic enough to see first to the business end of Co-operation. In 1863 there had been inquiries into the possibility of launching some kind of insurance venture, but nothing was done because of the preoccupation with the nourishment of the infant Wholesale Society until early in 1867, when William Cooper sent out a questionnaire to determine whether or not co-operators were still interested. The response was so favourable that a conference was called which followed the usual procedure, selecting a small committee to carry out a thorough investigation of the subject and concoct a workable scheme. A fortnight later the committee met to consider a plan submitted by Neale (the 'Memoranda and Articles of Association of the Co-operative Insurance') and the new company was born on 29 August 1867, when his plan, essentially as submitted, was officially registered.[50]

The redoubtable old pioneers, Greenwood, Smithies, and Cooper became respectively manager, treasurer, and secretary of the Insurance Company; it was for the latter two, who were nearing the end of their lives, a last significant work.[51] Neale, however, continued to be indispensible – and finally when he attended his last Co-operative Congress (at Rochdale in 1892), William Barnett, the Insurance Company's Chairman, presented him with a long congratulatory address in recognition of his services.[52] For sixteen out of the twenty-five years of the Company's existence, Neale was numbered among its Directors and appears to have been, of all the co-operators, one of those most acquainted with the insurance business. Again he had learned the hard way, having had the trying experience of having to wind up in failure a branch of the Albert Insurance Company with which he had been closely affiliated; but having survived this hard experience, success greeted his personal efforts as a Director of the Co-operative Insurance Company.

In retrospect it is of some significance that one of the first moves made by the Company was to insure the Wholesale Society for the amount of £1,000 on its stock-in-trade. Those who had called the CWS into being and continued to direct it were now launching the Insurance Company and determining its policy — however independent their newest co-operative offspring might appear, its ultimately subordinate relationship to the Wholesale was never in doubt. In 1913 the two bodies overtly became one when the Co-operative Wholesale Society assumed complete control of the Co operative Insurance Society.[53] Gargantua's appetite was insatiable. Neale was fortunately spared the spectacle.[54]

It is clear that the restraints contingent upon having a comparatively limited income complicated life for Neale's entire family; indeed his wife never really adjusted to them. The relationship between Frances and Edward was not infrequently strained. They often took their holidays away from each other's company, he visiting friends or relations on his own side of the family, and she going either to the Farrers at Ingleborough or more frequently to Corfe Castle in Dorset, or Encombe, where all comers fell under the influence of Lord Eldon.

But it was most difficult for Neale's son Henry.[55] The third Earl of Eldon was Henry's first cousin — three years younger and a good friend — with whom he frequently socialised. They went to steeple chases, boat races, and the theatre (once to the Adelphi 'to see Miss Bateman in the Hunchback which was very fairly got up') and played a lot of cricket together.[56] With a companion such as Lord Eldon, it is little wonder that Henry found it very difficult to remain the poor relation. Eldon had been elevated to the peerage at the early age of eight, and the entire family with all of its branches took part in the festivities when he turned 21, on 8 November 1866. Consumed with jealousy, Henry found it very difficult to pay his respects to the young Lord and confided bitter feelings to a Journal he kept during these years.[57] Wistfully, a few days after the young Earl's birthday, he solaced himself with the thought that 'hardships, and trials of poverty of an inferior station in life ought to strengthen the mind, even if they rather imbitter, the temptations of an easy luxurious life, of great wealth, of high station must often enchain the soul.'[58]

The examples of great wealth and social position found among near relatives, especially the Eldon connection, heightened Henry's bitterness in the knowledge that his father had heedlessly abandoned both; however, the words in his Journal are far from being all bleak. Despite the fact that Henry found it difficult to have confidence in his father's financial acumen, their relationship with one another was affectionate. Moreover, it is clear that Henry was torn in two directions: while bitter over the loss of money and status, his most serious thoughts on religion and philosophy followed patterns set by his father. Both men were addicted to taking long walks for pleasure and on the many occasions when they journeyed together, they communicated intimately. One such time, Derby Day in May 1866, they walked on foot some twenty-two picturesque miles of Surrey countryside: they went through Addington and Warlingham to Marden Park, which the elder Neale fondly remembered from his having visited the Wilberforces there over forty years before. After enjoying the magnificent hilltop view of Redhill Valley, they took lunch at Godstone and then finished their exercise by traversing the top of the chalk hills to Merstham.[59] Doubtlessly, on walks such as this Neale explained to his son the plan for the new society which he hoped to build by means of associative effort, and Henry, as his own future work for the Co-operative Movement would indicate, was apparently convinced. But Henry lacked the dogged, often reckless, will-power which drove his father to throw absolutely everything into the cause; he lacked the nerve to stand against the social demands of his rich relations, and ultimately, after his father's death, he entirely abandoned his labours on behalf of the Co-operative Movement.

During the years that are carefully recorded in Henry's Journal (1865—68), there was a revival of interest in Producers Co-operation propitiously accompanied by, and to a certain extent resulting from, massive unrest in the Trade Union Movement and political discontent. This was a sequence of events not without resemblance to the early 1850s just before Neale's investment in the doomed engineering associations. Despite his earlier misfortunes, however, Neale was so greatly influenced that by the summer of 1868 he was once more to be found taking a position of leadership and making decisions that would direct the future course of Co-operation as an organised movement. He would never again be out of the limelight.

Notes

The opening quotation is from Abraham Greenwood, *The Educational Department of the Rochdale Pioneers Society Ltd.: Its Origin and Development. A Paper Read . . . Before a Conference of Delegates from Co-operative Societies held at the Co-operative Hall, Toad Lane, Rochdale, July 14 1877* (Manchester, 1877), pp.3–4.

1. H. W. Lee, *Edward Vansittart Neale: His Co-operative Life and Work* (Manchester, 1908), p.4.
2. Florence Vansittart Neale, MSS account of Bisham Abbey.
3. E. O. Greening, 'Memories of Edward Vansittart Neale', *Co-operative Official* (1923), p.72.
4. Masterman, *op.cit.*, pp.95–96.
5. See e.g., E. V. Neale to E.R.A. Seligman, 21 March 1885, where Neale writes: 'Incidentally, the only matter that I regret in respect to my connexion with this movement is, that I was in too great a hurry. Led away by the enthusiasm proclaimed by the efforts of the Parisian workers to raise themselves by their united efforts, I advanced considerable sums to various bodies of workers, who were to have all the profits on their work, after paying me 5 per cent on the capital, without having succeeded in setting up one society which lived; and in consequence only crippled my own power without benefitting permanently those whom I desired to benefit.' Available in Seligman Collection, Columbia University.
6. Margaret E. Dickinson to P. N. Backstrom, 1966. This letter is in my possession.
7. Pitman, *op.cit.*, p.42.
8. *The Analogy of Thought and Nature Investigated by Edward Vansittart Neale* (London, 1863), p.10.
9. *Ibid.*, p.87.
10. *Ibid.*, p.10.
11. *Ibid.*, p.158.
12. See *Labour and Capital* (London, 1852), p.33.
13. *The Analogy, op.cit.*, pp.189–190.
14. *Ibid.*, pp.190–191.
15. *The Reader*, II (1863), 217.
16. The first references to socialism appeared in Neale's Journal, August 29 and 30 1841, where he spoke of reviewing Fourier s system in a book. Ten years of sporadic work resulted in *The Characteristic Features of Some of the Principle Systems of Socialism*, only an extended lecture printed as a pamphlet. His later works on the subject are similarly brief.
17. *The Co-operator*, III (1862), 21.
18. E. V. Neale to Stephen Hawkey, 13 May 1860. Neale Papers.
19. E. V. Neale, *Associated Homes: A Lecture . . . with Three Engravings of the Familistère at Guise, and a Biographical Notice of M. Godin, its Founder* (London, 1880), p.vi.
20. See Thomas Hughes and E. V. Neale, *A Manual for Co-operators Prepared at the Request of the Co-operative Congress Held at*

Gloucester in April, 1879; and Revised 1888 (Manchester, 1888), pp.23–32. Only the preface to this book was written by Hughes.

21. E. V. Neale, 'The Relation of Co-operation to Socialism', *Co-operative News*, X (1879), 145, 161. *Co-operative News* hereafter abbreviated as '*C.N.*'

22. *Manual, op.cit.*, p.31.

23. 'The Relation of Co-operation to Socialism', *op.cit.*, p.161.

24. *Manual, op.cit.*, p.230.

25. *Ibid.*, pp.229–230.

26. 'The Relation of Co-operation to Socialism', *op.cit.*, p.145.

27. *Manual, op.cit.*, p.230.

28. *Ibid.*, p.25.

29. *Ibid.*, p.48.

30. *Ibid.*, p.61.

31. *Ibid.*, p.71.

32. William Nuttall, 'E. V. N. As a Conservative', *C.N.*, XIII (1882), 28.

33. E. V. Neale, 'Reform, Political and Social', *C.N.*, XI (1880), 225–226.

34. Nuttall, *loc. cit.*

35. From Gladstone's speech introducing Earl Russell's Reform Bill to the House, as reported in The *Co-operator*, VI (1866), 237.

36. Northcote to Neale, 7 March 1867; 20 March 1867; 20 May 1867; 25 July 1871. W. Gladstone to Neale, 14 March 1867. Neale Papers.

37. Henry Fawcett to E. V. Neale, 17 November 1883. Neale Papers. 'The Guild of Co-operators and the Land Bill', *C.N.*, XII (1881), 331.

38. Thomas Hughes to Edward Owen Greening, 23 December 1892. Edward Owen Greening Papers (package entitled 'E.O.G. Letters'). Library, Co-operative Union Limited, Manchester, Lancs.

39. Edward's activities from 1854–59 are frustratingly difficult for the historian to follow because of the dearth of source materials, but the period from 1860–71 is quite a different matter for during the later time the movement again had a newspaper to testify to the continuity of his efforts called The *Co-operator*. First published in 1860 by the Manchester and Salford Equitable Society, it came to be dominated by Henry Pitman, an odd man with a great deal of influence who was a leader of the Anti-Vaccination Crusade and a brother to Sir Isaac Pitman, the originator of the widely known shorthand system. The publication was an extremely important co-operative clarion until Pitman himself, more polemicist than editor, inadvertently destroyed it: on 1 January 1870, he changed its title to The *Co-operator and Anti-Vaccinator* and crowded out most responsible news with viscious, ever-escalating attacks on Dr. Jenner's 'inflammatory fermentive brute virus'. In the following year the publication was slain in this retrogressive battle against smallpox vaccine.

40. See e.g., The *Co-operator*, II (1861), 34–35; and III (1863), 129.

41. See G.D.H. Cole, *A Century of Co-operation*, p.156; and

W. H. Brown, *A Century of London Co-operation*, p.72.

42. 'Soiree of London Society for Promoting Co-operation', The *Co-operator*, V (1864), 4–6.

43. Thomas Hughes to John Ludlow, undated. Ludlow MSS, Cambridge. Date can, however, be deduced from the contents to be some time in 1854.

44. For a short but thorough account of the origins of the Co-operative Wholesale Society consult G.D.H. Cole, *A Century of Co-operation*, p.133ff. Percy Redfern's *The New History of the CWS* (London, 1938), is, of course, indispensible. Neale's interest in changing the national laws relating to co-operative societies was of long standing. Several years earlier he had led a deputation to the doorstep of E. Cardwell, who, as President of the Board of Trade, was then first introducing the Bill which ultimately granted limited liability to ordinary joint-stock companies. Neale enjoined Cardwell to extend the privilege to co-operative associations, but he had gained access to a deaf ear. Yet, despite failure, he never gave up hope and thus welcomed the opportunity to join the northern co-operators in making another attempt in 1860. *Co-operative Commercial Circular*, No. 16 (1 February 1855), 116.

45. See Redfern, *op.cit.*, p.22.

46. Neale letter dated 27 July 1862, Library, Co-operative Union Limited, Manchester.

47. *C.N.*, VI (1875), 381.

48. W. Henry Brown, *The Rochdale Pioneers: A Century of Co-operation* (Manchester, n.d. [1944?]), p.43.

49. In later years a contingent of idealists within the Co-operative Movement who realised how great a part Neale had played in the creation of the CWS blamed him for not having 'fixed more definite and narrower limits to the functions of the society'. Thomas Hughes defended Neale as follows: 'The fact is, that in the first place he was not free to follow his own judgment, but had to frame, not a constitution which he thought the best, but one which the representatives of the societies proposing to federate would accept and work under; and, again, although his own ideas as to what the Wholesale Society should become – viz., an agency for buying and distributing all the societies needed, and for collecting and employing their funds in strengthening and advancing the cause of Co-operation – were perfectly clear, the experience which alone could indicate in what directions limitations would be needed was not in existence.' Thomas Hughes, 'Edward Vansittart Neale as a Christian Socialist', The *Economic Review*, III (1893), 175.

50. Brown, *The Rochdale Pioneers*, p.73.

51. *Ibid.*, pp.73–74.

52. Pitman, *op.cit.*, p.11. R.G. Garnett, *A Century of Co-operative Insurance* (London, 1968), pp.88–89.

53. The Co-operative Insurance Company was reorganised in 1899 and its name changed to the Co-operative Insurance Society.

54. Cole, *A Century of Co-operation*, pp.146–147; 258. Garnett,

op.cit. pp.136–148.

55. In 1860, Henry decided to leave Eton at least partly for financial reasons and later secured an appointment to the Admiralty. See E. V. Neale to Henry V. Neale, 6 October 1860; Oliver Farrer to Henry V. Neale, 10 August 1862. Neale Papers.
56. See e.g., Henry's Journal, p.106. Neale Papers.
57. *Ibid.*, p.151.
58. *Ibid.*, p.149.
59. *Ibid.*, p.135.

PART TWO

CONFLICT AND CO-OPERATION

IV

UNION AT LAST
1865–1870

What shall hinder, in the coming year, the commence-
ment – to use the words of Mr. Neale – of 'an experiment to realise *now* what must ultimately come as the
fruits of Co-operation'?

William Pare, 25 January 1868

On 1 July 1865, an industrialist, Henry Briggs, became a great source of
inspiration when he initiated a system of sharing profits with the
labourers in his Yorkshire collieries. Co-operators responded enthusiastically, including those who, like John Watts, were usually indifferent to
any effort not directly involving co-operative consumers; even the old
Chartist, Ernest Jones, praised Briggs. Almost everyone appeared to
overlook the fact that Briggs' motives left something to be desired:
indeed, he had initiated profit sharing only as a last resort, an economic
expedient to end a series of strikes at his mines which were of such
turbulence as to ultimately necessitate the calling out of troops. He
even publicly admitted that the purpose of the new plan was pecuniary,
the addition to a miner's pay under its blessings 'more apparent than
real'.[1] The scheme was symptomatic of the revival of interest in
co-operative production during the late 1860s and early 1870s, and was
all too typical. This and other similar ventures were called industrial
partnerships'. They were, for the most part, simple joint-stock
companies where the owner, on his own initiative, merely allocated a
proportion of the profits and, less frequently, some of the responsibilities of management to his workmen, although sometimes labouring
men from other workshops held shares in such industrial partnerships
or even owned them entirely as working class capitalists.

As demonstrated at Briggs' mines, the term 'partnership' could be
very misleading since the regular labourer in these establishments
usually did not hold shares nor did he participate in either profits or
management. Thus even with the best will in the world, such industrial
organisations represented, on balance, only a small advance over strictly
private enterprise – they were, nevertheless, exceptionally influential.[2]
Aside from Briggs, the new enthusiasm for co-operative production
in England was a result, to a large degree, of the widespread publicity
given to the efforts of Edward Owen Greening. The partnerships he

established during the lean economic years from 1865–67 were to
provide the model for a host of similar enterprises which multiplied
extravagantly, particularly in the coal industry, during the years of
economic boom which followed. An egotistical, yet warmhearted and
friendly Mancunian industrialist, Greening was a political radical
already noted as a founder of the Emancipation Society and the
Manhood Suffrage League.[3] He had been indirectly involved with the
profit-sharing scheme at Briggs' collieries, but of more importance, even
while it was being initiated, he himself decided 'to establish a few
examples of the principle of industrial partnerships in the leading trades
of the country'.[4] He began the work alone but soon enlisted the aid of
Thomas Hughes and Walter Morrison, and their joint efforts were
greeted with unusual success, at least as business ventures. First
Greening had turned his own workshop, which manufactured all kinds
of bric-a-brac in iron from chicken coops to vases, into an industrial
partnership: next he launched the South Buckley Coal and Firebrick
Company along similar lines; and finally, in 1866 and 1867 respectively, he established the famous Cobden Mills (formerly owned by
Cobden himself) and the Agricultural and Horticultural Association.
Neale became a prominent member of the latter two companies and
contributed substantially to their success despite ideological misgivings.

The Agricultural Association was the most significant of the new
partnerships. Designed to supply members with first quality farm
machinery, seeds, manures and manufactured food for livestock, it was
destined to survive as a healthy company until the First World War.[5]
Because of the prevalence through the nineteenth century of adulteration, overcharging and downright fraud in agricultural dealings, there
was a great demand for a thoroughly trustworthy company, and the
Agricultural and Horticultural Association had arisen to meet this
demand. Neale had been interested in Agricultural Co-operation for
many years, his initial concern dating back to at least 1849 when he
had had long discussions on the subject with Charles Kingsley. Thus this
Association was of major importance in reviving some of his old
dreams.

The relative repose of the past few years, during which he offered legal
advice to co-operators but shunned leadership, had been in conflict
with Neale's natural inclinations. While at university he had been deeply
moved by some of Byron's lines on Napoleon in 'Childe Harold';
possibly he still remembered a few of them.

But quiet to quick bosoms is a hell,
And *there* hath been thy bane; there is a fire
And motion of the soul, which will not dwell
In its own narrow being, but aspire
Beyond the fitting medium of desire;
And, but once kindled, quenchless evermore,
Preys upon high adventure, nor can tire
Of aught but rest; a fever at the core,
Fatal to him who bears, to all whoever bore.[6]

The new industrial partnerships were born at a time when the national scene was filled with commotion as the events of Neale's youth and early manhood appeared to be repeating themselves. Latent violence charged the atmosphere. The old question of the respective rights of employer and employed came back into the limelight, even as franchise extension became the most important issue to challenge Parliament Moreover the major political leaders had hardly begun to consider the 'shooting Niagara' of workingmen's franchise – with many of those in favour basing their arguments on the practical ability, common sense and good behaviour evidenced by workingmen involved in the Co-operative Movement – when a bomb exploded under the home of a worker in Sheffield who had stubbornly refused to join a trade union. A few such violent incidents in that city came to be known, collectively, as the 'Sheffield Outrages' – a war cry on the lips of those Parliamentarians like J. A. Roebuck who wished to repress unions. Restrictive legislation threatened as a Royal Commission was established to investigate the Labour Movement. It was fortunate that two men who were considered friends of labour were appointed to its number (the Positivist, Frederick Harrison, and Thomas Hughes) for it was at least partly due to their influence that the Royal Commission recommended no repressive action inits Majority Report.

Violence, strikes, lockouts and the threat of legal retribution against labour unions provided a discordant accompaniment to the simult-aneously reviving interest in co-operative production; and perhaps as in the past, had much to do with causing it (in any case, the connection between striking and profit sharing was clear enough at Briggs' collieries). Although Neale was essentially negative in his response to the demands of the trade unions, a characteristic stemming in no small part from his past disappointments, he was still very intrigued by their potential. Indeed there could hardly have been a series of events more calculated to awaken his imagination than those which had occurred during these few years. Even his interest in co-operative stores dwindled somewhat as he felt himself again confronted with dramatic proof of the eminent need to implement co-operative production in order to counteract the harsh climate of labour unrest. Hostile employers and union leaders must be made to recognise this need: co-operators must synchronise their efforts. The attempt to construct a federal union of co-operative associations comprehensive enough to absorb all kinds of workingmen's organisations must be renewed at all costs. Thus the gears of Neale's compulsion to design instruments of social harmony were re-engaged; but he was still cautious as he moved back towards the centre of activity, and he may not have moved at all had it not been for E. O. Greening.

Greening was a new bolt of lightning in the co-operative world and his efforts were brightening the darkness in exactly those areas which were of greatest interest to Neale. In 1867 he started a propaganda organ to herald the progress of the newly-launched 'partnerships' in industry called *The Industrial Partnership's Record* (continued under the title *Social Economist* from 1868 to 1869), and his office in Manchester, at 4 Warren Street, became a major centre wherefrom calls for co-operative unity were issued on an ever-increasing basis. Most relevant to Neale was Greening's demand that a national conference be held in Manchester. The object of the conference, Greening stated years later in retrospect, being 'to bring together the practical men who had made Co-operation successful in the Manchester district and the old leaders of the schools of Robert Owen and Frederick Denison Maurice. My idea was that such a union would lay the foundation of a national movement.'[7] And so it did. The Industrial Partnerships Conference was duly held in the last week of September 1867, and Neale not surprisingly was drawn irresistibly to attend. The week involved a whole series of special events: the Main Conference Session which was held in Manchester on Friday, the 27th, in the Assembly Room at Free Trade Hall, lasted only one day; whereas the important related meetings kept the principal participants planning, speaking and debating for several days. The significance of the Conference must not be underestimated – taking all the sessions collectively, it constituted the initial and most important gathering in the series which led to the First Co-operative Congress of 1869 out of which Neale's long-awaited Co-operative Union finally emerged.[8]

Indeed, because of his action in promoting the Industrial Partnerships Conference, Greening later claimed to have been the real father of the Congress of 1869 and the Co-operative Union.[9] The claim is not

without substance. William Pare, who is usually given the credit for
these developments, had for some time been calling for a Congress in
the pages of the *Co-operator*, but he did not appear on the scene
actively involved until 1869. Greening was, as he claimed, the most
important man in reviving the spirit of union: he acted as a strong
stimulant within the Co-operative Movement when he launched his
industrial partnerships; and then he brought all interested Englishmen
together in one body at the Conference in the last week of September
1867. There were in attendance such notables as Professor Jevons, the
economist, Henry Pitman, the editor, Reverend Molesworth, 'the
co-operative parson', Thomas Hughes, Neale, Walter Morrison, Ludlow,
Holyoake, Lloyd Jones, Malcolm Macleod of the ASE, and the
Equitable Pioneers of Rochdale.[10] A few, like 'old Gruff' Ludlow, who
wrote letters to Greening complaining that the new partnerships were
too profitable, came to the Conference almost as opponents,[11] but
they came nonetheless, and their interest in Co-operation was rejuven-
ated. Ultimately Greening even rounded up the old Redemptionists to
his cause: after he moved to London, James Hole worked closely with
him – as his 'chief associate', Greening later claimed – and Edward
Hole, James's son, became the only clerk at the Agricultural and
Horticultural Association.[12]

In his major address at the Industrial Partnerships Conference at Free
Trade Hall, Edward Owen Greening spoke out for co-operative unity in
words that must have strongly recalled to Neale's mind his own efforts
to the same end – efforts which dated back to his work as a Christian
Socialist, now almost two decades in the past. Greening informed his
listeners that the times were right for some action; he was receiving at
his office up to thirty letters a day from people interested in
Co-operation; and he proposed that an Annual Conference be established as well as a permanent Co-operative Union.[13] But had the matter
rested with him entirely there would have been little responsive action,
for he was at this time too narrowly interested in a union merely as a
means of promoting industrial partnerships. Indeed, he and Thomas
Hughes were totally blinded by Briggs and Co., whose profit-sharing
efforts overshadowed the whole Conference and were, unfortunately,
too transparently self-serving to provide a proper focus for any kind of
enlightened action.

The conference week had begun at the Whitwood Colliery where
Archibald Briggs gave a most delightfully revealing speech, inadvertently branding his so-called co-operative scheme for what it really was.

His theme seems to have been 'Co-operation forever, and no strikes'. All
the worker had to do to collect bonuses was to work well; that is to
say, as Briggs bluntly put it,

> 'by working how and when the managers wanted them to work.
> That was of great importance. To increase their prosperity they
> would have to give a long pull, a strong pull, and a pull altogether;
> but whatever they did, he hoped they would never take any pull at
> the beer-pot'.[14]

And there was a hearty laugh, but not a few, having looked into the
mathematics of Briggs' bonus, saw that owner and stockholder were the
real beneficiaries, as always, of the workingmen's obediently offered
long, strong pull. William Pare for one questioned why the extra profits
resulting from the long, strong pull should not belong *entirely* to the
labourer.[15] Also, Ludlow intensely disliked such partnerships, later
branding Briggs' scheme as an attempt 'to extract from the worker the
largest possible amount of labour for the smallest possible bribe in the
way of bonus.'[16]

Neale agreed with Pare and Ludlow: as early as 1852, when
discussing employers who were willing to share profits, he had guarded
his praise;[17] and not even the self-governing workshops fully pleased
his socialist inclinations, for unless they were regulated by being in
some sort of federal association with other co-operative bodies,
particularly stores, they would tend to follow the stern law of
competition. Moreover, he considered that the mere provision for
working-class shareholding, so common in many industrial partnerships,
served only as a dangerous temptation in the path of the co-operative
pilgrim's progress.

> 'If workers are shareholders also, no doubt they will be better off
> than if they were workers only; and I hope they will make good use
> of their improved means. But this will not make them *Co*-operators.
> This system leaves *labour*, as labour, where it found it. It is the side
> way over the fields, pleasant to walk in at first, and beautiful with
> the flowers of dividends ... but leading away from the straight
> highroad, to end, sooner or later, in the dungeons of Giant Despair.
> Let all earnest Co-operators beware of trying it.'[18]

Although Greening was the most idealistic of the builders of industrial
partnerships, even he was activated by motives which Neale rejected.
'The impression one gets of Greening at this time,' his biographer later
asserted, 'is that of a man trying to graft Commerce onto Co-operation.'

' "Give me your best," one can imagine him saying to the workers, "and I will not forget you when the profits are being divided." There is also the further suggestion that a share in the profits was dependent upon the utmost efficiency in the workshop and maximum production.'[19]

More important than Neale's scepticism about industrial partnerships was the fact that he was now no longer certain of the consumers co-operative ideal either; and his opinions in this area came obtrusively to light as the conference week closed with a tea at Rochdale to celebrate the Pioneers' new central store. During the festivities, William Cooper humorously introduced Neale, who was about to deliver a speech, as 'a very good sort of lawyer', telling the story of his having demanded only £7.7.0 for drafting the Industrial and Provident Societies Act of 1862. Neale responded rather negatively, both to Cooper's humour and to the hospitality of the Equitable Pioneers Society. He reminded the men of Rochdale that the real strength of the movement was that 'it was not started by those who looked forward merely to shopkeeping upon a better system; not to merely putting a little more profit into their pockets; but who looked to this movement as being the first practical step forward in a great social and moral advance.' Neale chided them for their mercenary spirit in abandoning profit sharing with workers at their cotton mill. This he felt had been a great mistake.[20]

Greening and Hughes were doubtlessly instrumental in convincing him that his old confidence in the consumer had been misplaced; in any case, he now became alive to the fact that there were dangers endemic to the stores which equalled those he observed in the workshops. He realised that the growing number of consumers advocates, who cared more for dividends than for the old transcendental ideals, were of the same mercenary bent as the Messrs Briggs. If it were argued that worker-owned workshops and industrial partnerships tended to generate only a few working-class capitalists. then it could with equal validity be maintained in retort that the consumers movement, in producing a new generation of working-class shopkeepers, was doing no better. The danger lay in the fact that neither side appeared to treasure the old idealism. The generation had changed and many men were finding it convenient to abandon the socialistic ethics which had undergirded the early Co-operative Movement, using the excuse, if any were offered, that they must adapt themselves to new conditions. The waning 1860s even witnessed the anomaly of a strike among the employees (shoemakers in this instance) of a co-operative store.[21]

While conducive to disillusionment, the commercial success of Consumers Co-operation and the related loss of idealism most certainly
heightened Neale's yearning for a meaningful Co-operative Union.

The most important aspect of the Industrial Partnerships Conference
was completely unplanned. As noted above, trade societies were in the
national limelight. Labour unrest tended to add weight to the
arguments of the promoters of industrial partnerships, and simultaneously caused a few trade union leaders to look with interest in the
direction of Co-operation. For example, Malcolm Macleod of the
Amalgamated Society of Engineers reported, while at the Conference,
that 'the leading men in their society believed that co-operation was the
only way out of the present muddle'.[22] Not unexpectedly it was
Ludlow who took the most advantage of these propitious circumstances; he had written a paper which at Holyoake's suggestion was
belatedly read at a special 'adjourned conference meeting' in Greening's
new offices at Albert Square. Entitled *Trade Societies and Co-operative
Production*, it played old Christian Socialist music. He advocated
utilising the ever-accumulating resources of trade societies to establish
co-operatives – but added a new turn to this old theme. Ludlow
maintained that while any attempt to convince the unions to use their
funds directly in the creation of co-operatives would be tantamount to
breaking one's head against a brick wall, their credit was a different
matter; and he innovatively concluded that trade societies could be of
great service if they would merely make their funds available, as Lloyds
of London commonly did in the sphere of private enterprise, for the
purpose of backing or underwriting co-operative ventures.[23]

Neale participated prominently in the important discussion which
followed. He agreed substantially with Ludlow's ideas but hesitated at
the word credit, which brought to mind all the common dangers which
beset speculative undertakings, such as overextension; its misuse could
lead not only to the collapse of the new co-operative ventures, but to
the termination of the hapless trade societies as well. Business ventures
based on credit were best left entirely to bankers. Therefore Neale
suggested that co-operators and trade unionists set themselves the more
basic task of 'founding a central association, that might serve as a bank
of credit to labour'.[24] This, of course, was no new theme so far as
Neale was concerned, for he had been a strong proponent of banking at
the first Christian Socialist Conferences in the early 1850s. His position
was strongly backed by the Rev. William Molesworth, 'the co-operative
parson', vicar of Spotland parish, Rochdale, who argued with feeling
that the French *Credit au Travail* was exactly the needed system, and

Molesworth's words again brought Neale to his feet to further amplify the theme. Trade unions could not be persuaded directly to utilise their funds in co-operative work, and using them as collateral was dangerous; but they could put their money in a Labour Bank to gather interest, and leave the matter of its investment to that organisation: he insisted that this was 'only asking trades unions to do what they do now. They invest their funds now; why should they not invest their funds in a society specially appointed to secure its safety and profitableness?'[25]

Neale's ideas were too close to Pierre-Joseph Proudhon's to be a coincidence, especially as the latter's notion of public credit banks was then at the height of its popularity. There had been resolutions in favour of Proudhon's scheme at recent Congresses of Marx's First International. Indeed, the Congress which had met less than a month before (2–8 September), at Lausanne, was seriously concerned with exactly the same questions as was the Industrial Partnerships Conference. The Lausanne Congress declared itself in favour of co-operative production (with reservations similar to those expressed by Neale), showed great scepticism about co-operative consumption (again similar to Neale), generally agreed that the trade unionists should support Co-operation, and recommended the establishment of credit banks. The matters which were taken up at the Industrial Partnerships Conference were thus, simultaneously, of international significance. Indeed this was true even of the industrial partnerships themselves, as several such schemes were attracting attention on the Continent a full decade before the Messrs Briggs got underway in England: in the 1850s knowledge of the work of Edmé Jean Leclaire in Paris and J. B. A. Godin at Guise was widespread. Leclaire employed a company of profit-sharing house painters, and Godin, in his own iron foundry, initiated a system which ultimately turned his employees into joint owners. Doubtlessly these experiments influenced the renewed emphasis on co-operative production in England. It is also reasonably certain that the vigorous efforts of Proudhon's disciples in the First International stimulated John Ludlow, Edward Vansittart Neale and others to reconsider the matter of establishing a co-operative bank.

In any event, banking was the most important issue to be raised at the Industrial Partnerships Conference, transcending in its pertinence both the question of profit sharing and that of the consumer's purported overemphasis on the dividend. Moreover, the insistence upon the need for establishing a banking society, more clearly than any other factor, called for the holding of another national meeting – one sufficiently representative seriously to contemplate such action. All of the friends of labour must be contacted and asked to attend: economist and philosopher, unionist and co-operator. At this point, the centre of action shifted to London and the initiative passed into Neale's capable and ready hands. If the new commercial spirit had pervaded the atmosphere in the North, as evidenced at the Industrial Partnerships Conference by the inordinate influence of the Messrs Briggs, such was not the case in London where the old idealism was more firmly entrenched.

Finally, after a lapse of eleven months, on Friday evening, 28 August 1868, Neale presided over a meeting at the offices of the Agricultural and Horticultural Association, held to determine the exact time and place for the prospective conference, with the result that a date was set for early in February 1869.[26]

Actually it was only in retrospect that Neale would realise the importance of the meeting in the offices of the Agricultural and Horticultural Association on 28 August, for it came very near failing in its purpose. Although a few stalwarts like James Hole, Greening and Holyoake were present along with delegates from the principal societies in the London area, the attendance of the northern co-operators, who represented the main strength of the Movement, was disappointingly slight. Even the proposed time for the holding of the national conference was soon abandoned in favour of an unspecified later date, despite all of Neale's efforts.

Yet the meeting had served its purpose. It did attract the interest of a few important northern consumers; and William Pare, although abroad in Norway at the time of the meeting (from which country he sent a note of encouragement) was totally enthused by the new work. He soon returned to England calling upon co-operators to make at least one more attempt to realise the great objective of co-operative union: he insisted that a national congress should be held at all costs. This was a call from the Movement's aging grand-dean – he was Robert Owen's literary executor, the erstwhile Governor of the Queenwood community in Hampshire, and his years of service made his voice irresistible. Thus Neale agreed to preside over yet another preliminary meeting, scheduled in early spring, at Stubbs' Mercantile Offices in Gresham Street, London, 'to consider the best means by which the benefits of Co-operation may be diffused, and extended to higher objects than those now attained'.[27]

This plea for 'higher objects' must be understood in terms of the uneasy awareness among many of the older co-operators, of the fact that the northern consumers were gradually abandoning the old ideals. The move to convene a national Congress was conceived, at least in part, as a rescue operation; its sponsors would recall co-operators to their original utopianism. If necessary, as a last resort, the Congress could provide a rival influence to counteract those who were primarily interested in the dividend, and who were even then beginning to crystallise their efforts in the Co-operative Wholesale Society.[28] To look into the future, an unhealthy rivalry did ultimately develop between the directors of the CWS and the old idealists who came to manage the Co-operative Congress, which persisted until Neale's death in 1892. This division between the leaders of the two most important organs of Co-operation – the administrative and economic centres of the movement – was the locus of its difficulties and disappointments in the formative years, and on not a few occasions threatened to entirely destroy it.

The spring meeting, with Neale presiding, was duly held on 2 March 1869, at Gresham Street, followed shortly afterwards on the 10th by another at Westminster. It was decided, at Pare's insistence, to call the coming national co-operative get-together by the American term 'Congress'; a new date (in May) was set for its meeting, and a General Committee was established to make the necessary arrangements.[29] This time there was to be no flagging of interest and the Congress convened as scheduled. Pare's charisma and Neale's organisational genius together constituted an unbeatable combination.

Despite the disappointments preceding Pare's appearance on the scene, Neale had been extremely active, especially in contacting and securing the support of old friends. Owenites as well as Redemptionists were once again corralled: Dr Henry Travis had been working with Neale at least as early as January 1868; James Hole and George Holyoake were brought in by August; and E. T. Craig was enlisted as of 10 March 1869. Furthermore, thanks largely to Ludlow's inspiring efforts at the Industrial Partnerships Conference, Neale had also been working hard to bring the major figures from the world of organised union labour into the Co-operative Movement. He was, in the beginning, very successful as the trade unions were substantially represented at the two preliminary meetings on the 2nd and 10th of March. When at the first of these meetings a permanent arrangement Committee was formed to prepare for the Co-operative Congress, its most prominent members included Robert Applegarth and Daniel Guile; and George Odgers was added to its number at the second meeting on the 10th. Indeed, of the group which Beatrice and Sidney

Webb labelled the trade union 'junta' because of their combined power, only Edwin Coulson of the Bricklayers was absent from involvement. The General Committee also included William Allan, William Newton and Malcolm Macleod of the Engineers. All of these labour leaders were appointed to a special subcomittee which, it was hoped, would obtain widespread support from trade unions for the upcoming Congress.

The majority of the names appearing on the General Committee were there for propaganda purposes and had very little to do with the drudgery of advertising and organisation. It appears that Pare and Neale did most of the planning and co-ordinating, while those men who had been prominent at the Industrial Partnerships Conference were their co-labourers in working out the details. Under their guidance the Committee was thorough, to say the least, and at its meeting on 30 April, Pare reported that advertising circulars had been sent to all trade societies and co-operatives with a known address, and to a myriad of foreign co-operators and sympathizers as well. The latter list was impressive and included such notables as Prof. Francesco Vignano, Prof. V. A. Huber, Hermann Schulze-Delitzsch, Elie Reclus, A. Desmoulins, Dr Hubert Valeroux and Louis Blanc.[30]

William Pare had been chosen by the Gresham Street meeting to act as the Honorary Secretary to the coming Congress, and, unlike the holders of most honorary offices, he worked very effectively writing propaganda material and corresponding extensively. Pare died in 1873 and the successful Congress stands as a monument to his last efforts. But the Congress was also Neale's monument. His genius lay behind its organisation, and it was he who ultimately engineered the branching of an effective Co-operative Union out of the stem of the Congress' Executive, thus bringing to full fruition Pare's dream as well as his own.

In view of the very significant support from the trade unions, it is noteworthy that northern co-operators continued to be slow in their response. The Wholesale moved with crablike indecisiveness towards the acceptance of what may have been recognised by some of its leaders as a potential rival. Were not some of the Congress's promoters already outspoken in criticism of the Wholesale's business services to the co-operative community? When it was suggested that the General Committee seek to form an immediate bond with the Conference Committee of the Lancashire and Yorkshire co-operative societies, there was some question as to whether this northern body — representing the strongest union of co-operators then in existence — would be willing to act with them in making arrangements for the forthcoming Congress. Although Co-operation was already financially strong, it was not yet by any means a Movement with anything resembling a central authority.

When the First Co-operative Congress finally met on Monday, 31 May 1869, at the Society of Arts, John Street, Adelphi, in London, it was strikingly reminiscent of the old Christian Socialist Conferences of the early 1850s. The resemblance was no accident; it was dominated by the same men and took up the same issues as those earlier gatherings. The meeting of the Congress represented a clear victory for all of those who, like Neale, sought to inject new life into Co-operation.

This gathering (again like those held in the early 1850s) occurred during a period of increased trade union activity and a burgeoning economic boom. Disraeli referred to the times as 'a convulsion of prosperity'[31] and this had manifested itself in a spirit of optimism, a renewed faith in progress, and an extensive revival of the old yearnings for co-operative union. Interest in projects that might be of benefit to the working classes was widespread; and, perhaps because Co-operation had been sanctified by Gladstone's 'Rochdale argument' for franchise extension, many prominent Liberals were attracted to it. A. J. Mundella attended the Congress on its second day and his name is only one of a group of Liberals present and speaking at this and subsequent yearly sessions. To compile a list of subscribers would be to call together such widely differing persons as Louis Blanc, John Ruskin, Dr Hodgson of Edinburgh University, Stanley Jevons, John Stuart Mill and even the Hon. Auberon Herbert whom Sidney Webb once described as 'serving the function of a stick by the side of a glacier to measure progress'.[32] Some of the leading lights of the Liberal-Labour-Co-operative world were thus corralled into loaning, temporarily in most cases, at least their names to the cause of co-operative extension and advance.

Neale, being abroad, was unavoidably absent from the first two Congress sessions. Consequently it fell to Thomas Hughes and John Ludlow to revive, in speeches and discussion, the same schemes the Christian Socialists had propounded unsuccessfully in the past. Hughes was President on the first day of the Congress and his inaugural address made it quite clear that there would be friction, as he chose to criticise the dull, plodding materialistic path taken by the co-operative consumers of Lancashire and Yorkshire, especially since Rochdale's abandonment of profit sharing.[33] Those who opposed Hughes' views also made themselves heard. One of the most important discussions turned about the inevitable, and after this time perennial, issue of the Wholesale's relation to the Co-operative Movement in its entirety –

how it could be of the most service – and the representative of the
Scottish Wholesale Society set a prophetic tone when he asserted
candidly 'that persons having the interests of Co-operation at heart
should divest themselves of all transcendental ideas as to principle.'[34]

John Ludlow proved to be the central figure, his ideas on banking,
involving as they did the question of the use of trade union funds,
providing one of the most ardently discussed issues. He made the old
appeal to those trade union leaders present, to join together in common
effort with co-operators, but the times had not changed for the better.
He had failed in the past, and would fail again. While the Congress was
supported in its idealistic resolutions by some of the most significant
names in the Labour Movement, nothing practical resulted as they too
had accommodated themselves to the new individualistic economic
beliefs current in mid-century England. Labour unionists like co-
operators would attempt no transcendental excursions into utopia.
William Allan of the Engineers, whom Ludlow labelled the representative of the 'Toryism of trade societies,' was no more willing at the
Congress in 1869 than he had been in the 1850s to see the funds of his
union risked by investing them in co-operative schemes, even if
accomplished through the facilities of a co-operative bank.[35] The wary
Allan's hesitation spoke most eloquently of the difficulties: while
willing to see their names enscribed on the rolls as supporters of the
Congress, most union leaders were unwilling to take more definite
action. In addition, they were soon to be irrevocably antagonised when
Co-operation's committeemen determined to exclude working men
from a share of the profits in co-operative workshops, after which they
proudly withdrew themselves to the isolation of their own movement in
which the primary concern was to raise wages.

Unhindered now by loyalty to any competing organisation, Ludlow
rivalled Neale in his enthusiasm for union. He called for the
establishment of a permanent central representative body and suggested
that it be organised regionally to cover the whole of England. But this
idea had to wait, his fellow delegates thought, for the Congress to gain
more headway; as well attended as it appeared to be, it still lacked the
wholehearted support of the northern co-operators. More realistically
they set up a London committee, very similar to the one which had
planned the Congress in the first place (Neale, in absentia, was voted to
its membership), which was enjoined to act in concert with the old
Lancashire and Yorkshire Conference Association. Finally in the spring
of 1870 the latter association agreed to merge itself into a national
body, which development resulted in the creation of the Central

Board — the desired central representative organ which some years later evolved into the Co-operative Union. Not unexpectedly, however, Ludlow's multi-regional plan was again passed over, the new Board being instead divided into only two sections, one for the North and the other for London and the South.

The basic mission of the Congress, as conceived by its founders, was more evident than ever in its Second Annual Session held in the heart of co-operative country, at Memorial Hall in Manchester. William Pare read an Address by Neale entitled 'State, Prospects, and Objects of Co-operation', which set the stage for the future conflict between the dividend-seeking shop-keepers representing the northern stores and the worker-oriented advocates of the old socialist dogma of Association.[36] The focus of the conflict would be a bid by the newly-emerged Congress and its Central Board to take over control of the Co-operative Movement and re-dedicate it to the regeneration of society. Repeating many of Thomas Hughes' warnings made the previous year at the Congress in London, Neale quoted from the Equitable Pioneers' utopian 'Declaration of Objectives' made in 1844, and compared it to the increasingly familiar statement of a new generation in Rochdale who less idealistically declared the aim of their society to be the accumulation, through members' voluntary subscriptions, of 'a fund for better enabling them to purchase food, firing, clothes, or other necessaries, by carrying on in common the trade of general dealers, both wholesale and retail'.[37] Neale then voiced his growing fear that this change of wording indicated only too clearly a change of thought:

'The noble idea of regenerating society from top to bottom, by an effort springing from the united exertions of those whom it consigns to its lowest rooms, has given way to the idea of obtaining good articles at the cheapest possible price.'[38]

In the words that recalled the 'manifesto' which he delivered at the Manchester Conference in 1853, Neale elaborated upon what he still conceived to be the true principle of Co-operation and the necessary steps toward its accomplishment. Despite the fact that the years since the collapse of Christian Socialism in 1854 had been, for the Co-operative Movement, years full of half-resolves and compromises Neale's ideal was more comprehensive than ever. Stores were, in his view, still the necessary first step; then wholesale centres should be established capable of supporting a vast and growing number of workshops through their ability to marshall a great and growing co-operative market. Thus far Neale only paced himself to the cadence of his old arguments, but the march of the times had quickened his imagination, for he next drew the outlines for a new international dimension. The wholesale centres should enter the sphere of foreign trade – he suggested founding a 'Co-operative Export Society', organised on the same federal basis as the Congress and the CWS, to provide new markets for a wider variety of products. He urged that since Ludlow's plan for a co-operative bank would facilitate these expansive endeavours, it should be immediately implemented. Lastly, he was yet a community builder: Co-operation must think beyond the purse, interesting itself in the quality of living by building healthy, roomy, pleasant homes for its working people as a prelude to realising at last the dreams of Plato, Owen and Fourier – the final creation of whole townships of people 'where the present isolation of our family life may be removed without destroying its sacredness' and where the 'separation of rich and poor shall vanish before the equalising influences of instruction and refinement'.[39] It is certainly curious to observe in a generation which came, as one historian stated as the title to a book 'before the socialists', that despite the existence of scepticism (characteristic of those who rested their minds in the assurance of mid-Victorian capitalism's ever-progressing victory over working class want), the response of great numbers of working and middle-class Victorians to these millenarian nostrums was not the expected nay-saying but hearty approval.

Neale's new emphasis on international Co-operation is perhaps easier to account for in the context of the times than his lingering utopianism: England's foreign trade was then entering a period of unprecedented expansion; he himself was spending an increasing amount of time abroad; and William Pare's recent and well-publicised foreign perambulations undoubtedly had their enlivening effect as did the widespread popularity of Marx's First International.

It is quite possible to over-emphasise the potentially schismatic differences of opinion in the Co-operative Movement, at least prior to 1873. As Pare delivered Neale's Address to the Manchester Congress, the loss of the older associationist idealism, although evident in the Northwest, did not appear to be an irrevocable phenomenon. The major opponents of profit sharing, for example, stepped forward only on an *individual* basis to meet Neale's carefully calculated challenges; and until these men totally captured the CWS, causing it to abandon profit sharing entirely, and giving it an almost anti-labour hue, the struggle was not joined along institutional lines. Indeed, the Wholesale under the presidency of James Crabtree often contested the materialistic direction of some of the Rochdale men and was hesitantly responsive to the revitalisation injected into the Movement through the efforts of the old Christian Socialists. Neale's plans included the Wholesale, his scheme for the establishment of co-operative banks and workshops depending upon the willing co-operation of that organisation and its business leadership. If the new Congress with its Central Board was to provide administrative and moral direction, he sincerely hoped the Wholesale would be its most important economic component; and therefore when the Wholesale in1872 decided to launch factories of its own, Neale was by no means in opposition. His chief concern was that these manufactories would be run on the basis of truly co-operative principles: they should be afforded not only the benefits of profit sharing but given a great measure of local autonomy. From the outset, the workers themselves should be allowed the lion's share of their own management, and ultimately complete independence. The attack on the Wholesale for pursuing what Neale later termed a policy of 'Caesarism' was still in the future. He was at this time actively trying to extend its functions: at the Wholesale's Quarterly Meeting in November 1872, he persuaded the directors to drop the qualifying 'North of England' from its title and urged them to open a branch in London to give much-needed help to the struggling co-operators in the South. Neale almost carried the Wholesale with him, or so it seemed, in his attempt to bring the movement onto a higher moral plateau, for its members also 'heartily affirmed' their commitment to the principle of profit sharing.[40]

William Pare himself in one of his last articles (part of a series he entitled a 'Trumpet-call to Co-operators') wrote enthusiastically:

'Although in feeble health, just recovering from a painful illness, I cannot refrain from expressing to you the high gratification I have felt at the perusal of the proceedings of the last quarterly meeting of the North of England Wholesale Society.'[41]

But within a year Pare died, and an obituary article by J. C. Farn entitled 'Mr Pare and Communistic Co-operation' proclaimed the 'high gratification' of the old Owenite to have been premature. The idealists now entrenched in the new Congress were in for some rough seas. Farn wrote prophetically:

'Here we leave the matter in the hope that the memory of Mr Pare will be considered none the less valuable because he was the

advocate of plans and purposes which the co-operators of 1873 do
not think it desirable even to attempt to realise.'[42]

Had it not been for the growing pre-eminence of 'Billy' Nuttall, John
Watts and J. T. W. Mitchell (the latter soon succeeded Crabtree as head
of the CWS) in the co-operative councils of the North country, Neale
and his fellow hopefuls might have been successful. But these three men
proved too powerful. They spoke a practical message – of making
profits not sharing them – which was attuned to the times: under their
direction the Wholesale's temporary, if significant, flirtation with
idealism was not destined to last more than a moment.

Notes

The opening quotation by William Pare may be found in the
Co-operator, VIII (1868), 56.
1. Mack and Armytage, *op.cit.*, p.155.
2. Benjamin Jones, *Co-operative Production* (Oxford, 1894) deals
   extensively with most of the 19th century experiments in
   co-operative production including the industrial partnerships. The
   book is indispensable; Jones' facts and figures are generally reliable
   (after 1871 taken primarily from the *Co-operative News* and
   Congress Reports) though too often manipulated in such a way as
   to favour his own views. Using virtually the same sources, I would
   take issue with many of his conclusions.
3. W. M. Bamford, *Our Fifty Years (1871–1921), a Jubilee Souvenir
   of the 'Co-operative News' the First Number of Which was
   Published on September 2nd, 1871.* (Manchester, 1921), p.80.
4. *Supplement to the Industrial Partnership's Record, November 1st,
   1867* (London [?], 1867), p.6.
5. Margaret Digby and Sheila Gorst, *Agricultural Co-operation in the
   United Kingdom*, 2nd ed. (Oxford. 1957), p.21. On the origins of
   the Association see also Tom Crimes, *Edward Owen Greening: A
   Maker of Modern Co-operation* (London, 1924), p.54; The *Co-
   operator*, VIII (1868), p.176; and *Agricultural Co-operation.
   Prospectus, Memorandum, and Articles of Association, of the
   Agricultural and Horticultural Association, Limited, Formed to
   Supply its Members with Implements and 'Machines' by the Best
   Makers, and with Unadulterated Seeds, Manures, and Feeding
   Stuffs, at Wholesale Cost Prices, on the Co-operative System*
   (Manchester, n.d. [prob. 1867]).
6. Canto III, XLII.
7. E. O. Greening MSS entitled 'Notable Congresses', E. O. Greening
   Papers, package marked 'E.O.G. Letters'.
8. The Conference as a whole was reported in the previously cited

Supplement to the Industrial Partnership's Record.

9. E. O. Greening, *A Pioneer Co-partnership: Being the History of the Leicester Co-operative Boot and Shoe Manufacturing Society Ltd.* (London, 1923), p.9. See also 'Notable Congresses' cited above

10. Crimes, *op.cit.*, p.62.

11. Mack and Armytage, *op.cit.*, p.156.

12. Crimes, *op.cit.*, p.36.

13. *Supplement to the Industrial Partnership's Record*, p.6.

14. *Ibid.*, p.16.

15. Benjamin Jones, *op.cit.*, pp.792–793.

16. Donald Wagner, *The Church of England and Social Reform Since 1854* (New York, 1930), p.129.

17. *Labour and Capital, op.cit.*, pp.22–23.

18. E. V. Neale, 'Co-operative Profits', *Co-operator*, I (1860), 78.

19. Crimes, *op.cit.*, pp.47–48.

20. *Co-operator*, VII (1867), 556. Neale's criticism must have come as a surprise, for prior to this time he had been a forthright defender of the consumers' position even on the delicate question of profit sharing, see e.g., *Co-operator*, VI (1866), 241–242, 261.

21. J. M. Ludlow, 'True and False Co-operation', *Co-operator*, VIII (1868), 593–595.

22. *Supplement to the Industrial Partnership's Record*, p.6.

23. *Ibid.*, p.7ff.

24. *Ibid.*, p.10.

25. *Ibid.*

26. *Co-operator*, VIII (1868), 586, 588. *The Social Economist. Industrial Partnership's Record and Co-operative Review*, II (1868). 119. For a good summary account of this meeting and subsequent events leading up to the First Co-operative Congress, see the *Proceedings of the [1st] Co-operative Congress Held in London at the Theatre of the Society of Arts, May 31st, and June 1st, 2nd, and 3rd, 1869. Reprinted Chiefly from 'The Co-operator', and Edited by J. M. Ludlow* (London, 1869).

27. The *Social Economist*, III (1869), 6, 13ff. *Co-operator*, IX (1869), 205.

28. Hughes, 'Neale', *op.cit.*, pp.175–176.

29. See The *Social Economist*, III (1869), 25; *Co-operator*, IX (1869), 205; and the *Fifth Annual Co-operative Congress, Held at Newcastle-upon-Tyne, April 12, 14, 15, 16, 1873* (Manchester, 1873), Preface, p.vi.

30. *Co-operator*, IX (1869), 305.

31. Disraeli cited by Asa Briggs, *Victorian People* (New York, Harper, 1963), p.296.

32. Helen Lynd, *England in the Eighteen-Eighties; Towards a Social Basis for Freedom* (Oxford, 1945), p.74.

33. *Proceedings of the [1st] Congress, op.cit.*, p.10.

34. Hughes, 'Neale', *op.cit.*, p.176.

35. *Proceedings of the [1st] Congress, op.cit.*, p.32.

36. E. V. Neale, 'State, Prospects, and Objects of Co-operation, with
    Special Reference to Production', *Co-operator and Anti-
    Vaccinator*, X (1870), 675–676, 701, 716, 745. Also available in
    *Proceedings of the [2nd] Co-operative Congress Held in Manchester at the Memorial Hall, Albert Square, June 6th, 7th, 8th,
    and 9th, 1870* (Manchester, 1870), pp.43–48.
37. *Ibid.*, p.675.
38. *Ibid.*
39. *Ibid.*, p.745.
40. See report of this Quarterly Meeting in *C.N.*, II (1872), 592–593.
41. *C.N.*, II (1872), 613.
42. *C.N.*, III (1873), 346.

V

THE ASCENDANCE OF BUREAUCRATISM:
INDIVIDUALISM VS. FEDERALISM
1870–1876

The errors of good men ought to be treated with respect.
Neale's 'Journal', 15 October 1831

The infant Congress was unquestionably in good health, Neale's work on behalf of co-operative union having at last borne fruit. But as the decade of the 70s got underway it became evident that the greatest effort of his life still lay in the future. The Movement was soon to be rocked by a serious disagreement about the conduct of co-operative production, a disagreement characterised by the widespread use, or misuse, of the terms 'federalist' and 'individualist'. Briefly stated, the trouble first arose when the administrators of the northern stores determined to eliminate entirely individual shareholding within the Movement's many workshops; there was a strong and growing current of opinion that factories were truly co-operative only if owned collectively by the stores and worked solely for the consumers' benefit. Here Neale and his idealistic friends dug in their heels: how could workers ever come to be self-employed under such a system? In addition, the stores threatened to boycott any independent workshop which refused to share profits with them in proportion to purchases; this was certainly inconsistent behaviour considering the fact that in their own workshops (such as the mills founded by the Rochdale Pioneers) they sharply contested the principle of profit sharing with labourers.

By 1873 the profit-sharing question was uppermost, and a major controversy on the issue was impending as the spotlight descended upon the CWS. In that year the Wholesale launched the Crumpsall Biscuit Works and the Leicester Boot Factory. Why, some co-operators queried, should the Wholesale, in operating these factories, parcel out profits to individual working men which rightfully belonged to its members, the federally organised consumers who had provided all of the initial capital? Two things were evident to all observers: firstly, that the Wholesale was the unrivalled and almost unquestioned business centre of the Co-operative Movement; and secondly, that its conduct in the sphere of production would determine the future course of Co-operation. Consequently it was a turning point of the utmost significance when that organisation, in 1875, abandoned all profit

99

sharing. The term federalist reached its definitive meaning as the Wholesale's apologia. From this time forward the word was most frequently used narrowly to refer to that system whereby the Wholesale would own and control all productive establishments, managing them on a strictly profit-making basis and turning all of the benefits over to the stores in the form of a dividend on purchase. This was federalist only in the sense that the Wholesale itself was a federal organ — stores not individuals were its sole constituents.

In short, under federalism, production was totally subordinated to consumption. The stigma of individualism was stamped upon those who wished to emphasise the primacy of the producer and who sought to bestow upon the co-operative workshop the same semi-autonomous position enjoyed by the co-operative store. They were accused, in most cases falsely, of merely advocating the multiplication of industrial partnerships and individualistic, self-governing, isolated and frequently competing workshops. In the view of the Wholesale Society and its defenders, the individualists would deny to the consumer his rightful profits while establishing, as so-called co-operatives, a myriad of joint-stock companies.

Edward Vansittart Neale's basic ideal was to bring together into one movement all the very diversified efforts to advance the cause of labour. This would include workingmen's clubs and institutes, friendly societies and trade unions, as well as co-operatives; the great unifying work of Association must be neither exclusive nor sectarian. He desired that each of Co-operation's great federal centres — the Congress, the Wholesale, the Insurance Society, the projected Bank and Newspaper — should work together harmoniously and with all other similarly motivated organisations. Although it is doubtful, given the practical mindedness of the labourers in Lancashire and Yorkshire, that Neale's hopes could ever have been fully realised, it does seem reasonable that, had the Movement remained true to even a semblance of the 'old virtues' and retained its focus on the wage earner without being diverted by the shopkeeper, it could have led all others in its time and become an important economic weapon in the struggle for the realisation of socialist principles.

The most significant items on the agenda of the first few sessions of Congress turned about the task of launching a newspaper (the *Co-operative News*) and a bank. A short history of the origins of these institutions provides a valuable aid in understanding the nature and development of the conflict between the self-styled federalists of the

Wholesale Society and the so-called individualists led by Neale and his old Christian Socialist friends. It would be difficult indeed to overestimate the importance of the *Co operative News*, as it constituted the most intimate contact the national leaders had with the rank and file. Therefore it was especially disappointing that the *News* never became what Neale wished it to be — a national organ representing the views of all co-operators, producers as well as consumers. Instead, by means of what in effect constituted an interlocking directorate, it soon fell within the burgeoning administrative sphere of the narrow coterie of committeemen who dominated the Consumers Movement. Such an outcome was predictable from the very beginning of the newspaper's existence: in 1871, when the pledges of money were fulfilled and the venture launched, it was called, significantly, the North of England Newspaper Company Limited; and at least nine of the original fourteen members of the Management Committee were at the same time affiliated with the Wholesale.[1]

In a short while, as might be expected, there was mounting complaint that the company was dominated by a faction — the special instrument, in Neale's words, of 'Lancashire, with a dash of York-shire' — and E. O. Greening, the most outspoken critic, was stridently insisting that something must be done to make it more representative.[2] Like Greening, Neale had always been of the opinion that the Movement's official newspaper must be operated with complete impart-iality, especially as it was designed to have a compulsory circulation; and ultimately he made specific proposals to this effect in a long letter to William Nuttall (15 February 1874).[3] He suggested that a member of the Central Board, as such, as well as a delegate from each of its sections (five were created by the Newcastle Congress in 1873, South, Midlands, North, Northwest and Scotland), should be elected as representatives to the Newspaper's Management Committee, thereby giving that body a national rather than a sectional disposition. The letter was an extremely important one; its recommendations, substant-ially unchanged, were incorporated into official resolutions passed by the Halifax Congress (1874) and subsequently implemented. Winning Nuttall's support had insured success in this instance.

But there is a pyrrhic quality to all of Neale's victories and this one was not destined to be an exception: short of excommunicating the consumers of Lancashire and Yorkshire, it was impossible to draw up any Constitution which would not ensure their ultimate predominance. The societies of the Northwest, being not only more numerous than in the rest of England, but individually larger and richer, would certainly continue to hold the greatest amount of share capital in the newspaper and thus would be assured the predominant voice in its management. Unfortunately, the sectional representatives never had any real influence in either the choice of executive officers or in matters of the balance sheet.[4] Indeed, the General Meetings of Shareholders grew steadily smaller and more Lancashire-Yorkshire in character — a trend which was in evidence within two years of the Resolutions made at Halifax. The outcome was that the editorial policy of the *Co-operative News* became consistently 'federalist' and remained so.

Meanwhile, the banking controversy had come to dwarf all other issues. Unwilling to see his earlier efforts wasted, John Ludlow had again become the prime force when he delivered an inspirational address at a special conference in Bury on Good Friday 1870, recommending the initiation of a full scale co-operative banking scheme to function in close conjunction with the CWS.[5] Ludlow's paper notably reinforced the general consensus that such a move was an ultimate necessity, but co-operators were nothing if not cautious and it was still necessary for more than two years to elapse before action was taken on his proposals. Indeed it would have taken an even longer time had not Neale joined the cause: at the Birmingham Congress in 1871 he contributed a paper on 'The Amendment of the Law as to Banking'; he and Ludlow afterwards collaborated in securing the passage, on 16 August 1871, of a Parliamentary Bill which greatly encouraged the expansion of co-operative activities by enabling societies to deal in land and buildings with little risk.[6] Under its provisions many restrictions on buying, selling and mortgaging were lifted and as a result the bigger societies undertook extensive building projects. Cottages, cotton and corn mills were erected on an unprecedented scale, and it was the stimulus afforded by this rush of capital development that finally turned the demands for a co-operative bank into reality; early in 1872 it was realised by most of the important English societies that their caution in this sphere was costing them money.[7] The Wholesale was the logical place to begin; aside from Neale and Ludlow, Dr J. H. Rutherford, a flamboyant co-operator from Newcastle, was the most energetic in pressing that body to make the necessary move into banking.

Unfortunately, Rutherford's motive differed markedly from that of the other banking enthusiasts. He was then well known as the managing director of the Ouseburn Engineering Works near Newcastle (one of the new industrial partnerships) which produced marine engines of superior quality, but was, nevertheless, proving a source of anxiety to co-operators. Rutherford, a medical doctor and sometime Congregationalist minister who admitted to having no business qualifications, had taken on orders at such low prices that the company was faced, almost from the beginning, with serious losses. Subsequently, when he encouraged the Wholesale Society to commence banking, it was not for the sake of the Co-operative Movement alone; he had visions of an endless supply of ready money for his own troublesome Ouseburn Works. The Wholesale, however, while under the leadership of James Crabtree, moved with great caution, and Rutherford's natural impatience quickly mounted to the point of indiscretion. Unwilling to wait upon events, he called together a group of northern co-operators, obtaining their sanction, and founded a bank of his own on 8 July 1872.

The new creation was called the Industrial Bank. It opened for business in Newcastle, portentously asserting itself to be co-operative and demanding the loyalty of co-operators, while its claim to such loyalty was questionable. Opponents pointed out that it was simply a profit-making concern; membership was open to individuals and they were promised an extravagant return on their share capital. Rutherford responded to criticism by insisting deviously that some place in the Movement must be reserved for bodies 'not co-operative in form but truly co-operative in spirit.'[8] In spite of its obvious shortcomings, he propagandised the Industrial Bank as a reasonable fulfillment of Ludlow's ideas; and even Holyoake, who should have been wiser, commented in his preface to the Congress Report for 1872 that Ludlow 'must have been gratified' by the interest taken in a co-operative bank and its subsequent establishment in Newcastle.[9]

In fact, Holyoake's enthusiasm for Rutherford's project was not shared by either Ludlow or Neale. The latter had been very concerned to restrict membership in any new bank to societies, this being one of the major reasons why he had joined those who tried to press the CWS, as the financially strongest federal organisation in existence, to take the initial action. Heretofore individual ownership in anything but the productive societies (where it was necessary to insure workmen's participation) was advanced only as a temporary expedient. There had been all but universal agreement that where individual shareholding existed in federal organs (in bodies like the Union, the Wholesale and the Newspaper Society), it must as soon as possible give place to shareholding by societies alone. Ludlow was frankly appalled to see such an apparent distortion of his banking proposals and denounced Rutherford's scheme in the pages of the *Co-operative News*: 'The longer

I live,' he wrote angrily, 'the less do I believe in bodies "not co-operative in form but truly co-operative in spirit" .'[10] He supported Neale's view that the admission of individual shareholders into the large federated institutions was a dangerous practise. It is of some significance that on this issue Ludlow and Neale stood staunchly by the side of John Watts, the major theoretician of Consumers Co-operation, who also was severe in his criticism of the Industrial Bank.[11]

Then new complications developed. John Watts, supported by the most powerful CWS committeemen – notably J. T. W. Mitchell and William Nuttall – finally prevailed over Crabtree's caution and in September 1872, the Wholesale opened a Deposit and Loan Department. The Movement had, it seemed, proceeded from famine to feast, now being blessed with two banks.

There was certainly room enough within the Co-operative Movement to accommodate both; but a controversy arose between them which owed largely to Rutherford's antagonistic approach to the CWS. At first the antagonism was not reciprocated. The Wholesale directors harboured no ill will for Rutherford's Newcastle schemes – neither for the Ouseburn Works, nor for the Industrial Bank. Indeed, William Nuttall had so heavily invested in the Ouseburn Engineering Works that he made a strenuous effort to drum up support for the continuously failing company. Rutherford, however, utilised the opportunities afford by every public speech and co-operative get-together to downgrade both the CWS and its new Deposit and Loan Department. Moreover, despite Neale's and Ludlow's strong disapproval of individual shareholding in essentially federal schemes, Rutherford continued to propagandise his efforts as truly representative of the Movement's oldest ideals; he claimed that 'true unity of co-operation is a unity in diversity', and therefore requires 'both individualism and federalism'.[12] To the detriment of the views held by Neale and Ludlow, and causing general confusion, Rutherford tied two basically separate questions into one package by identifying profit sharing and individual stockholding in producers co-operatives (which all the old associationists thought to be a necessity) with individual stockholding in his own banking venture, which was quite another matter. His efforts had the deleterious effect of helping to affix the brand 'individualism' not only on himself but upon all those who advocated profit sharing with workers. More than anyone else, Rutherford must bear the blame for the division of co-operators into federalists and individualists, the dichotomy that was to plague the Movement for the next twenty years with one round of devastating controversy after another.[13] But then it is likely the division would have occurred anyway, for the seeds of the struggle over profit sharing, sown many years earlier, were now beginning to germinate.[14]

Late in the summer of 1871, Lloyd Jones made a co-operative tour of the northern counties; in York, Lancaster, Chester, Stafford, 'nearly everywhere,' he reported, 'Co-operation as *mere* retail trading had become an unmistakable success.'[15] He was not encouraged by this development, indicating that in place of the old enthusiasm for the emancipation of labour, there was now apathy. Changes in the ideals of northern co-operators had inevitably accompanied success. At first these changes went undefined and undefended, but finally, tired of being reminded of their shortcomings by southern idealists, *mere* traders generated theoreticians of their own to defend their interest-begotten preference for consumption. Particularly sensitive on the issue of profit sharing with working men, they moved to counteract the ever-escalating charges that they were mercenaries without ideals and in the process fully developed the concept of Federalism.

William 'Billy' Nuttall fired the opening salvoes on behalf of the retailers. Nuttall (who advertised himself in the columns of the *Co-operative News* as 'Accountant, Auditor and General Financial Agent, Exchange Chambers, Bottom-o'th'-Moor, Oldham') was then known as the statistician of the Co-operative Movement because of his intricate statistical tables showing the progress of the societies which he regularly published in the *News*. In the spring of 1872 he argued that as both labour and capital made their gains at the consumer's expense, productive co-operation would be best organised by consumers alone. He would countenance neither profit sharing nor a bonus to labour. Consumers should provide the capital themselves (when borrowing, paying the least possible interest) and employ the needed labourers at the usual rate of wages, retaining all the profits to be parcelled out as dividends on purchase.[16] By the fall of the year, he was enunciating his theories more bluntly:

'Once put the labourer in the position where he commands a bonus . . . and he would command it by electing men who would give largely to labour, little to capital, and little or nothing to the consumer.'[17]

He demanded an end to all individual shareholding whether by working men co-operators or otherwise. Ownership, he reasoned, should be limited to federations of consumers. In implementing his ideas, Nuttall first aimed his gun at the Co-operative Printing Society, which he successfully forced to commence a system of sharing profits with consumers. Under attack, even the Hebden Bridge Fustian Society (an industrial partnership launched in the autumn of 1870) took a step towards this new federalist position by finally closing its share list to individuals.[18]

As Nuttall had first introduced the case for the consumer, so it was Dr John Watts of Manchester who accustomed co-operators to the use of the term 'federalist' to represent the exclusive dogma of the Wholesale Society. Goaded by Rutherford's mounting attack, Watts argued that not only banking but, ideally, all co-operative production should be carried on exclusively by the CWS – a truly federal body disallowing individual shareholding – for the sole benefit of the stores. If Rutherford represented one extreme, then Nuttall and Watts were his opposites.

Co-operators began to take sides on the issue as the *News* added a new column to its statistical section, indicating which societies gave a 'Bonus to Labour'. E. O. Greening wrote a tirade against the consumer under the title 'False Federalism',[19] and finally Neale sent a contribution to the *News* entitled 'Individuality and Federation' which, unlike most preceding articles, attempted to disarm both sides; the problem, he felt, must be treated with 'calm, reason and impartial investigation'. Neale did indicate, however, what he considered to be the defects in the plan of federation advocated by Watts and Nuttall while declaring himself to be, according to his own understanding of the term, an advocate of federalism. 'The danger arises now,' he pointed out, 'when the consumers, supplying at once the capital and the custom, threaten to convert the worker altogether into the condition of salaried servants.' On the matter of excluding individuals from co-operative ownership, he felt that there should be no hard and fast rules; the necessary thing was to word the constitutions of societies so that it would be impossible to divert them from their common co-operative objects toward private ends. Neale agreed with Nuttall and Watts that the consumer had a genuine claim to some of the profits on production, 'but participation,' he concluded, 'is not identical with absorption.'[20]

It had become evident, especially since the Congress at Bolton in 1872, that the Movement's administrative machinery was due for a major overhaul in the interest of greater efficiency; a Central Board with only two sections – one in the North, the other in the South – could not effectively co-ordinate the work of Co-operation for the whole of

England and Scotland. Indeed, from the time of its establishment the Board's sphere of activities had steadily expanded until William Pare, the Honorary Secretary, found it virtually impossible to keep abreast of the burgeoning amount of correspondence, and William Nuttall had been brought in to function as an additional paid secretary. Ultimately, the complexity of the problems resulting from the Movement's otherwise encouraging physical growth and organisational development led Neale to propose to the Newcastle Congress (1873) that it be remodeled along regional lines. The subsequent division of the Central Board into five representative sections was the tangible result of this proposal. When implemented, Neale's plan combined a great measure of regional independence with overall central administration. Each section, while locally autonomous, was tied to all other sections by common membership in a United Board, which met periodically and served as the supreme co-ordinating body. Neale hoped thereby to make the Movement centrally effective as well as thoroughly representative. He and Ludlow both had agreed on the desirability of some such change since 1870; but it had taken the events of the past year, particularly the problems which arose as a result of the controversy over banking, to make its necessity evident to all co-operators. Holyoake, following Neale's line of reasoning, was one of those at the Newcastle Congress who readily associated the banking dispute with the wider question of creating a more effective Central Board: 'The only thing they had to do,' he maintained, 'was to strengthen the hands of the Central Board, so as to enable them to bring the two banks into harmony.'[21]

Holyoake was overly optimistic. Unable to resolve the controversy between the banks, the Board itself stumbled on the issue, divided by a discouraging amount of personal animosity. On 23 August 1873, the *News* contained the following announcement: 'Mr Nuttall has given notice of his intention to withdraw from the secretariat of the Central Board. Mr Farn [then editor of the *News*] has offered himself as his successor.'[22] The resignation caused a stir of questioning within the Movement as angry letters to the editor followed in its wake, a typical one complaining that as most members of the Central Board held views differing from Nuttall's, he had most surely 'been cramped in his power to advocate the right co-operative principle — ''societies interests'' — and because he refused to teach principles not in harmony with his views he was placed in a very awkward position.'[23] Neale rushed to explain that while it was probably true that Nuttall's resignation was due to his holding views opposed to most other members of the Central Board, there had never been any attempt to crush him; his resignation was his own spontaneous act. Fortunately, in this case the anger died away as quickly as it had arisen, and the decision was made to hold a meeting at Barnsley on 13 September to determine Nuttall's successor. Out of twenty-seven candidates, six were selected for submission to the United Board; with some reservations on account of his age, Neale was the final choice. This proved to be another major turning point in Neale's life: at the age of 63 he was at the start of a new career.[24]

His work in designing and installing the organisational apparatus of Co-operation was almost complete; to be placed in charge of its maintenance was the crowning recognition of his years of service. For Neale did not merely replace Nuttall, his accession to the office of General Secretary resulted in its being decisively changed. Prior to this time there had been no one who could legitimately be thought of as a Chief Executive. Pare had served only as Honorary Secretary with Nuttall functioning as his paid assistant, and when Pare had died earlier in the year, Nuttall's position had become somewhat anomalous. At that time Neale had volunteered to succeed Pare as Honorary Secretary; now with Nuttall's resignation he enlarged the offer, and agreed to take on not only all the secretarial duties of the Union, but its legal business as well, combining it all into one office and for less pay.

Neale's appointment was initially for only one year, as there were those even among his supporters (including Thomas Hughes) who were sceptical about an old man taking on so many burdens. Several co-operators had steadfastly opposed his election for that reason, one of whom was Henry Whiley, a member both of the Wholesale Committee and the Congress Board. But Neale quickly proved himself capable of handling the job, and by the end of the year's probation, Whiley could state without hesitation that 'he had never worked with a more indefatigable secretary.'[25] Considering the way Neale devoted all of his life's energy to the cause, it was little wonder he was so successful. Eight years after his appointment Holyoake wrote in praise, 'I know of no movement in which the secretary is so uniformly conclusive and accurate in the solution of the difficult questions often submitted to him.'[26] A short time later, Dr Watts, with whom Neale had been battling in the pages of the *Co-operative News* (as E.V.N. vs. J.W.) on almost a monthly basis, paid him the highest tribute of all: 'Co-operation owes more to Mr Neale,' the Doctor wrote, 'than to any other dozen — he thought he might say any other twenty men, unless it were the original pioneers.'[27] With such eloquent support, Neale was perpetuated in office until the year before his death when, in poor health, he finally submitted his resignation: he was then eighty-one.

Gathering testimonials is the usual biographer's blunder, but the fact was that as General Secretary Neale did do the work of several men. No detail was too small to escape his careful attention. His untiring efforts as legal advisor, organiser and propagandist had indeed made him all but indispensable to the Co-operative Movement prior to his acceptance of the General Secretaryship, and afterwards, despite the added burden of official work, he was even more of a prolific contributor. By 1874, in collaboration with Ludlow, he had added another *Co-operator's Handbook* to his publications. Even a partial listing of his efforts commands respect: he drew up several Acts of Parliament; he wrote explanatory articles simplifying legal questions for the benefit of the general reader, as well as articles and pamphlets of all sorts to propagandise Co-operation; he compiled Congress Reports, penned pungently idealistic prefaces to them and also drafted the Reports of the United Board; Neale assembled detailed travel instructions for deputations to various Co-operative Conferences, made arrangements for speakers and then attended almost every major conference himself, even when the travelling involved hardship; finally, he continued to give legal aid of the most detailed kind, and to prepare prospectuses, passbooks and model rules for new societies – the latter being all neatly printed up in a standardised form so that a society need only fill in some blanks, and send the rules off to the Registry of Friendly Societies. Neale's lingering compulsion to bring unity was evidenced by the escalating burden of work he took upon himself, and successfully completed.

Neale was appointed General Secretary at Barnsley, 13 September 1873. That same day, as scheduled, representatives of the rival banking schemes met with the Central Board to attempt a final resolution of the controversy through the magic of amalgamation.[28] After investigating the question a special committee had recommended severing all of the banking business from the Wholesale and amalgamating it with the Industrial Bank to form one central organ with principal offices in London. More in line with co-operative principles this essentially new entity would, by its constitution, prohibit individuals from holding more than one-third of the total amount of shares; and it was reasonably certain that it would be only a matter of time before individual shareholding was eliminated entirely. Neale, although favouring amalgamation, had attended the meeting at Barnsley with a mind to compromise and so, surprisingly enough, had Thomas Hughes, but they were the exceptions. Rutherford came with his usual hostile propaganda against the Wholesale Bank, and J. T. W. Mitchell, by now the most vociferous of the Wholesale's bureaucratic leaders was adamantly unwilling to yield. Mitchell was a person of strong words and equally strong action, who could rise 'like a lion' at CWS meetings[29] to roar out his point of view. A tall, heavy-set, clean-shaven, balding man with an innate sense of never being wrong, Mitchell, like Ernest Bevin a few generations later, was a practical man with a practical man's contempt for social theory and theorisers. He drew his dogma from Dr Watts, and once he had clearly comprehended the federalist idea, he never departed from it for the rest of his life. Like a few future leaders of note, also in the Labour Movement, he had struggled to the top by the hardest route, beginning his life in Rochdale as the son of a working-class mother with no known father; no greater contrast to Neale could anywhere be found. It is a tribute to Mitchell's utter determination to succeed – and his business acumen – that despite his poverty, he rose to great prominence in the Co-operative Movement. His contribution, however, was in no sense creative; he lent to the Movement the talents of an exceptionally good Victorian businessman, dogged stubbornness, a complete indifference to the labourers who worked for him, willingness to take a risk and an abundance of luck. Mitchell took the most intransigent position at the Barnsley meeting when he rose to state categorically that 'The Wholesale was the bank of Co-operative societies; it was established by themselves for their own requirements, and amply fulfilled them, and he would not be a party, in any sense, to disturb the arrangements.'[30]

The final outcome of this argumentative meeting was a disappointment to all those who wished for a settlement. The men at Barnsley supported a CWS plan to enter upon general banking business and open new branches while recommending, without enthusiasm, that the Wholesale make an effort to amalgamate with Rutherford's Industrial Bank at some unspecified time in the future. J. T. W. Mitchell had won. Later, on 22 May 1874, still basking in the limelight of his victory over Rutherford, he was elected Chairman of the CWS.

After his promotion to the position of General Secretary, Neale appeared to spring into new life as the apologist for the doctrine mislabelled 'individualist'. Heretofore most of the rough-and-tumble of ideological conflict had been left to Ludlow, Hughes and Lloyd Jones. As the interrelated problems surrounding the questions of profit sharing and the bank had continued to grow more perplexing, Neale had expressed himself forcefully only on general principles, leaving the specifics to his colleagues, and sometimes it was not certain to all the

parties in the controversy precisely where he stood. Indeed, as in
Christian Socialist days, it may have been Ludlow who was the chief
figure during the period 1867–1873: as he had been the force behind
Maurice, so he may have been the force behind Neale. However, in the
autumn of 1873 Neale took the direction of affairs into his own hands:
breaking the chrysalis of his vague generalisations and compromising
imprecision on controversial issues, he emerged with a clarity and
certainty consistent with his new executive position.

There was a special urgency about the question of co-operative
production in 1873, for in that year the Wholesale Society opened the
Crumpsall Biscuit Works and the Leicester Boot Factory. As previously
indicated, Neale welcomed this development, for he had always thought
that the Wholesale Society, with its huge marketing facilities, would
serve as the most effective launching centre for co-operative workshops.
However, he also felt it to be of the utmost importance that that great
federal body manage its new factories for the benefit of the working
man, in strict accordance with the old co-operative ideals. The threat of
a federalism which could justify the exploitation of labour for the sole
benefit of consumers had to be counteracted at all costs. In an address
entitled 'On Federative Production', Neale finally made specific
proposals which he hoped would settle the issue. He did not make out a
case for the complete independence of the co-operative workshop (as,
indeed, some of his opponents on the Wholesale Society's Board of
Directors expected him to do) but instead argued for equity between
labourer and consumer, both in the amount of their respective capital
holdings and in the sharing of profits. Neale felt that this equity could
be quickly achieved by requiring that the labourers' share of the profits
be added to their account within the association until it balanced the
capital contributed by the consumers. In addition, he insisted that
workers must participate effectively in the management of their own
workshops, and also be represented on the board of the distributive
centre (whether the CWS or an individual society like the Rochdale
Pioneers) with which they would maintain a federal connection similar
to that existing between the CWS and its member stores.[31] The fact
that when Neale became Secretary he had replaced Nuttall — one of the
major consumers' polemicists – added a dramatic poignancy to his
literary activity. He could not be ignored. Consequently 1874 proved to
be a prolific year indeed as Neale was forced to write article after article
in response to the criticism of the federalists in the pages of the *News*.
The most formidable of his literary opponents were Nuttall himself and
an anonymous author who chivalrously styled himself 'Bayard'.

The most interesting of Neale's undertakings in 1874, however, was the establishment of a small union of independent productive societies called the Co-operative Chamber of Commerce. It was brought into being primarily to compensate for the fact that the Wholesale took little interest in those workshops not under its direct control, especially where products were involved which had no market within the Movement and therefore could offer nothing in the way of dividends to co-operative consumers. Although short-lived and of little lasting significance, Neale put much thought into the design for the new body which was remarkably sophisticated. It anticipated some of the basic elements in the modern concepts of industrial rationalisation and national planning, such as facilities for market research and control; systematic advertising; the provision of capital for expansion; the pooling of information relative to the improvement of industrial processes; control over quality and price (although this facility was largely limited to the settlement of disputes); and arbitration machinery designed to prevent competition between the individual productive societies within a specific industry.[32] In the Co-operative Chamber of Commerce, Neale again revealed his prescience; when he brought his imagination to bear on practical problems, he frequently came up with ideas that were well in advance of his times.

Yet, despite his imaginative genius, all of Neale's efforts to counteract the gospel of Consumers Federalism proved inadequate, for in the summer of 1875 the CWS made that most consequential move in its history when it entirely abandoned profit sharing, referring to it variously as a 'pet theory' of an 'Oliver Twist nature' and a bribe: If we could not get men to give us their services for wages,' went the argument, 'it was time we changed the men.'[33] The London Branch of the CWS had opposed the move, the Newcastle Branch blew hot and cold, but Manchester, with the overwhelming balance of power, and that now wielded by J. T. W. Mitchell, prevailed.

If there were still some lingering questions in the minds of co-operators as to precisely what issues were at stake in the struggle between federalists and individualists they were clearly dispelled when Dr John Watts finally followed the precedent set by Nuttall and 'Bayard' and carried on an open controversy with Neale in the *Co-operative News*. They disputed with one another disguised as 'E.V.N.' and 'J.W.', the use of initials, common enough in polemical discourse, releasing them from some of the necessities of official courtesy. Neale now lifted the bar of temperance and combatively declared the Co-operative Wholesale Society to be pursuing a policy of

Caesarism in an article entitled 'Caesarism and Federation'.[34] It was a valuable effort, for its clarity of line, logic of development and deftly exaggerated analogy, as the perfectly balanced propellants of a point of view, demonstrate that Neale had fully mastered the art of polemical writing. And although his terminology is readily understandable only in the context of the Co-operative Movement, some of the patterns which underlie his work have universal application:

> 'If I have given to the system the name of Caesarism, it is not in order to create prejudices against it, but because I know of no name which so accurately expresses its true character — its tendency to centralisation, which unavoidably accompanies despotism — though attended in this case, as in many other cases of so-called fraternal government, with the assumption that this despotism is only for the common good. I have been the more induced to give it this name from the "gross misapplication" of the name federalism, by which the advocates of the system have disguised its true features.'[35]

Neale admitted that the relationship between the Wholesale and the stores, its member societies, was one of true federalism, its delegate meetings examples of pure democracy, but, he insisted, that was not the system by which the Wholesale Society proposed to conduct its productive works. The federal ideal had been completely rejected by the Wholesale when establishing workshops; practicing 'Caesarism' in its stead, they established a central authority which would regulate everything without giving to the producers, as such, any voice at all in the matter.

If the word 'individualist' referred to those who advocated establishing isolated, autonomous, competitive, worker-owned workshops, then the Wholesale magnates had created a paper tiger to fight with, for there were no individualists, least of all any led by Neale. In this article he again took great pains to indicate that he had no intention of depriving the CWS of the ownership and control of its factories — at least not in the near future. Wholesale societies (and Neale thought there should be many such centres) should act as wet nurses for infant co-operative workshops. In the beginning the workshop would be very dependent; the Wholesale, having supplied the capital would exercise the predominant authority, and standing 'above the influence of local jealousies, and the factions of the workshop' could impose upon it the necessary degree of moral order. Yet, since the ultimate goal was to turn it into an autonomous component of a great federal union, the workman must be gradually weaned to self-government. The first

managers of the new productive establishment would logically be of the
CWS's choosing; but these managers would know that their actions
would be subject to review, for the workers would have delegate
representation at the Wholesale Society's Quarterly Meetings. The
present behavior of the CWS, Neale concluded, was unjust and
inexcusable, differing in no way from that of competitive employers
who, though they couldn't buy a man outright, hired him on the lowest
possible terms appropriating all the advantages to themselves.

> 'There is no trouble about the division of the spoil, if the lion takes
> it all. Profit on capital, because I buy the materials; profit on work,
> because I pay the wages; profit on consumption, because I am the
> consumer. It is a case of simple division with a quotient satisfactory
> probably to those who bring it out in their favour.'[36]

In his answer, J. W. claimed to be closer in principle to E.V.N. than
it might appear, for he too was in favour of the democratic
participation of labour in the profits of co-operative work. But, he
reasoned, it must be assumed that every worker is a member of a
co-operative store, which store is in its turn a member of the Wholesale;
consequently, he is 'a partaker, not only of the profits which he helps
to produce, but also of those made by the producers of all the
commodities which he purchases at the store.'[37] The most controversial of Ricardo's ideas he made his own and turned them against
E.V.N.; workers frequently got so much of a share in the fruits of
production, J.W. complained, that some were forced out of employ-
ment because the limited amount of capital available for wages and
materials was exhausted. He chided E.V.N. for not making a distinction
between the 'idlers and slovens' on the one hand, and the 'industrious
and careful' workmen on the other, when to the latter alone belonged
any of the credit for a company's prosperity. As for E.V.N.'s appeal for
justice to labour, J.W. had some moral arguments of his own. He told
the story of a factory where the observance of 'St Monday' (that is to
say, the habit of the indolent to stay out of work on Monday) had
become a standing nuisance, but where an easy solution to the problem
had been quickly found; namely, the wages of the absentees were
docked for the day of their absence and the money so gained
distributed among those willing hands who had showed up for work.
J.W. concluded prosaically, 'the result was that St Monday lost its
votaries. This was, as I think, *just*, and the result was *moral*.'[38]

While the federalists could defend their business practices as
financially sound, their logic failed completely when in arguing with

Neale and his friends they tried to show that their system was capable of working a great work of social transformation. J. T. W. Mitchell (Watts' apt pupil) was particularly naïve in this respect, and doubtless believed that it was actually possible to mitigate all the evils of capitalism by the laboriously gradual procedure of offering to countless thousands of Englishmen a few shillings a year in dividends on their purchases at co-operative stores.[39] Neale was impatient with such patent nonsense. At Oldham in January 1876, Mitchell spoke of profits which, 'instead of going into the hands of 500, might be divided amongst 10,000 or 15,000 people. What was meant by Co-operation was that every man and woman should feel in their own homes the benefits of the industrial enterprises in which they were engaged.'[40] Neale could only interpret this as saying, in effect, that the money so necessary for the work of co-operative propaganda, the expansion of co-operative educational facilities, the establishment of more work-shops and stores, was to be unconscionably dissipated in shillings and pence to thousands of people who, in most cases, were the very ones who needed it least. In speaking of the profit made from co-operative production he argued that if it were

' . . . distributed among the consumers according to their purchases, six-tenths of it would go into the pockets of the 23 per cent of the population who now receive, according to the calculations of Mr. Dudley Baxter and Mr. Leone Levy [sic], 60 per cent of the yearly income of the United Kingdom, and four-tenths only into those of the 77 per cent of the population who now receive the remaining 40 per cent of income, *since income and purchasing power are necessarily commensurate*; while of the 40 per cent, for the same reason, the largest share would always go to those who had the largest means, who thus would be continually gaining an advantage at the cost of a class generally poorer than themselves, by whose labour the profit thus distributed had been produced.'[41]

Taken in perspective it would seem to be the Wholesale federalists who were the most unrealistic co-operators in envisioning a social revolution based on the dividend.

Holyoake had at first supported the federalist position, his pamphlet, *The Logic of Co-operation* (1873), being a classic in defense of 'the poor consumer'. But 'logic' ultimately necessitated a change in direction. After the Wholesale Society had abandoned the bonus, Holyoake made a complete about-face, a dramatic change of opinion, which spoke very eloquently against his erstwhile fellow champions of the consumers' gospel; his expatiations on their behalf were of less than three years duration. At the Eighth Congress at Glasgow in 1876, when charges of 'sentimentality' were lodged against Neale, Holyoake, with his usual caustic humour, moved entirely over into the camp of the 'individualists'. He denied that sentiment was the basis of Neale's schemes and quipped wittily at Neale's accusers, 'Why, there was nobody more sentimental than speakers of that class, only their sentiment was concentrated upon dividend. (Hear, and laughter).'[42]

Notes

1. W. M. Bamford, *op.cit.*, p.5.
2. *Ibid.*, p.12. See also E. O. Greening, 'A Plea for a Truly Co-operative Press', *C.N.*, IV (1874), 229–230; and E. O. Greening to Neale, 19 November 1873 (in Greening Papers, the letter books). Unless otherwise stated all succeeding letters from E. O. Greening may be found in his letter books.
3. *C.N.*, IV (1874), 39. Bamford, *op.cit.*, reprinted the letter, pp.11–12.
4. Bamford, *op.cit.*, pp.12–13.
5. Percy Redfern, *Story of the CWS, The Jubilee History of the Co-operative Wholesale Society, Ltd., 1863–1913* (Manchester, 1913), p.65. For a brief but valuable commentary on Ludlow's address at Bury, written by Thomas Hughes, consult the *Ninth Co-operative Congress, Leicester, 1877* (Manchester, 1877), pp.12–13.
6. The Bill became law as 'An Act to Explain and Amend the Law Relating to Industrial and Provident Societies' (34 and 35 Vict. c. 80). See Hughes, 'Neale', *op.cit.*, pp.177–178.
7. *Fourth Annual Co-operative Congress, Held at Bolton, April 1st. 2nd. and 3rd. 1872* (Manchester, 1872), p.9. As the titles to the Annual Congress Reports vary, I shall hereafter abbreviate them uniformly as follows: *Fourth Co-operative Congress, Bolton, 1872* (Manchester, 1872). On the second citation it will be further abbreviated as *Fourth Congress*.
8. See John Ludlow, 'The Industrial Bank', *C.N.*, II (1872), 517. With this article Ludlow became the most outspoken critic of Rutherford's bank.
9. *Fourth Congress*, p.x.
10. Ludlow, 'The Industrial Bank', *loc. cit.*
11. Rutherford answered his critics in an extensive letter to the editor, *C.N.*, III (1873), 37–39. He specifically dealt with Ludlow's arguments in *C.N.*, II (1872), 541.
12. *C.N.*, II (1872), 541.
13. I believe Benjamin Jones to have been incorrect in attributing the origin of the term 'individualist' to an article by Neale written in

the *Co-operator* in 1862. The term is properly understood only in
the context of the 1870s. See Jones, *op. cit.*, p.738.

14. The origins of the profit-sharing controversy can be traced back at
least to the 1850s, see e.g., *Co-operative Commercial Circular*,
No.12 (1 October 1854), 85; also, *Report of the [2nd] Co-
operative Conference Held at Manchester... 1853* (London,
1853), pp.18–19. In the early years Neale always attempted to
accommodate the consumers' position: *C.C.C.*, No.6 (1 April
1854), 33–36; E. V. Neale, *The Co-operator's Handbook...*
(London, 1860), passim; *Co-operator*, I (1860), 94, II (1861),
86–87, III (1862), 82–83.

15. *Fourth Congress*, p.17. I have added the italics to emphasise his
negative reaction.

16. *C.N.*, II (1872), 268.

17. *Ibid.*, 495.

18. Fred Hall, *History of the Co-operative Printing Society,
1869–1919* (Manchester, 1919), pp.103–109. See *C.N.*, II (1872),
591 for Joseph Greenwood's comments on Federalism and the
Hebden Bridge Fustian Society.

19. *C.N.*, III (1873), 98.

20. *Ibid.*, p.122.

21. *Fifth Congress*, p.70. For general background material consult
E. V. Neale, *The Central Co-operative Board: Its History, Constitution and Use* (Manchester, n.d.) See the *C.N.*, IV (1874),
134–135 for extracts from and a discussion of this paper.

22. *C.N.*, III (1873), 426.

23. *Ibid.*, p.459.

24. Curiously enough it was G. J. Holyoake who first suggested to
Neale that he make a bid for the position even though the
relationship between the two men had, in the past, left much to be
desired. See Neale to Holyoake, 3 September 1873, Holyoake
Papers (from Brown Bundle).

25. *Sixth Congress*, p.64.

26. *C.N.*, XII (1881), 397.

27. *Ibid.*, p.840.

28. *C.N.*, III (1873), 480–481.

29. Percy Redfern, *John T. W. Mitchell; Pioneer of Consumer's Co-
operation* (Manchester, 1923), p.39.

30. *C.N.*, III (1873), 480.

31. E. V. Neale, 'On Federative Production', *C.N.*, III (1873), 586. See
also Neale's 'The Position of the Individual in Co-operation', *C.N.*,
III (1873), 529; and 'On the True Spirit of Co-operative Propaganda', *C.N.*, III (1873), 624.

32. See *C.N.*, V (1874), 160.

33. Abraham Howard, erstwhile President of the Pioneers Society,
backed the motion to abandon profit sharing retorting that,
'Honourable and upright men did not want bribes to do their duty';
and Samuel Stott agreed, rudely commenting that '... great
sympathy was due for those gentlemen who spoke so pathetically

for their pet theory . . . . Somebody said it was a pity it was
allowed to drop; he thought it a pity it was ever introduced. He
ventured on the prediction that it would never succeed, because it
had a great deal of the Oliver Twist nature, and was ever asking for
more.' *C.N.*, VI (1875), 352. Thus time had brought a remarkable
change in the views of many of the Movement's leaders: in 1855 as
the Rochdale Pioneers accepted Neale's suggestion that they
establish a Wholesale Department, they idealistically spoke of
'attaining that point where each man will be his own employer'.
Co-operative Commercial Circular, No.17 (1 March 1855), 126.

34. *C.N.*, VI (1875), pp.378–379.
35. *Ibid.*, p.378.
36. *Ibid.*, p.379.
37. *Ibid.*, p.390.
38. *Ibid.*
39. *C.N.*, VII (1876), 137.
40. *Ibid.*, p.44.
41. *Eighth Co-operative Congress, Glasgow, 1876* (Manchester, 1876),
    p.21. Italics are my own. See also E. V. Neale, 'The Hebden Bridge
    Manufacturing Society', *C.N.*, VIII (1877), 54–55.
42. *Eighth Congress*, p.56.

VI

THE CO-OPERATOR AND THE LABORER: INDIVIDUALISM VS. FEDERALISM 1873—1879

> You talk of 'working men' . . . but what are you? Are
> you shopkeepers? Are you members of the 'upper ten
> thousand'? What are you?
>
> Lloyd Jones, 1879

Although the negative attitude towards workmen expressed by some of the leading theoreticians of Consumers Co-operation was neither newly arrived at nor related to any one specific incident, certainly the collapse of the Ouseburn Works as well as the critical economic conditions after the depression of 1873 tended to exacerbate their prejudices.

Stimulating the dramatic business boom of the late 1860s and early 1870s had been a great surge of economic development centring in Eastern Europe and the United States, accelerated by the increasing demand for British products resulting from the Franco-Prussian War. On the home market prices had soared and profits increased commensurately, spurring a rush of investments and the proliferation of new business schemes.[1] Labour demanded more and got it by striking; the industrial partnership was one response to their increased demands. While generally motivated by high ideals, partnerships had been often used as a sort of industrial opiate to disarm labourers and render them quiescent while the employers reaped the gains. This, it may be recalled, was the case with the coal mines of the Messrs Briggs. Co-operation had also expanded to meet the challenge of the boom phenomenon with its greater profits; for example, as coal prices had risen steeply, co-operators responded by launching a plethora of ill-fated collieries. In the year 1872 alone, when the mining mania first began, collieries had been opened by them in Eccleshill, Darwin, Leeds and Newcastle-on-Tyne.[2] Even London's co-operators had responded. In 1873 Neale, Greening and Hughes established a Coal Co-operative Society in Westminster for the purpose of retailing coal supplied by the new co-operative collieries.[3]

The economic bubble burst in 1873 with a world-wide effect. Panic began at Vienna in May and quickly spread to Germany; the climax came on 18 September when it reached New York where the firm of Jay Cook and Company crashed, and the shock waves bowled down other great economic barons like Jay Gould. There was no panic in

England to compare with that seen in Vienna and New York City, but there was no escape either: prices fell, profits dwindled and then dried up: wages were cut and in the co-operative world talk of profit sharing, or bonuses, became reckless talk. This time, unlike past economic disasters, the country refused to recover, and the carcasses of dead and dying business enterprises dotted the economic landscape until the decade's end. Most of the industrial partnerships dissolved completely, or reverted to simple joint-stock companies. Typically, the Messrs Briggs, faced with a strike in 1874, cut off their own deceptive profit-sharing scheme. The new co-operative collieries died slowly but surely; while there was certainly enough co-operative coal consumption to make the pits remunerative under normal conditions, they had all been launched on the basis of the high, boom price of coal, and proved impossible to maintain during the long years of slump. It is clear that attitudes toward labour stiffened as a result of the depression. The walls that separated the lower from the middle classes were raised a little higher and co-operative committeemen, who must be numbered with the latter, hardened their hearts.

It is paradoxical, however, that the most disheartening failure in the co-operative world, the collapse of the Ouseburn Works in the summer of 1875, stemmed less from conditions resulting from the business recession than from the sheer mismanagement of Dr Rutherford. This failure was to have a most profound effect on opinions within the Movement, for Rutherford's widespread propaganda efforts had conspicuously woven the Ouseburn Engineering Works into the fabric of the so-called 'individualist' argument for co-operative production. Although they were too busy counting their own losses to realise it at first, the collapse of this company provided the federalists with precisely the excuse needed to end, for good and all, the talk of worker-control, individual stockholding and profit sharing. Ironically, Rutherford himself supplied the federalists with their most damaging argument when he claimed that the collapse of the Ouseburn Engineering Works had been due solely to his labourers' demand for a 10 per cent increase in wages.[4] William Nuttall, who had most heavily invested in the Ouseburn scheme, was eager that the CWS should take it over and lost no time in backing Rutherford's point of view. Like Rutherford he would prove the company sound by attributing its losses to labour.[5] And John Watts too, used the Ouseburn labourers as a moral illustration of the truth of his own preconceived ideas. In one diatribe entitled 'The Working Man: A Problem', Watts charged that they had, through their demand for more pay, 'helped the company into liquidation and themselves into the streets', concluding with some passion, 'and yet if one could drive a grain of sense into workingmen in general, what a future is within their grasp!'[6] Lloyd Jones, who had been barnstorming the co-operative countryside off and on for years as an advocate of Producers Co-operation, was the outstanding pro-claimant against the view that labour was at fault in the Ouseburn failure. In the pages of the *Beehive* he petulantly replied to Watts, 'The grain of sense is, we fear, wanting in other heads besides those of working men.'[7]

Unfortunately co-operators were not the only ones with ears to hear the new negativistic gospel of the co-operative industrial titans; as a result the friendly intercourse with trade unions, so evident in the first few Congresses, was by the middle of the 1870s drawing to an end. Proposals for a closer alliance between unions and co-operatives were still occasionally heard — from such as Lloyd Jones — but in the central organs of both movements these proposals were consistently defeated by substantial majorities. In 1877 the Parliamentary Committee of the Trade Union Congress reported to the labourers assembled at Leicester:

'There are men amongst us who, your committee venture to say, do not fully appreciate the power for good possessed by the co-operative system. On the other hand, we consider that there are men in the co-operative movement whose anxiety for large profits needs considerable force to impress them with the just claims of labour even in their own works.'[8]

The federalist titans like Mitchell, Watts and Nuttall, however, were not entirely alone in holding opinions displeasing to the TUC. Neale had a few prejudices to overcome in this area himself, one of his permanent blind spots being an antipathy to Trade Unionism.[9] Just as Marxists often damned unions for deflecting attention from the necessary revolutionary struggle and (by the process of their being ever accessible to the middle class embrace) for lulling workers into the acceptance of a capitalist society, so Neale reasoned that the workers' belief that unions were beneficial 'naturally tends to make them indifferent to that kind of union by which they may be permanently benefitted.'[10] The same difference of opinion which divided Sir Stafford Cripps from Ernest Bevin in the 1930s divided Neale from the trade unionists of the 1870s. Both Cripps and Neale worried about Trade Unionism as a *conservative* force. Nevertheless, having made his opposition explicit, Neale conceded that given the present capitalistic society, strong trade unions were a necessary evil; this may have weakened his argument a little but testifies again to his basic common sense.[11]

Indeed, one significant aspect of trade union activity always drew Neale's unmitigated praise. This was their function as mutual assurance societies making provision for members when they were beset by unemployment, sickness, and death.[12] He believed that in the course of moving toward the Co-operative Commonwealth, it would be necessary to transform each labour union into a friendly society. Organisations for mutual assurance would find an easy place as integral components of the new social order – organisations for fighting employers would not. As in 1852 his advice to unions was that they should use their funds, now saved for striking, on mutual assurance and the establishment of co-operative workshops.

To implement his ideas, on 20 January 1877, at Barnsley, Neale submitted a plan for a broadly based Co-operative Friendly Society. His scheme was intended to provide benefits similar to those afforded by membership in the great orders like the Foresters and Oddfellows, that is insurance against sickness, old age and death, as well as such other services as endowments for children when they reached a specified age. Enthusiastically received, the Co-operative Friendly Society was, in due course, registered as a federal organisation composed of a central headquarters with a number of regionally located branch lodges, and Neale obtained the full support of the Co-operative Insurance Society which became largely responsible for its management. The new organisation was carefully designed. Dependable actuarial tables were calculated from the rates recently published in the report of the Actuarial Commission; no member would be called upon to contribute more than a fixed amount paid in regular periodic installments. However, the co-operative rank and file showed no disposition to take advantage of the new body – even with the backing of the prestigious CIS, Neale simply could not get them to see beyond the store – and its winding up was officially announced at the Congress at Edinburgh in 1883.

Unlike so many of his contemporaries Neale was not a supporter of friendly societies because they encouraged working class thrift. He could envision their becoming the basis of a federally unified, nationwide system of social insurance under the auspices of the Co-operative Movement. Nevertheless, the fact that the Victorian upper classes accepted their social utility without question was of the utmost importance to Neale. Because the majority of mankind were essentially slow to appreciate innovation, he once wrote, a new course of action 'must be presented to them under an aspect not far removed from that which previous custom enables them to appreciate.'[13] Like most of Neale's creations the Co-operative Friendly Society was of little significance by itself – it was but a small dab of paint on the large canvas of his plans for the Co-operative Commonwealth. Sadly enough, friendly societies, labour unions, and co-operative stores and work-shops, all went their separate ways during the last quarter of the nineteenth century, remaining relatively ineffectual organisations on the periphery of the capitalist system rather than becoming, as Neale had intended, integral and necessary components of a socialist federation. Had he been successful in carrying out his grand design there need not have evolved a paternal system of welfare capitalism based upon instruments of social and economic reform wielded by men interested in alleviating distress rather than in dealing with its causes. Had workingmen caught Neale's dream, perhaps they could have managed to carry out for themselves, by the means of a unified movement with a consistent social philosophy, the measures that were later carried out for them by classes interested only in ironing out the kinks in the status quo.

Neale continued to champion the cause of the worker (not the unionist) in the pages of the *Co-operative News*, taking stronger issue with John Watts month by month. 'But the new federal system,' he wrote in the summer of 1877, 'of which "J.W.", if not the author, is at least the skillful advocate, turns our machinery for elevating the condition of the worker into a scheme for cheapening the results of his work.'[14] Up to this time Neale appeared willing to accept a three-way division of industrial profits with a view to conciliating the opposing forces of capital, labour and custom. He now changed his mind, concluding that ultimately 'all division of profit must be abandoned, and the whole, beyond the wages of capital, be given to one of the three claimants – that one, however, being, not the capitalist, as the joint-stock system contends, nor the purchaser, as what I take leave to call the Wholesale system maintains, but the worker.'[15] As the decade drew on towards its end Neale began to evidence in his words and actions a growing frustration; early in 1879, when charged with doing harm to Co-operation by always talking about what was desirable without properly considering what was possible, he responded with a new and unusually immodest virulence:

'If he was in the time of life at which Mr. Nuttall was he might wait for fifty years perhaps – (applause) – but if he were to wait now he should only have an audience of worms to speak to, and that was not worth much. Plato spoke a great deal above the heads of the people, but his words have been echoing through the ages ever since, and a great deal of what we are enjoying now we owe to him.'[16]

Shortly after this outburst Neale even took George Holyoake to task for what the latter had recently published in his celebrated *History of Co-operation*. Holyoake had compromisingly tried to mean all things to all men, his history praising without discrimination the workingmen's partnerships, and also upholding the necessity of sharing with the consumer. 'Capital and labour,' he stoutly maintained, 'would have a poor time of it were it not for the consumers who pay for their produce.'[17] Holyoake had once referred to Neale as 'so kindly-natured a gentleman that I believe he would apologise for doing what was right – if anyone objected to it.'[18] While this may have been generally true, Neale's review of the *History of Co-operation* showed little, if any, respect for feelings; he attacked Holyoake strongly for holding some of the very same compromising views he had himself expressed but a few years before. Holyoake praised the Hebden Bridge Fustian Society, one of the most eulogised of the new profit-sharing concerns. Neale denounced it: '... out of a sum of £1,110.17s.8d. divided on six balance sheets lying before me, £869.12s.10d. went to those who simply used what other people made, and £241.4s.10d. only to the workers who made what was thus used.'[19] His views on sharing with the consumer were again made explicit: he would give the consumer nothing.

The course of events in 1879 tended to further exacerbate tensions, widening the gap between federalists and individualists. Private retail traders had launched an offensive against civil service stores and co-operative associations which had led to the appointment of a Parliamentary committee of investigation;[20] and when Dr Watts came to be interviewed by this committee, in July, he surprised some of his fellow co-operators by blandly describing Co-operation as 'a scheme for getting commodities at wholesale prices, selling them at retail prices, reserving the difference as quarterly dividends, and encouraging the members to leave these dividends to accumulate at 5 per cent interest. He looked upon it as a very important element in teaching provident habits, and preventing poverty and pauperism.'[21] Watts was at the time making frequent public appearances, speaking on Co-operation and related economic topics. On one such occasion before the Social

Science Congress in the late fall of 1879 he made the well-known assertion (still to be heard today in some quarters) that government expenditure tends to depress the labour market. Indeed he did not hesitate to contend that the ratio between 'excess' government expenditure and unemployment was a matter of simple arithmetical calculation:

> 'In the last five years . . . our national expenditure has exceeded by £34,086,983 that of the five years immediately preceding, which lessens our means for productive employment by 340,869 men; and the expenditure of 1877–8 exceeded that of 1869–70 by £14,140,241, thus lessening our means of productive employment by 141,402 men. Surely there is room for retrenchment here; and the Government has only to turn back to the expenditure of 1869–70 in order to reinstate all these men, and feed their families.'[22]

Neale's reply, in an article entitled 'Taxation and Government Expenditure' warrants a quotation of some length for his ideas were well in advance of those of most other economic thinkers in that day. Neale maintained that Watts' logic required a belief that the Government *buried* its money and he elaborated on the point as follows:

> 'Is not Dr Watts aware that, with the exception of the small sum applied by Sir Stafford Northcote to the reduction of the national debt, every penny of the income received by the Government is paid back again to the nation, either as interest on the debt, or as salaries, or wages, or for the purchase of materials, and so goes, in some shape or other, to stimulate productive employment and "feed the men employed and their families?" . . .
>
> 'The Government employ it, suppose, in building an ironclad: they give employment to ironworkers, miners, smelters, engineers, smiths, carpenters, etc., etc., and all whom these persons help to employ – again an endless list . . . .The case is obviously . . . one not of loss, but of transfer of property. What is withdrawn from A is given to B. A may grumble at the diminution of his private means, but if he tries to give dignity to his selfishness by big talking about this diminution as a "loss" to the nation, and a lessening of its productive power, he talks nonsense . . . But if we wish to fulfill that indispensable condition of all sound judgment, to "free our minds from cant," we must carefully distinguish the question whether any Government exercises a wise economy in the use of the funds at its

command for the objects which it proposes, from the question whether we approve of these objects or not; and the more so because these two questions are very apt to get mixed together. Still more carefully must we guard against the temptation to elevate our likings and dislikings into alleged scientific principles, and talk about loss of national resources, when what we really mean is, "We don't like the purposes for which they are used". '[23]

When ten years later J. A. Hobson in *Physiology of Industry* made a similar defence of public expenditure, he was in consequence denied permission to speak at London University.[24] In 1879 Neale had made something of a first.

The decade's final blow to the sensibilities of that coterie of co-operative intellectuals who stood with Vansittart Neale – the scandal of the Congress at Gloucester's Corn Exchange in 1879 – was the outbreak of a strike in the CWS shoe factory at Leicester. Holyoake wailed to the delegates at the Congress that it was a disaster and 'simply disgraceful' that the CWS had not made provisions for sharing profits with workingmen; and in the course of lively discussion one Mr. Hemmings stated that he was 'not against bonus, but he objected to making too much of working men.' This was more than Lloyd Jones could bear; taking the floor he denounced such 'loose talk'. His extemporaneous peroration was executed with mastery:

'When men threw off the principle that should make them saviours of society, it was the devil in the saint's doublet, and a bad business for the world . . .You talk of "working men" . . . but what are you? Are you shopkeepers? Are you members of the "upper ten thousand"? What are you?'[25]

Although nowhere near as dramatic an issue as a strike in a co-operative factory, it was the old question of the bank which was the most important to the Movement's future, and the controversy over this question also had reached flash point as the 1870s drew to a close. As early as the First Congress in 1869 it was clear that the success of Neale's plans depended on the creation of a co-operative bank. Stores had been established, the Wholesale had properly followed as desired, and the capital that the old Owenites had sought to obtain through the medium of these organisations was now in hand. It only remained to establish banks to direct that capital to the desired ends – the emancipation of labour from economic thralldom through the establishment of self-governing workshops, associated housing facilities, and finally, home colonies. The Wholesale, when it began banking, appeared to be moving in the right direction, but then unexpectedly the flaw had appeared in Neale's master blue-print; the Wholesale arrested progress at this stage of its own success and turned means and ends upside down by refusing service to any but the 'poor consumer'. Many of Neale's projects, for example the friendly society scheme, could fail without unravelling the whole skein, but lacking credit facilities broadly available to labour unions as well as to any other groups of labourers who wished to practice Co-operation, there was no chance that the Movement could proceed to the highest level of social achievement.

At first Neale had strongly supported the CWS in its banking venture, but the years since 1873 had been crowded with events which served to change his mind. The collapse of the Ouseburn engine works had drowned the Industrial Bank in its wake, leaving the field to the CWS alone; and the Wholesale had almost simultaneously abandoned profit sharing. As Nuttall maintained correctly, it was at this juncture that Neale, Hughes and Greening commenced deliberation on how best to 'take the sinews of war from the Wholesale'.[26] In their view it then became a matter of life or death for Co-operation to detach banking from the consumers' side of the Movement. It was time to establish a separate bank, open to the patronage of all labour organisations, including workingmen's clubs and institutes, friendly societies, and labour unions, the purpose being to draw together 'the accumulated resources of the industrial population into a great federative centre.'[27]

By 1877 it had become apparent that Neale and his fellow idealists in the South — a group which could now justifiably be called the co-operative junta — wielded the power of the Central Board and through it controlled the Congress. Neale even turned the Annual Congress Report into a vehicle of his own propaganda, a sort of weak counterpoise to the federalist-dominated *News*. Year after year, far into the future, the Congress would call co-operators back to the true principles under the guiding hand of 'E.V.N'. There were always overwhelming votes for idealism; the Wholesale was perpetually reminded of its sin by the yea-saying congregation. But, like Sunday churchgoers, the co-operators when they left their Christian Socialist preacher and his assembly, left to follow the leadership of mammon. And Benjamin Jones always made a cynical point of this: Congress decisions never seemed to influence policy at all.

The Congress at Leicester in 1877 fulminated threateningly at the CWS and Neale commented gravely in the Preface to the Congress

Report that if the function of that body were only legislative, the system of Federalism would vanish.[28] Hughes contributed a paper in advocacy of a separate banking institution, a ponderous tome entitled 'Banking; Should it be carried on by a Distinct Central Institution, or as a part of the business of any other institution for trade or investment, as now carried on by the Wholesale?'[29] It was an exceedingly valuable and informative paper especially as it traced the history of the banking question from the beginning. Indeed, it proved to be the highlight of the Congress and after a prolonged discussion, which Neale and Nuttall dominated as antagonists, the delegates at Leicester resolved to recommend to the Wholesale the 'desirability of working the banking business by a separate board of directors.'[30] Ideally, Neale and Hughes wanted an entirely separate bank, so the Resolution of the Congress was another distinct attempt to compromise.

Recent developments appeared to indicate that Neale, despite his instinctive libertarianism, was trying to manoeuver the Congress and the Central Board into a position of legislative authority within the Movement — but he lacked the necessary support. Indeed, even his hold over the Board was uncertain. Only the Southern Section was fully dependable; consequently his moves to force the Wholesale into line met substantial opposition. The Newcastle Section, for example, sounded a note of rebellion when they resolved 'that this board is of opinion that the consideration of the banking business as at present carried on by the Co-operative Wholesale Society does not come within the functions of the Congress or the United Board.' Newcastle's co-operators concluded by referring to the Congress as 'a mixed and irresponsible body'.[31] Neale did not take this challenge to his plans lightly but reminded the Northern Section of its pledge under the Union's constitution loyally to 'carry out the policy laid down by the Congress and the United Board.' He argued, making a major point of it, that such an objection as that taken by the Newcastle co-operators, if admitted to be valid, would 'reduce the action of Congress to a nullity'.[32]

As far as Mitchell and the CWS directors were concerned the Congress may as well have already been a nullity, for they would certainly refuse to implement any of its decisions which they deemed adverse to the Movement's business interests. The Wholesale had taken to acting for itself and would continue to do so in the future; thus the banking question ultimately ended with the federalists having it entirely their own way. On 9 November 1878 (probably more out of deference to the small but vocal minority of idealists within his own organisation

than any sympathy for the authority of Congress), Mitchell gave the
issue of a separate committee for banking a final mock trial by
submitting it to the popular vote at a General Meeting of the CWS. The
spirit of the meeting was evident, and Crabtree almost stood alone
when he insisted that both sides be heard. The motion in favour of a
separate committee for banking was defeated; the final vote, including
ultimately the branches at London and Newcastle, was 264 against
32.[33] On into the 1880s, refusing to give up the struggle, Neale and
Hughes read papers and preached about the necessity of a separate
bank, but it was still as much if not more of a dead loss in the 1880s
than it had been in the autumn of 1878. The sometimes strident
character of Neale's propaganda during these years is easy to understand, for although he tenuously continued to control the Congress, on
every other front that really counted he had gone down in defeat.

Neale's greatest disappointment in the 1870s came as a result of the
failure of one of his life's most ambitious undertakings. In 1875 he
founded the Mississippi Valley Trading Company, a scheme for
International Co-operation primarily designed to facilitate a large scale
exchange of products between the American Patrons of Husbandry
(commonly called the Grange) and British co-operators.[34] The
company was especially important to Neale as conflict developed
around the issues of individualism and federalism, for he hoped it
would open in America a vast new market for British manufactured
goods, thus serving to stimulate the establishment of new producers
associations which might help to turn the balance of power in the
Movement away from mere consumption. 'It will supply, in the United
States,' he reasoned, 'precisely that *market for his goods which the
co-operative producer requires*.'[35] In an article entitled 'How to
Promote Co-operative Production', Neale enthusiastically listed some of
the products which could be exchanged:

> ' . . . they will require, in exchange for the enormous amount of
> their products with which they can supply Great Britain – the
> "cotton, grain, flour, pork, beef, hides, tallow, cheese, butter, and
> timber," which form their staples, a vast amount of the articles
> which we can supply – our "cotton, silk, hosiery, linen, and woolen
> fabrics"; our "jewelry, machinery, cutlery, iron, and shoes, station-
> ery, china, or earthenwares and chemicals".'[36]

Through the agency of the MVTC, all of the English manufactures
might eventually be produced by co-operators; in any event the

Wholesale's power over the movement would surely dwindle as the weight of combined producers increased within the Co-operative Union.

The MVTC failed for a variety of reasons, perhaps the most important being that Neale had initially been misled into believing the company could lucratively export cotton from New Orleans, and that the Grange was a powerful, unified movement of American farmers who were successfully practising Co-operation in marketing their products.[37] He did not long remain in ignorance, however, for a journey to the United States in the summer of 1875 proved disillusioning indeed.[38] Neale discovered that the merchants in New Orleans had already gained a virtual monopoly on the cotton trade, and that the national Grange, far from being a powerful farmers' co-operative organisation, constituted only a multitude of loosely-united state and local groups, scattered over a great area and more character- ised by anarchy than order. With the exception of cotton, the products that Neale wanted for co-operative mills in Britain were dispersed in individual farms throughout the Mississippi Valley. If, for example, the company were to attempt to export wheat, an efficient internal system of transporting it and collecting it in depots would have to be implemented; and conversely, for English imports, there would have to be an effective organisation of wholesales and stores for distribution.[39] It was thus evident that before the MVTC could effectively commence its operations, he would have to bring into being an entirely new American co-operative organisation out of practically nothing but good will.

At this juncture only the warmth of the Grangers' enthusiasm prevented Neale from giving up the whole project; though they were not already practising Co-operation, they wanted to begin. Con- sequently, before Neale returned to England he drew up for the Grange a complete plan, including model rules, for the implementation of Consumers Co-operation along the lines pioneered by the distributive societies of Great Britain: 'a plan for a systematic organisation of wholesale and retail stores by the state and county Granges.'[40]

For the next two years Neale struggled to keep the company alive but the circumstances of the times were inhospitable. American farmers were too impoverished to raise the necessary amount of capital to begin trading, and the British stockholders (themselves still suffering from the effects of economic depression) lost confidence in the venture and withdrew their support in 1877.[41] Yet Neale had not laboured in vain, as the creation of the Mississippi Valley Trading Company ultimately proved to be the most decisive event in the history of the American

Co-operative Movement. The designs he had submitted to the Patrons of Husbandry, for the purpose of installing a thorough-going system of Consumers Co-operation, were officially adopted at their tenth national meeting in Chicago (November 1876).[42] Within a year Judge John T. Jones, the Master of the National Grange, wrote optimistically to Neale: 'There are few members of our order who do not expect to become members of a co-operative society on the Rochdale plan.'[43] And Jones was not exaggerating.

Neale had sown seed in fertile ground. For the first time in America on a national scale, the Rochdale Plan provided the ubiquitous pattern for co-operative undertakings; and the Grangers' efforts were so successful that early labour unions such as the Sovereigns of Industry and the Knights of Labor also enthusiastically adopted the Plan. Indeed, where the idealistic objectives of these unions are enumerated, it may be observed that the doctrine of Co-operation stands high in the order of priorities.[44]

In the long run it was the American farmer who benefited most. Solon Buck contends that the co-operative stores founded after 1876 probably were 'efficient factors' in preserving the Grange during the late 1870s and early 1880s, when, with national power extinguished, its continued existence was subject to grave doubt.[45] As for benefits to the individual farmer, the establishment and management of co-operatives taught him the power of organisation, gave him business training valuable to his future dealings with middlemen, stimulated him to free himself from the debts incurred through farming on credit, and enabled him, as well as all others who patronised co-operative societies, to actually save money during years of severe depression.

Notes

1. For an excellent brief account of the events leading to the business boom of the late 1860s and the subsequent depression, consult S. G. Checkland, *The Rise of Industrial Society in England, 1815—1885* (New York, 1964), p.45ff.
2. Cole, *A Century of Co-operation, op.cit.*, p.161.
3. 'The Coal Question', *C.N.*, III (1873), 467—468. See also p.310.
4. *C.N.*, VI (1875), 487.
5. *C.N.*, VII (1876), 51.
6. *Ibid.*, p.87.
7. *Ibid.*, p.157. Lloyd Jones placed the blame on the management, where it belonged: 'The Ouseburn failed because it was managed by men who did not know their business, and who took contracts

upon which there were serious losses; the men had nothing to do with it. It broke down under a blundering management, and they ought at once to acknowledge it.' *Ibid.*, p.153. Ultimately Nuttall also emphasised the failure of the management. *Ibid.*, p.187. For information about Rutherford's all but dishonest activities relative to the winding up of the Ouseburn Engineering Works, see *Ibid.*, pp.625–627.

8. As quoted by the *C.N.*, VIII (1877), 503.
9. See e.g., *Eighth Congress*, p.v.
10. *C.N.*, VII (1876), 480.
11. See L. Jones, 'Preface to Congress Report', *C.N.*, VII (1876), 429. E. V. Neale, 'Trade Unions and the Congress Report', *C.N.*, VII (1876), pp.443–444.
12. *Ibid.*, p.444.
13. E. V. Neale, *The Distinction Between Joint Stockism and Co-operation* (Manchester, 1874), p.3.
14. *C.N.*, VIII (1877), 393.
15. *Ibid.*, p.394.
16. *C.N.*, X (1879), 119.
17. *Ibid.*, p.129.
18. *C.N.*, VII (1876), 506.
19. *C.N.*, X (1879), 129. For a similar expression of opinion see also E. V. Neale, 'The Sun Mill Company', *C.N.*, IX (1878), 82.
20. The civil service stores were then popular in London. While seeking the benefits of registration as industrial and provident societies, the civil service stores – unlike the Rochdale-type societies – closed their membership to outsiders and sold to themselves at cost. The main charge made against the legitimate co-operative stores was that they were not bearing their fair share of the tax burden.
21. *C.N.*, X (1879), 468.
22. As quoted by E. V. Neale in 'Taxation and Government Expenditure', *C.N.*, X (1879), 706.
23. *Ibid.*
24. Asa Briggs, *Victorian People, op.cit.*, p.136.
25. *Eleventh Co-operative Congress, Gloucester, 1879* (Manchester, 1879), pp.38–39.
26. *Ninth Congress*, p.22.
27. E. V. Neale, 'Co-operative Banking', *C.N.*, VII (1876), 467. See also E. V. Neale, 'Banking with the Wholesale', *C.N.*, VII (1876), 383.
28. *Ninth Congress*, p.iv.
29. *Ibid.*, pp.12–18.
30. *Ibid.*, p.23.
31. *C.N.*, IX (1878), 231.
32. *Ibid.*, p.241.
33. *Ibid.*, p.740.
34. For a brief but detailed account see P. N. Backstrom, 'The Mississippi Valley Trading Company: A Venture in International Co-operation, 1875–1877', *Agricultural History*, XLVI (1972), 425–437. The primary source of information is the large collection

of documents (MVTC Papers) at the Library, Co-operative Union Ltd.; also an extensive amount of material is available in the *Co-operative News* and annual Congress Reports, 1875—77. For general information about the Grange, consult Solon J. Buck *The Granger Movement: a Study of Agricultural Organization and its Political, Economic, and Social Manifestations, 1870—80* (Cambridge, Mass., 1913).

35. E. V. Neale, 'How to Promote Co-operative Production', *C.N.*, VI (1875), 258.
36. *Ibid.*, p.259.
37. *C.N.*, V (1874), 255, 267, 301, 304. See also Thomas D. Worrall, ed., *Direct Trade Between Great Britain and the Mississippi Valley, United States. 1874* (London, 1874), passim.
38. E. V. Neale, 'Mississippi Valley Trading Company. Diary of Deputation to United States', *C.N.*, VI (1875), 563—564, 575—576, 588, 599, 611—612, 624, 636, 648—649; *C.N.*, VII (1876), 5, 20, 27, 55—56, 67—68, 79—80. See also, 'Mississippi Valley Trading Company Limited; Report of the Deputation to the Directors of the Mississippi Valley Trading Company Limited', *Supplement to the Co-operative News*, VI (December 25, 1875), 4 pp.; esp. p.4, 'Report of Mr. Vansittart Neale'. These are the most important single documents relating to the venture.
39. Neale to Joseph R. Buchanan, 3 July 1876. MVTC Papers.
40. *C.N.*, VI (1875), 596; 'Report of Mr. Vansittart Neale', *loc. cit.* See also Joseph K. Knapp, *The Rise of American Co-operative Enterprise, 1620—1920* (Danville, Ill., 1969), 52—53. Neale's scheme, complete with model rules, became the substance of a report presented to the Ninth Annual Session of the National Grange which Knapp contends was 'destined to become one of the most influential documents in the history of American Co-operation'.
41. Neale to J.W.A. Wright, 10 July 1877; John T. Jones to Neale, 15 December 1877, MVTC Papers. *C.N.*, VIII (1877), 642.
42. E. V. Neale, 'The National Grange Meeting', *C.N.*, VII (1876) 691—692. See also Buck, *op.cit.*, p.260ff., on importance of the meeting at Chicago.
43. John T. Jones to Neale, 12 October 1877.
44. Clifton K. Yearley, *Britons in American Labor: A History of the Influence of United Kingdom Immigrants on American Labor, 1820—1914* (Baltimore, 1957), pp.257—265. Neale was also directly influential in promoting Co-operation within these trade unions. John Samuel, the most important co-operator in the Midwest, was Neale's protegy. Operating out of St Louis, Samuel was a vital force within both the Knights of Labor and the Sovereigns of Industry. In 1883, a year after the Knights of Labor had established their own General Co-operative Board, he became its principal member. His record as a co-operator is remarkable. He was responsible for creating or advising at least twenty-four associations between 1881 and 1883, and in the period 1883—88, increased his activities to include a minimum of 104 organisations

(Yearley, *op.cit.*, pp.285–286). Samuel's contacts with Neale were very close: in 1882, Neale arranged for his appointment to membership in London's Guild of Co-operators – he was frequently referred to as the Guild's 'sole agent in America' – and thereafter reams of co-operative literature were sent to him and widely circulated. Yearley wrote of the relationship between Samuel and Neale: 'Samuel felt that the Englishman had rendered signal service to self-help in America, in part because Neale had ... [awakened] "the workingmen of St Louis" and in part because of the masses of information and advice he had sent across the Atlantic. On the other hand, Neale appears to have looked on Samuel as a Welsh missionary at work in virgin territory, and he consequently relied upon him for the latest word of the potentialities, the conversions, baptisms, and backslidings in the industrial wilds of North America.' (Yearley, *op.cit.*, p.282). Neale also supplied many other Americans with information and propaganda material. Numbered among those with whom he corresponded was Professor Richard T. Ely, the labour historian and economist and Imogene Fales, of the Sociologic Society of America. Thus long after the failure of the MVTC, Neale's influence on the American Co-operative Movement continued.

45. Buck, *op.cit.*, 260–267.

VII

OLD WINE IN NEW BOTTLES: THE GUILD OF CO-OPERATORS AND ASSOCIATED HOMES

Ring out, wild bells, to the wild sky . . . .
Ring out the feud of rich and poor,
Ring in redress to all mankind.

Tennyson, *In Memorium*

Frustration and impatience are the most appropriate words to describe the way Neale felt in 1877. He had debated earnestly and at length at the Congress in Leicester, but there was little hope that the issues which divided the Movement could even be glossed by compromise let alone resolved. Neale stubbornly predicted the disappearance of the federal system — which gave everything to the consumer — but was indulging in wishful thinking. The balance of power, due to the overwhelming number of societies in the Northwest, was securely in the hands of the Wholesale Society, while in the South of England Co-operation languished. This was, doubtlessly, a major reason for both the popularity and the progress of the Guild of Co-operators, an organisation set afoot in London in 1878, the primary function of which was to propagandise the cause of Association through lecture and discussion, and to promote the establishment of co-operative stores. Although *inspired* primarily by the simple desire to spread Co-operation, the *success* of the Guild stemmed from the feeling of many of the southern committeemen that London must rise to balance the colossus at Manchester. The latter feeling, minimal at the time of the Guild's origin, became more significant as time went on.

It was Hodgson Pratt, the mentor of the Working Men's Clubs, who initiated the new work when in 1877 he suggested to the Southern Sectional Board the establishment of an auxiliary body to propagandise Co-operation in the South, enlisting in the effort 'the services of men and women of all classes who are in sympathy with the principle of association'.[1] Directly, a Committee of the Board, consisting of Pratt himself, Neale, Benjamin Jones and Robert Newton, was appointed to consider the idea and, if desirable, to prepare a Prospectus for the new enterprise. Their efforts were crowned with success. The organisation was launched in June 1878, by a series of four lectures delivered at Exeter Hall by Neale, Thomas Hughes, Lloyd Jones and Edward Owen Greening respectively.

On the 22nd of that month, with Hughes presiding, the first meeting of enrolled members took place, which approved the Constitution and settled on the Guild's official title. The new body was to be called, cumbersomely, 'The Guild of Co-operators, established to investigate the principles and to promote the practice of Co-operation, Productive, Distributive, and Social'.[2] It was the old Christian Socialists who provided the backbone of the venture, especially those delivering the lectures which launched it — Neale, Hughes, Jones and Greening. Thomas Hughes became the first chairman and John Ludlow was also active in the work, duly subscribing the sum of ten guineas for his lifetime membership. Included among the life members were such other notables as the Earl of Ducie, Miss Helen Taylor, the step-daughter of John Stuart Mill, and Neale's son, Henry. It was deeply gratifying to Neale that his son was now working at his side; indeed, Henry soon became one of the Guild's most important supporters and remained so until the organisation wound up in 1894.

As the Guild developed Neale shaped it to the pattern of his own ideas: at his suggestion (in 1882) five separate committees were established, each with a special Honorary Secretary, to promote specific areas of co-operative work:

(1) distribution;
(2) production ('either in manufactures or agriculture');
(3) 'participation of labour with capital in the profits of manufactures or agriculture';
(4) 'formation of associated homes, either independently of or in conjunction with industrial establishments';
(5) propaganda ('discussing and diffusing a knowledge of the principles relating to economic and industrial associations').[3]

It was clear from the nature of the committees' objectives that Neale's dedication to the old idealism was unrelenting, and equally clear that the Guild, if it lived up to these stated objectives, would be in conflict with the federalist committeemen of Lancashire and Yorkshire, especially as it found itself in support of the principle of profit sharing.

Fortunately, balancing the power of the northern co-operators by multiplying societies in the South never became the Guild's chief *raison d'etre*, for this it did not accomplish. After nine years of extensive work (as a result of which the number of southern co-operative associations increased by over 100 per cent), the Northwest still led the South in the number of societies, 475 to 211.[4] While the Guild doubtlessly was nurtured in the area of London by the desire to counterbalance

Manchester and Rochdale, its popularity ensured by the sectionally-oriented controversy between federalists and individualists, this was certainly not Neale's basic motive when he first affiliated himself with the work. The Guild became a prime political tool of the southern idealists, but it did not specifically originate as such: Indeed, Neale personally was more concerned to convert than to counterbalance the more numerous, and consequently politically powerful, northern co-operators; he promoted such organisations primarily because he wished to secure new platforms from which to proclaim the old community building ideals. Indeed, before he turned to support Pratt's initiative in London, Neale had first tried to promote the establishment of co-operative guilds in the North where, he felt, such organs were especially necessary.

Another basic reason why Neale wanted to establish new propaganda vehicles arose out of his desire to end the damaging isolation of the Co-operative Movement from the other great movements of labouring men. More than ever before, in his view, there was a need to carry the gospel of Co-operation to labour unions, friendly societies, and working men's clubs and institutes; for all of these organisations seemed to be pulling in different directions.[5] The Guild therefore, like all institutions which aroused Neale's enthusiasm, was primarily designed as an instrument of unification, and this design was revealed in the names of its earliest members. Successful in its intention to recruit from 'all ranks and classes', the Guild's first elected Governing Council included men such as Benjamin Jones, manager of the London Branch of the CWS; George Howell and Daniel Guile, the well-known trade union leaders; E. T. Craig, who was a very old and very eccentric Owenite, prominently known for his work with the Ralahine Community; and a latter-day Christian Socialist, the Reverend Stewart Headlam. Several years later, as part of the same effort to reach the widest possible congregation of people who might be interested in the Guild's work, Neale even arranged for a deputation consisting of himself, his son Henry, and Thomas Hughes, to visit the Council of the Charity Organisation Society.[6]

Ben Jones was by far the most important of the Charter Members. He became the first Honorary Secretary and (doubtlessly to Neale's great satisfaction) overflowed with idealism when expressing his ideas about the purpose of the new venture. 'The great bulk of the members of the various stores,' he maintained, 'had not yet got beyond the point of looking at Co-operation as a mere shopkeeping, dividend-making machine. The original idea was that the shopkeeping and the dividends

were means to an end; that end was the more equal distribution of
wealth among the wealth-producers, and the moral and social elevation
of the workers. It was extremely desirable these views should be spread
widely and rapidly.'[7]

As the director of the London Branch of the CWS, Jones was a
particularly significant ally, but his loyalty to that body ultimately
proved too strong; after a short time he left off helping the Guild,
changing from a most important friend to an exceedingly wily
antagonist. He came to describe himself as belonging 'to the middle
school of co-operators', and attempted to straddle both sides of the
profit-sharing question, expressing the opinion that whichever was the
best method of conducting co-operative production (federalist or
individualist) would with freedom of choice win out in the end. This
was a predictable course of behaviour: Ben Jones had begun working
for the CWS as an office boy and had risen to become manager of its
London Branch while still only twenty-four years of age; to him the
Wholesale represented more than just a job, it was a way of life. While
he continued, for some time, to pay lip service to the theories of his
idealistic friends on the Southern Sectional Board, his strongest
inclinations held him firmly in line behind J.T.W. Mitchell. Nevertheless, until 1881 it seems that he was a sincere champion of profit
sharing, and when the issues were clear, he always rose to the defense of
the labouring man, a practice which occasionally brought him into
conflict with other prominent directors of the Co-operative Wholesale
Society. Jones was quick witted in debate, a good administrator, an
able businessman and a first rate propagandist.

In the Guild's Fourth Annual Report, its members expressed the hope
that through the means of the new committees organised at Neale's
insistence 'many persons may be enabled to find opportunities of
rendering service to the general cause of social welfare' — and the report
continued by praising Neale as the 'able and unwearied friend of human
welfare'.[8] The Guild's emergence had been timely: since the outset of
the great depression in 1873, the problem of poverty had increasingly
intruded itself into the minds of the middle and upper classes; and in an
atmosphere of concern, which contrasted strongly with the indifference
of mid-century, the 'general cause of social welfare' claimed its
champions.

Christian Socialism (of a more Christian and less Socialist variety)
was revived in the pulpits of England. The Reverend Stewart Headlam,
who it will be recalled was a member of the Council of the Guild of

Co-operators at its origin, founded the Christian Socialist Guild of St Matthew in 1877, edited a paper called the *Church Reformer*, and later affiliated himself with the Fabian Society. Some seemed to have discovered poverty for the first time, and there was a growing conviction that it was more a consequence of bad environment than bad behaviour. Popular opinion seemed at last to be vindicating Robert Owen's views on environmental conditioning; indeed, William ('General') Booth, who in 1878 founded the Salvation Army, was to make the point quite explicitly, 'Placed in the same or similar circumstances, how many of us would have turned out better than this poor, lapsed, sunken multitude?'[9] Neale, in the past always a doubter of the doctrine of circumstances, had also changed his position considerably: 'The doctrine on which Robert Owen insisted, he wrote, 'is true to a degree which those who are occupied with the realities of our spiritual being are prone to overlook. Man is, to an enormous extent, the creature of circumstances. His character is so influenced by the insensible continuous action of his surroundings, that in instances without number, it may be said to be practically formed by them.'[10]

The new generation of Englishmen were eager to do social work and Neale realised that Co-operation was in a unique position to exploit the situation. Young Arnold Toynbee, now well known as the Oxford scholar who popularised the term 'Industrial Revolution', and who was without doubt, a most typical spokesman of the times, addressed himself to the working classes: 'We have sinned against you grievously . . . not knowing always, but still we have sinned, and let us confess it; but if you will forgive us . . . we will devote our lives to your service.'[11] Before his early death in 1883, Toynbee began his penance by moving towards Co-operation. Participating prominently in the work of the Congress held at Oxford in 1882, he supported Neale in calling upon co-operators to remember their old mission to the labouring classes, and one of his last efforts was to help the Guild to establish an Oxford branch.

Certainly Neale welcomed these changes in social attitudes — changes which fructified in the 1880s with the origin of the Social Democratic Federation, the Fabian Society and the Socialist League — and he could even review with some satisfaction the decade of government intervention launched in 1870 by the passage of Forster's Education Act. He welcomed the end of laissez faire, the general acceptance, even by the national government, of responsibility for the condition of the poor:

'Other questions are now coming to the fore, and claiming to be
considered as true functions of the State. Education for those who
cannot educate themselves; protection for those who cannot protect
themselves; sanitary regulations for the mitigation or extirpation of
disease; the reformation of criminals in place of simply punishing
them; removal of temptations to excess; care for the dwellings of
those who are too poor or too ignorant to exercise this care;
provision for public recreation. These, and other similar efforts . . .
show that the idea of a higher class of objects belonging to the State
than only the protection of life and property, and the introduction
of equal laws, is springing up in men's minds. Beyond the
maintenance of the institutions which enable everyone to take care
of himself, we feel the want of institutions by which the strong may
take care of the weak.'[12]

Neale could speak of such state intervention in terms of approval, but
he by no means ascribed to these changes the importance that was given
them by many of his contemporaries – and by later historians. Neale
would not be consoled by the token reformism of capitalism; he looked
forward to no welfare state. Social benefits which, as he would have it,
were superimposed by law 'upon a form of society to which they are
not natural' were not sufficient for him.[13] He still claimed that he
wanted nothing more from the capitalist state than the liberty of action
to form co-operatives. Neale feared strong central government and in
consequence hesitated to add to its power. He could tolerate its
extension into the area of welfare, but no further. This was the reason
why he objected to modern, or 'political', socialism, preferring what he
sometimes called 'social' socialism, another name for the panacea of
voluntary association.[14]
    Neale, however, did not carry his belief in political non-intervention
to the point where he could even partially accept the individualistic
nostrums of the Manchester School. Indeed, one of the things that most
aggravated Neale was the thoughtless adoption by co-operators of the
crude phraseology of Samuel Smiles. In 1880, for example, the
President of the Equitable Pioneers of Rochdale proclaimed that human
society would attain its highest state of perfection when every member
of it had come to act upon the conviction that it is not only a right but
a duty to *do all the good that it is possible he can do to himself*. This,
he argued, was the best way to promote the general welfare. Neale took
umbrage in an article entitled 'Self-Help'. Such is the direction, he
lamented, that the Equitable Pioneers have taken, when only thirty-six

years ago their intention was to erect self-supporting home colonies; 'Does "self-help" mean to the co-operator anything more than it means to Dr Smiles, . . . whose interesting exposition of its results in the struggle of competition is said to have helped him to a handsome house?'[15] Neale defined 'self-help' in terms of the progress of organisations not individuals; that is to say, he consistently used the well-known appellation in the same way as it was used in Owenite days (prior to its perversion by Smiles) when it was understood to mean *collective* self-help. (Indeed, it appears to have been Holyoake not Samuel Smiles who coined the term.) Although the expression negatively implied the rejection of paternal aid from the state, its overall implications were socially dynamic as the following statement by Neale would indicate:

> 'This, indeed, is the true education from which great things are to be hoped for the people, – the education of self-help which shall be not selfish help, but mutual help of men united by the consciousness that they are working for a noble future, and by the firm faith that in promoting the general good they are doing what will most effectively promote their own well-being.'[16]

Above all, Neale's efforts on behalf of the Guild revealed his lingering utopianism, especially after he had brought into being the special committee to consider the formation of associated homes. Neale never questioned the ultimate desirability of communal living, and although he was always practical enough to avoid acting in this sphere without solid assurance of success, he was usually ready with a plan for applying Co-operation in the domestic sphere at the tip of his pen, awaiting only the proper moment for publication. 'For me,' Neale wrote (December 1878) in an article entitled 'The Old Path', ' . . . Co-operation will not have done her work until she has set this world turned topsy-turvey with its right side uppermost.'[17] The world 'with its right side uppermost', at the end of 'the old path', was a world full of co-operative townships, one example of which, he indicated, was the successful Oneida Colony in New York. Despite their complex sexual mores (Neale personally noted his preference for a community which would not disturb traditional family relationships), he frequently referred to the Oneida colonists in terms of deep respect.

A prospectus for a 'United Educational Home Company', (a project which grew out of an extended correspondence with Colonel Henry Clinton in 1860), was one early example of Neale's adeptness at

designing utopias in ink;[18] and although during the remainder of the
1860s Neale seemed almost to have forgotten the old path towards
associated dwellings, he more than compensated for this neglect in the
decade which followed.[19] After the establishment of the Co-operative
Congress in 1869, he applied himself with renewed determination to
the job of popularising Co-operation's old community building ideals.
Because of the Movement's trend towards materialism, he came to feel
that it was especially necessary to remind co-operators that the
Rochdale Pioneers, as Owenites, had originally intended to build
villages of Co-operation. It may be recalled that this was part of the
motivation for Neale's address on the 'State, Prospects, and Object of
Co-operation', which he concluded by calling forth visions of whole
townships full of pleasant, healthful homes for working men, communities 'where the present isolation of our family life may be removed
without destroying its sacredness'.[20] Actually the Congress at
Manchester (1870), where this address was read, was deluged with
propaganda on the subject of housing, for James Hole had entrusted
two hundred copies of his book on the 'Dwellings of the Working
Classes' to William Pare for free distribution to the delegates.

By 1872 Neale was adding new dimensions to his vision; considering
past failures it was unrealistic to contemplate the launching of fully
fledged villages of Co-operation and therefore it would be necessary to
begin more modestly. In an article which appeared in January of that
year he suggested that co-operators should build 'associated homes' —
great rectangular buildings five stories high, full of apartments and
enveloping spacious quadrangles.[21] Anyone familiar with the
architect's plans for the great utopian communities of the 1840s would
recognise their influence on Neale's thinking. He would turn each house
into a self-contained communal unit, placing a utility building in the
quadrangle, furnished on the ground floor with laundries and kitchen
facilities, and above with stores, dining rooms, conversation rooms, and
a library. Nothing was left out which might secure the character of
autonomy. Each unit provided school, nursery, and infirmary accommodations as well as room for such social amenities as smoking and
billiards. As far as the financing of such establishments was concerned,
Neale felt that expenses would not exceed that of erecting the present
inconvenient, unhealthy, and intrinsically wasteful separate
dwellings'.[22] Specifically, Neale estimated that one could calculate
costs at the rate of £50 per dwelling room, and about a month later
W. Morrison, a director of the Improved Industrial Dwellings Company
of London, wrote to the *Co-operative News* in confirmation of Neale's

figures. The latter concluded that there was no better mode of investment than dwellings which offered a good return on capital; then as now, within the framework of the capitalistic system, even charity had to be profitable.[23] Neale's was not an isolated interest; the Improved Industrial Dwellings Company, founded in 1863, was only one of a series of charitable societies established to deal with that most intractable Victorian stigma, slum housing. London was particularly blessed with the Metropolitan Association for Improving the Dwellings of the Industrious Classes (1845), the Central London Dwellings Improvement Company (1861), the London Labourers' Dwelling Society (1861), and the Peabody Trust — to name a few. Indeed, there was enough interest in the question throughout England to insure the passage of the Housing of the Working Classes Act of 1866, which facilitated the activities of such charities by entitling them to borrow money from the Public Works Loans Commissioners in order to purchase land.[24]

Neale's fellow co-operators were equally ready to voice opinions on the question of working class housing, and during the early 1870 s other articles appeared in the *Co-operative News* with such catchy titles as 'Co-operative Hotels', 'Palaces for the Poor' and 'Domestic Co-operation'. Nothing came of these endeavours but this did not seem to worry Neale who went on without faltering in his own propaganda efforts. Unlike Morrison, he was playing for much larger stakes than a good return on capital. If his efforts were to be successful, he realised that he must appeal not merely to the mercenary motives of his fellow co-operators but to their imaginations. With this in mind, in one of his more widely circulated pamphlets (*The Distinction Between Joint Stockism and Co-operation*, 1874) he wrote with chiliastic inspiration:

'I do not deny that this transformation is slow. Co-operators are still wandering through the wilderness. The Promised Land, with its many and varied blessings — the land of smokeless cities, the centres of industrial and intellectual life, beautiful with palaces occupied as dwellings for the men who make the goods which pay for their erection, not merely as storehouses for the goods made by them — of associated homes dotted over the country, seats alike of active industry and refined and manifold enjoyment — the land whence poverty has been banished by the union of scientific knowledge with the will to use it in promoting the common good — this true millennial land exists as yet only for the eye of faith.'[25]

Neale preached his sermon with dogged persistence and his belief in progress confirmed his confidence in ultimate success; as this confidence grew, what had been through life a passion became, by the late seventies, at the time of the Guild's creation, a most fervent obsession. Doubtlessly his renewed fervor was part of the ever-escalating idealistic response to the great depression – the same response that had brought Arnold Toynbee forward as a model for a class of guilt-ridden intellectuals turning, for absolution, to social reform. George Bernard Shaw wrote of a more militant variety of the phenomena:

'Numbers of young men, pupils of Mill, Spencer, Comte, and Darwin, roused by Mr. Henry George's "Progress and Poverty," left aside evolution and free thought; took to insurrectionary economics; studied Karl Marx; and were so convinced that socialism had only to be put clearly before the working classes to concentrate the power of their immense numbers in one irresistible organisation, that the Revolution was fixed for 1889 – the anniversary of the French Revolution – at latest.'[26]

Of those who were personally close to Neale, Thomas Hughes' behavior in these closing years of the 1870s is the most fascinating and revealing: he opened a unique English colony on the Cumberland Plateau in Eastern Tennessee called, significantly, Rugby. As might have been expected from its name, the colony was embodied nostalgia, an attempt to recapture an old England that was rapidly slipping by – the England of the public school, honour, deference and honest work. It was a carefully organised little community avoiding the plutocratic, competitive rat-race that life in England had become, and substituting for it the 'quiet comfort and repose' of an 'old-fashioned village'. Theoretically, all one needed in Hughes' community was a rod and gun, a little intelligence, and a willingness to get one's hands dirty. Rugby officially opened on 5 October 1880; a year later it was on the verge of failure, surviving only because friends like Lord Ripon (who contributed £1,000) and Goldwin Smith, were willing to rush to its financial rescue, but their help proved futile. Hopeless of success the adventure ended in 1891.[27] Neale was eminently more practical, having no desire to litter the co-operative landscape with yet another ruined community.

Because of all the failures, Englishmen tended to be sceptical of utopian socialist ideas. The old saying 'seeing is believing' was apropos and it was apparent that what Neale most needed was a really successful example of communitarian principles in action. The Oneida Colony was unsatisfactory because its practice of sexual freedom offended the Victorian frame of mind. The Shaker colonies were good examples of association, but the Shakers themselves were too ascetic, separating the sexes entirely; extinction of the human race was the condition for their success. Moreover, both of these examples were full-scale utopian experiments; Neale needed a practical model more in tune with the 'no nonsense' attitude of late-century England. As in the days of the Christian Socialist Movement, it was again France which provided him with it. In 1878 Jean Baptiste André Godin commenced the publication of a periodical called *Le Devoir* in which he explained his successful efforts to initiate a thoroughgoing programme of Co-operation in conjunction with his factory (an iron foundry primarily engaged in the manufacture of heating equipment) at Guise, a small town located 127 miles northeast of Paris. Godin called his social experiment the Familistère. When Neale read about the venture, he was completely captivated – it was exactly what he had been looking for.[28]

Neale's attention was drawn to France shortly before the right and final wing of the Familistère was completed, opening with fanfare and flourish in 1880. It was easy to see why he was elated about it; he could have drawn up the plans himself, they matched his own ideas so well. To begin with, the workmen at Guise shared in the profits of the factory to such an extent that in less than twenty years they actually became the owners. This alone would have generated Neale's enthusiasm, but Godin, in satisfaction of his Fourieristic instincts, had gone even further: the workers lived in associated homes or united dwellings (a separate residence for each family, but under communal jurisdiction); profits were used to establish co-operative stores which sold all the necessities of everyday life – beverages, food, furniture, fuel and clothing; and a free elementary education up to at least fourteen years of age was furnished for Familistère children, along with the fullest nursery accommodations for infants. Lastly, Godin worked out an ingenious system of mutual insurance against sickness, old age, disability, and death. As early as 1852, he had begun a Sick Fund in the iron foundry and almost immediately placed its direction in the hands of the workmen themselves. When he built the living quarters of the Familistère, he extended the insurance to include wives, a special portion of the Sick Fund being reserved for this purpose and administered by women – a surprisingly progressive move in the middle of the nineteenth century! The motive force behind all of his efforts, Godin once summed up in the following words: 'To respect, protect, develop all human life over all the world, as a means of serving God in men, by the worship of work and of peace and by the love of humanity.'[29]

Neale at last had found a practical model toward which he could direct the attention of co-operators. Unlike most experiments in communal living, Godin's Familistère did not involve a utopian escape from society or any breach in its conventional moral codes but could (and this was its greatest advantage) develop naturally out of existing manufacturing establishments. It was a kind of half-way house on the road to the Fourieristic phalanx or the Owenite village of Co-operation. Neale's enthusiasm for the Familistère was boundless; he visited the periodic festivals there and reported them in detail to English co-operators through the medium of the *Co-operative News*: he translated and republished articles from Godin's *Le Devoir* on a regular basis; and induced England's co-operative leaders personally (often accompanying them himself) to travel to France and see for themselves. Indeed, Godin and his social experiment figured prominently in Neale's co-operative polemic for the rest of his life. It was Godin's example which led Neale to introduce into the regimen of the Guild of Co-operators the special committee to consider co-operative housing; and it was under the Guild's auspices that he wrote his most popular pamphlet on the subject, published in 1880 under the title *Associated Homes*.[30]

Not unexpectedly, during the Congress at Newcastle-on-Tyne (May 1880) the idea generated controversy. Mr. Thirlaway read a paper entitled 'Co-operative Cottage Building and the Land Question' which responded to the growing interest, evidenced throughout the Movement, in the subject of dwellings for working co-operators. But Mr. Thirlaway and his supporters did not share Neale's enthusiasm for *associated* homes; they were interested in the means by which they could utilise co-operative capital, and credit, for the building of *individual* dwellings, which would be in no way related to any communal project, or for that matter dependent upon the Co-operative Movement per se. Some delegates argued that societies should use some of their surplus capital to buy up parcels of land and build cottages which could be made available to individual co-operators at reasonable prices. The societies could perhaps further facilitate the process by providing the credit to individuals for such purchases. Neale took umbrage at these suggestions, emphasising that the Industrial and Provident Societies Act of 1876 granted to societies a privilege enjoyed in no other country: they could form bodies, which in their *corporate* capacity had the right to hold land of any legal description, in any amount whatsoever. Did it make sense, then, for societies to waste this privilege by purchasing land in their corporate capacity only to parcel it out ultimately to individuals? Shouldn't the wealth gained through the collective efforts of the working class be used to further the work of Association?

Neale's opponents who were present at the Newcastle Congress warned, with good humour, that the French might make a go of associated homes, but it was unlikely that the English, individualistic as they were, would have anything to do with them. Mr. Crabtree of Heckmondwike chortled out that 'if it was intended to get Mr. Nuttall and himself, Mr. Pingstone and Mr. Mitchell, Mr. Holyoake and Mr. Lloyd Jones [all old enemies] to live together, he did not know how they would get on'.[31] It does seem that Neale's critics had rooted out a potential difficulty: it was problem enough to get the committee chiefs of Co-operation to work together amicably; could they ever be expected to share something as intimately private as the management of their own homes?

And in no other era of history had the word 'home' been fraught with so much symbolic meaning (Victorians pronounced it with reverence bordering on awe); no doubt it was Neale's old acquaintance and friend, John Ruskin, who most clearly enunciated the mood:

> 'This is the true nature of home – it is the place of Peace; the shelter, not only from all injury, but from all terror, doubt, and division. In so far as it is not this, it is not home; so far as the anxieties of the outer life penetrate into it, and the inconsistently-minded, unknown, unloved, or hostile society of the outer world is allowed by either husband or wife to cross the threshold, it ceases to be home; it is then only a part of that outer world which you have roofed over, and lighted fire in. But so far as it is a sacred place, a vestal temple, a temple of the hearth watched over by Household Gods . . . so far as it is this, and roof and fire are types only of a nobler shade and light, – shade as of the rock in a weary land, and light as of the Pharos in the stormy sea; – so far it vindicates the name, and fulfills the praise, of Home.'[32]

The idea of home and women's place in it served as a sort of moral pivot, upon the steadfastness of which turned the stability of society itself. It was the full implications of this which drove such intelligent and progressive women as Beatrice Potter, Mrs T. H. Huxley, and Mrs Arnold Toynbee to sign Mrs Humphrey Ward's famous manifesto,

'An Appeal Against Feminine Suffrage'. Beatrice Potter later felt that
she had made a 'false step' in signing it — but it is significant that she
waited some twenty years to publish her recantation.[33] Neale managed
to remain characteristically ambivalent (he seldom spoke with certainty
on political issues) about the matter of women's emancipation, while
uniquely relating the question to associated — or as he calls them in this
instance — unitary homes.

> 'I have long held with the advocates of women's rights that those
> who would be entitled to political votes if they wore coats should
> not be excluded from voting because they wear petticoats. Equally
> do I hold with them that women are not to be excluded from any of
> those intellectual pursuits or occupations which may place her on a
> level with man. But I hold also, with the opponents of such claims,
> that the true sphere of women's action is the domestic sphere. Her
> natural function is not to struggle but to charm. These views may
> appear inconsistent, but they meet in the idea of the Unitary
> Home.'[34]

Neale's view on feminine suffrage serves more in illustration of his
one-track mind than his practicality. With banal sentiment, he
expressed the opinion that a woman's mission in life would be best
realised in making a unitary home 'more attractive than its rival, and
thus to prepare the advent of general well-being'; and with benignity he
promised that 'if she exercises her social faculties to produce this social
good, whatever rights she may choose to claim mankind will willingly
concede to her'.[35] There is no question but that Neale was eminently
Victorian in his own idealisation of home, womanhood and love, yet
most of the time he lived like a bachelor in Manchester, his home life
manifestly less than satisfactory. Many Victorians in a happier family
situation would, because of it, tend to look with disfavour upon the
implied interference with their private lives suggested by the label
'associated home', and this is doubtlessly why, on occasion, Neale used
the expression 'unitary home'.

The idealisation of home, which must have driven most Victorians
away from communitarian theorising with repugnance, had precisely
the opposite effect on Neale. It was probably the emptiness, or, to use a
more appropriate term, the incompleteness of his own home life — its
failure to meet the rigid standard — which made Godin's community
seem so desirable by comparison. When he visited Guise he participated
in the lives of other, happier families than his own, as they went to
work or school, played games or made decisions, and participated in

festivals and celebrations. Neale's status in the social hierarchy, particularly after he acquired Bisham Abbey in 1885, also heightened his sense of isolation and stimulated his desire to imitate M. Godin. One Christmas, Neale wrote a revealing note to Holyoake about life with his family in the old Abbey:

> 'I suspect we, of the parlour side of the Abbey, are the smallest Christmas party in the village of Bisham, only three humans and a dog, in the largest house, and yet we have on the other side of the walls, under the same roof some ten persons with all of whom we are on very friendly terms, while if we tried to associate with them, we should spoil their society, and they would add nothing to ours. Here is the social question in a nutshell, but tuff [sic] to crack — creatures of circumstances — but circumstances hard to change tho easy to satirise.'[36]

'*The Associated Home*, Neale insisted, '*is the keystone of the social arch* — the indispensible condition of rational enjoyment and general well-being';[37] he was a lonely man, and this opinion is perhaps best understood in terms of his loneliness.

If the economic strength of Co-operation was due to the steady growth of the CWS and its subsidiary network of stores in the Northwest, the locus of Co-operation's strength of spirit is less easily pinned down. Many of the vitally innovative organisations of the late 1870s were first launched in London where the Movement was economically weak, the Guild of Co-operators being typical of this dynamism in the South of England. Neale himself was now spending most of his time in Manchester, but it would be fair to say that he looked to the men in the South — especially to Hughes, Holyoake and Greening — for inspiration and support. Indeed, it is sometimes difficult to be sure whether it was that junta-like coterie of idealists still dominating the Southern Section of the Central Board who motivated Neale, or whether it was he who was motivating them. In any event, the idea for his greatest work of propaganda was first proffered by Thomas Hughes: in December, 1878, hard pressed by the redoubtable old Rugbean, the Southern Section resolved that it was desirable that some kind of extended handbook or manual for co-operators be prepared. Two months later an outline for the manual (doubtlessly written by Hughes) was approved and he was chosen as its editor; Neale was brought into the project when Hughes proposed that some other member be associated with him as co-editor of the manual and recommended 'our General Secretary, whose knowledge of the theoretical and scientific sides of the movement, and experience in its practical working, is fuller and larger probably than that of any other living Englishman'.[38] This recommendation was accepted with the result that Neale wrote the entire book, save only its preface.[39] It remains one of the most complete, if controversial, expressions of the idealistic side of Co-operation.

The first two parts of the *Manual*, were concerned with co-operative theory and critically considered the views of a few of the major French and German socialists, including Marx.[40] Part III, 'The Practice of Co-operation', was more related to pounds and pence. The strictly business end of the Movement was here minutely and tediously scrutinised; and certainly Chapter 9 of Part III, 'The Practice of Co-operation in Social Life', is the most interesting for it sheds additional light on Neale's philosophy.

As indicated, his preoccupation with the question of model factories and villages was not an isolated phenomenon in these later years of the 19th century, but merely reflected a ubiquitous revival of interest in the labouring poor and their living conditions. He made it a point in the *Manual* to applaud the work of Sir Titus Salt, whose mill and model village founded in 1851 at Saltaire, was to provide a basic pattern for a series of such creations beginning in the late 1880s with Lever's Port Sunlight. But such benevolent attempts to improve working class conditions, however noble the motivating spirit (and more often than not the spirit was mercenary — contented labourers work harder and produce more profits) were not sufficient in themselves. Neale pointed out that the best model from his perspective was M. Godin, not Titus Salt. The workman must be more than a passive recipient of paternal aid, especially as this aid, often so ostentatiously bestowed, came out of profits which by right should have belonged to him in the first place. The well-kept apartments at Saltaire were beautiful, but they were filled with tenants rather than co-owners. While an individual workman could derive great benefit from such accommodations, they would do nothing to produce that spirit of communal solidarity which Neale felt was necessary before there could be any really comprehensive gains made in emancipating workingmen from their present state of thralldom to capital. In contrast, Godin's idea of the associated home represented, in microcosm, the objective towards which Neale was striving, and also served an immediate and practical function as a kind of training school in the spirit of Association.[41]

Such ideas were scorned as 'utopian' by co-operative realists. They lived the life and thought the thoughts of the dominant middle classes and were all but blind to the poverty and squalor which lay immediately beside them in their cities. The social cleavage between themselves and the very poor was so distinct that most co-operators were shocked by the revelations of Charles Booth in 1889. Unfortunately, Co-operation had become a Movement confined to labour's aristocracy and the *petit bourgeois*; instinctively its leaders found their place within the capitalistic society. They had lost the old desire to change it even if the schedule for change involved some far distant deadline, for their satisfaction with the present inhibited their concern for the future. Saint-Simon, the father of utopian socialism, in his 'Letters from an Inhabitant of Geneva to his Contemporaries' observed that 'Whenever a discovery, to be put into practice, requires a different outlook and habits from those prevailing when it appears, it is a treasure which can be enjoyed by the generation which has witnessed its birth, only through a feeling of affection for the future generation which is destined to profit by it.'[42] Looking ahead to this future generation, were Neale's ideas so very utopian, his critics so realistic? The same problems still remain to be solved. After more than a century of the accommodation to capitalism labelled 'realistic' and 'practical', working class slums still abound, and within them men are alienated when they should be united, are lacking in community spirit, take no pride in ownership for they own little or nothing of value, and are exploited by landlords, shopkeepers, even the forces of law and order. All of this increases their sense of frustration and anger at their own impotence, spawning a negative individualism damaging to the human relationships necessary for meaningful social existence. It is ironic that some social scientists now talk about generating a community spirit among the poorer classes by encouraging the initiation of co-operative projects; if details differ (although actually often uncanny in their similarity), Neale's concept of collective self-help has far from lost its voteries.

It is a useful task to explore Neale's beliefs, and to defend them from the misinterpretations which persist, in some instances, to the present time. However, in view of the way the *Manual* was written it is not too hard to understand the persistence of misunderstanding. Part IV, 'The Helps and Hindrances to Co-operation', was unduly recapitulative and apocalyptic; it contained only one chapter entitled 'The Perils of Co-operation, and How to Escape Them' and this chapter rambled back redundantly over ground already thoroughly explored in earlier chapters; poorly organised and developed, it obfuscated as much as it enlightened. Unfortunately, digressions within digressions and unnecessarily repetitive references to themes such as Christianity and Godin's Familistère at Guise abounded throughout the whole manual, but here they became particularly tedious. Actually, it is hard to escape the conclusion that either Neale was in too great a hurry to edit it properly, or his mind was so preoccupied with everyday affairs as to be unaware of the book's shortcomings. He likened his summary recapitulations to the barbed head of an arrow which might help to make the main thoughts of the book 'stick', a bad analogy, for arrowheads have the unfortunate tendency to draw blood. Despite the truth of his contentions, his closing words were caviling, and doubtlessly many co-operators who might otherwise have accepted the *Manual* with good grace, felt that it constituted the proverbial straw which broke the camel's back.

'The bridge which the profits on production would allow the workers to build over the river of poverty,' wrote Neale, 'is barred by the twin giants, Individual Self-seeking and Collective Indifference.'[43] One example given to illustrate the first giant was the English Wholesale deliberately diverting all of the profits of the Leicester Shoe Factory away from the workers who earned them; the remedy for this (one of the *Manual*'s main themes) was to direct the profits of production back to the worker. The other giant, Collective Indifference, Neale felt to be the most formidable obstacle. It was the indifference of the mass of the wealth producers (the working classes) that made socialism impossible of immediate realisation. Herein lay the work he set for himself. Before the millenium was possible, men's values had to be changed; they had to be curbed from their 'petty, ignoble, and unsatisfying' struggle after perishable objects, which was motivated by their competitive selfishness (a product of the capitalistic system) and turned toward the principle that gave direction to the whole course of human history, that principle being unity. It was always at this point that Neale, the practitioner of Co-operation, became the purveyor of Christian mysticism. This changing of men could best be accomplished by getting them to realise that they might become co-workers with the very God of creation in bringing his great kingdom of peace and love and brotherhood down to earth.

> 'The Jewish prophets look forward, with ever-brightening hope, to the glories of the reign of the Messiah . . . The New Testament takes up the same strain. The Lord's Prayer calls on us to hope, and desire that the will of God be done on *earth as* in heaven. The Apocalypse . . . brings down the Heavenly Jerusalem, the Temple of the living God, to earth, among the nations . . .'[44]

How would man best work with God in bringing down to earth this 'Heavenly Jerusalem' – how find his true fulfillment? Only in making 'earnest efforts to spread the kingdom of God over the earth, by creating such conditions of human life, as good men can feel to be worthy of this kingdom; the fit expression of the spirit of Him whose name is Love.'[45] This, of course, is where the panacea of Association comes back into the text – we are again returned to the co-operative workshops and the co-operative home – again back with Godin at the Familistère at Guise which Neale presents as a means as well as an end. With the spread of associative work, a new generation of working classes will arise, trained in selflessness and community spirit, and ready to realise at last God's will for man – that ultimate millenial brotherhood towards which all of history is directed. Christian Socialism *redivivus*!

This book, invaluable as a statement of Neale's faith, was unfortunately indigestible as a *Manual for Co-operators*. First conceived as a useful handbook both for the tyro as well as the long-time co-operator, it became an implement of war – an unrelenting attack on the federal system of Co-operation which doubtlessly alienated many who Neale sought to reach. Consequently, although the *Manual* did indeed become popular, its effectiveness was blunted. Actually had it not been for that very indifference of the average co-operator which Neale so deplored, the *Manual for Co-operators* might have split the Movement, despite its message of unity. It was designed to appease no one and evidences Neale's growing feeling that the issues had to be met head on; and the religious character of the book, although less controversial (most co-operators, having adopted the religious biases of the middle classes, were active Christians), was in a sense more tragic in consequence because it alienated allies.

When the question of the *Manual* came up for discussion in the Congress at Leeds (1881) Holyoake, that most militant secularist, was outraged at the idea that the Co-operative Union should publish, thereby abandoning its habit of religious neutrality, such an unmitigated piece of propaganda in favour of Christian Socialism. His reaction to the book was not surprising. Indeed, Neale himself later claimed with pride that the *Manual for Co-operators* was 'the most matured and complete exposition of the relation between Christianity and social reform, as it has been conceived by the Christian Socialists in this country'.[46] Recognizing the *Manual* as such, Holyoake took the offensive at the Congress, expressing the opinion that given its sectarian character the Board should not have published it. He then launched

into a highly spirited tirade which, as Hughes was Chairman of the
proceedings, came close to being a personal attack. 'The Co-operative
body,' he asserted, 'is asked for the first time to publish a theological
book.' As his speech rambled on, Holyoake warmed to the subject:
'Now what does the book do? It practically hands over the whole
co-operative body to the Church of England . . . Mr Hughes well
knows,' he lamented, 'that in raising the religious question he has a
majority on his side, and that if he proposed to add the Prayer Book to
the Manual he could carry it.' By this time delegates to the Congress,
doubtlessly good Christians, were crying, 'Time', and one of them rose
to order. Holyoake, however, doggedly clung to the floor and
concluded with a stinger:

> 'You may triumph today . . . you may expose the minority amongst
> us to the scorn of suspicion or the inferiority of defeat, but at the
> same time you lower and deface that noble quality of neutrality
> which has maintained respect and good-will amongst us hitherto . . .
> For myself, I do not object to creeds. I am friendly to the pursuit of
> religious truth, but I submit that the appointed place for it is the
> chapel or the church, and not the store.'[4 7]

When it was over, Lloyd Jones, who had been Holyoake's enemy
since the days when they were Owenite missionaries together, rose to
state with hauteur that he was sorry they should have to listen to this.
But the most revealing words seemed to prove Holyoake's worst fears
about the *Manual*: a Scottish delegate rose to proclaim that he was not
ashamed to say that he was a 'Christian man' and as for the *Manual*, 'Its
highest recommendation was that it had been condemned by Mr. Holyoake.'[4 8]

In the course of a long turbulent life Holyoake engendered much
controversy. He was always rather like Charles Kingsley in being too
ready for a fight, but there was a generous side to him as well, and
before the day had ended, Holyoake had apologised, explaining that he
had meant nothing personal; that, in fact, he had great respect for
Hughes and Neale. Any antagonisms that developed between Holyoake
and either Hughes or Neale were not of a character that deeply marred
their personal friendships. Indeed, in later years Holyoake loved to talk
about Neale's prodigious energy and was fond of relating the story of
those times when the two of them had been speakers at the same
meeting and afterwards faced the long journey home: waiting in the
rain and wind for a train and finally arriving exhausted back at the
station in Manchester, Neale would insist on seeing Holyoake, who

could not see well in the dark, to his flat at the Merchant's Hotel, even though he would then have a very long walk back to his own lodgings in Portsmouth Street. Despite the occasionally bitter falling out on the perennially difficult subject of religion, it was an unusual case where someone took issue with Neale without finding Holyoake standing at his side. Six years after Neale's death Holyoake recalled his long and paradoxical relationship with the Christian Socialists in a speech to the Chamber of Commerce:

> 'It is odd that the Christian Socialists regarded as their enemies among the co-operators those who held Free Thought views: yet they were the only co-operators who held their socialist opinions of the right of labour to share in profit. The constant opponents of this principle were Christian co-operators. They distrusted and derided Mr. Vansittart Neale and Mr. Thomas Hughes as "idealists." It was the heretics among the co-operators who shared their socialist principles who . . . stood by them stood up for them and vindicated them to the end of their days.'[49]

Notes

1. J. J. Dent, 'The Guild of Co-operators', *The Co-operative Educator* (no publication data given, included in a bound packet of papers, reports, etc.), p.111. Available in Library, Co-operative Union Limited, 'Guild of Co-operators Early Reports & Papers 1879 . . . ' Hereafter cited as Guild Papers. For more information on the Guild and Neale's views about it consult E. V. Neale, 'The Guild of Co-operators and Labour Exchanges', *C.N.*, VIII (1877), 691-692.
2. *Eleventh Congress*, p.28.
3. J. J. Dent, *op.cit.*, p.112.
4. Thomas Hughes and E. V. Neale, *A Manual for Co-operators, Prepared at the Request of the Co-operative Congress Held at Gloucester in April, 1879; and Revised 1888* (Manchester, 1888), Appendix, p.233.
5. E. V. Neale, 'The Guild of Co-operators', *C.N.*, VIII (1877), 603-604.
6. *The Guild of Co-operators, Third Annual Report* (February– March, 1881, Bibliographical data incomplete), p.4. The Co-operative Union Library has Reports 1–8, 11. Guild Papers. Nothing came out of the visit, nor should much have been expected. The Charity Organisation Society was an ultra-paternalistic body brought into being in 1869 in an attempt to harmonise the work of the numerous and continually multiplying Victorian charitable organisations. It made the crude distinction

between deserving and undeserving poor – consigning the latter to the tender mercies of the Poor Law – and its members once described Charles Booth's great study of poverty in London as an 'excursion into the pleasant dreamland of world making'. Bernard Shaw referred to the creations of the COS as 'abominable bastard Utopias of genteel charity.' Needless to say the goals of the Guild were rather far removed from those of the Charity Organisation Society, but nevertheless Neale could not resist making an attempt to enlist the Society's support.

7. *C.N.*, VIII (1877), 604. Jones spoke these words during a discussion which followed the reading of Neale's paper on 'The Guild of Co-operators', *op.cit.* See also *C.N.*, XII (1881), 710.

8. *The Guild of Co-operators . . . Fourth Annual Report* (1881–82), pp.10–11. Guild Papers.

9. From William Booth's *In Darkest England and the Way Out*; see Sydney W. Jackman, ed., *The English Reform Tradition* (Englewood Cliffs, New Jersey, 1965), p.156.

10. E. V. Neale, *Association and Education; What They May Do for the People . . .* (Manchester, 1882), p.7.

11. See Brian Harrison, 'Philanthropy and the Victorians', *Victorian Studies*, IX (1966), 359.

12. *C.N.*, IX (1878), 227.

13. *Ibid.*

14. E. V. Neale, 'What is Socialism?' *C.N.*, IX (1878), 385–386. See also E. V. Neale, 'The Demon of Socialism', *C.N.*, IX (1878), 294.

15. 'Self-Help', *C.N.*, XI (1880), 645.

16. *Association and Education, op.cit.*, p.15.

17. *C.N.*, IX (1878), 809.

18. See *Letters on Associated Homes, between Colonel Henry Clinton and Edward Vansittart Neale, Esq.* (London, 1861), passim.

19. During the 1860s, Neale compromised his utopian ideals defending the narrow views of the northern consumers; and in 1866, with unusual scepticism, wrote that attempts to apply the doctrines of Association to the sphere of domestic life should probably 'be postponed till society is so ripe for them that the failure of any trial may be attributed, not to the impracticality of the principle as would be the case at present, but to mistakes in its application'. *Co-operator*, VII (1866), 23.

20. *Co-operator*, X (1870), 745.

21. E. V. Neale, 'Associated Homes', *C.N.*, II (1872), 37.

22. *Ibid.*

23. *C.N.*, II (1872), 85.

24. W. L. Burn, *The Age of Equipoise; A Study of the Mid-Victorian Generation* (London, 1964), p.127.

25. *The Distinction Between Joint Stockism and Co-operation, op.cit.*, p.5.

26. G. Bernard Shaw et al, *Fabian Essays in Socialism* (Gloucester, Mass., Peter Smith, 1967), pp.228–229. From the essay entitled 'Transition' by Bernard Shaw.

27. Mack and Armytage, *Hughes, op.cit.*, p.227ff.
28. For information on Godin and the Familistère consult Aneurin Williams, *Twenty Years of Co-partnership at Guise* (London, 1903), 88pp. Also see 'Jean Baptiste André Godin; A Biographical Sketch', *C.N.*, XIX (1888), 109–110, 134–135. Most of the material which follows is from these works.
29. Williams, *op.cit.*, p.86.
30. E. V. Neale, *Associated Homes: A Lecture . . . with Three Engravings of the Familistère at Guise, and a Biographical Notice of M. Godin, its Founder* (London, 1880), p.3.
31. *Twelfth Co-operative Congress, Newcastle-on-Tyne, 1880* (Manchester, 1880), p.41.
32. As quoted by Walter E. Houghton, *The Victorian Frame of Mind, 1830–1870* (New Haven, 1957), p.343.
33. Beatrice Webb, *My Apprenticeship* (London, 1926), pp.341–342.
34. *C.N.*, XIII (1882), 513.
35. *Ibid.*
36. Neale to Holyoake, No date. Holyoake Papers.
37. *Fifteenth Co-operative Congress, Edinburgh, 1883* (Manchester, 1883), p.v. From Neale's 'Preface' to the Report of the Congress.
38. *Eleventh Congress*, p.28.
39. Hughes later insisted that his own name appearing as the *Manual*'s co-author was an example of Neale's selflessness: 'My part in it,' he wrote, 'was only the preface, and here and there a modification in the wording. It is only one example of his [Neale's] constant habit of self-suppression.' Hughes, 'Neale', *op.cit.*, p.181. In addition to the early influence of the Oxford Tractarians, Neale's conscious attempt to repress self owed much to the influence of Eastern religions. See E. V. Neale, 'Buddha and Buddhism', *Macmillan's Magazine*, I (April, 1860), 439–448. In a conversation with E. O. Greening, shortly after the death of the theosophist, Madame Blavatsky, Neale expressed great interest in the Brahminical idea of Nirvana as an ultimate objective, *C.N.*, XXIII (1892), 1121.
40. Some use was made of this portion of the *Manual* in Chapter III, see pp.60–63.
41. *Manual, op.cit.*, p.159.
42. *Henri De Saint-Simon; Social Organisation, The Science of Man and Other Writings*, ed. and trans. with a Preface and Introduction by Felix Markham (New York, Harper Torchbook, 1964), p.5.
43. *Manual*, p.211.
44. *Ibid.*, p.216. Neale here makes reference in a note to Revelations XXII:2.
45. *Ibid.*, pp.216–217.
46. E. V. Neale to Richard T. Ely, 29 November 1882. Richard T. Ely Papers, Wisconsin Historical Society, Madison, Wisconsin.
47. *Thirteenth Co-operative Congress, Leeds, 1881* (Manchester, 1881), p.49.
48. *Ibid.*, p.50. After Congress the controversy continued: see Neale's 'Preface' to the *Thirteenth Congress*, esp. pp.iv–vi, also

G. J. Holyoake, 'Impressions of the Co-operative Manual', *Supplement to the Co-operative News* (25 March 1882), 1–2.
49. From MSS entitled 'The Christian Socialists Explained', (Speech at Chamber of Commerce, 1898),Holyoake Papers, Manchester.

PART THREE

TRIUMPH OF BUREAUCRATISM AND THE FAILURE OF THE IDEAL

VIII

MARSHALLING THE FORCES OF CO-OPERATIVE PRODUCTION
1881—1886

> Were it not for the enthusiasts there would be no movement worth a rush.
>
> Thomas Hughes to Richard T. Ely,
> Christmas Day, 1886

English Co-operation recovered from the bad economic year of 1879, characterised in the *Economist* as 'one of the most sunless and cheerless of the century',[1] to face the new decade of the 1880s with a revived interest in the possibilities of co-operative production. The conflict between federalists and individualists had been maintained unabated through the economic trough of the late 1870s – E.V.N. continued to exchange blows with J.W. and William Nuttall on the same old issue of the Wholesale Society's 'Caesarism' in production and banking – but now both sides of this perennial exchange seemed to be revitalised. Indeed, Edward Vansittart Neale, his utopian, community-building instincts stimulated by the successes of M. Godin at Guise, and his hopes for new co-operative ventures heightened by the temporary upswing in the trade cycle (1880–83), was more on the offensive than ever.[2]

In the meantime a few of the important men who were Neale's chief supporters in the 1870s had come to be occupied elsewhere: John Ludlow, a dynamo in the earlier years of the past decade, was too busy as Chief Registrar of Friendly Societies to involve himself to any great extent with Co-operation's internal struggles; Thomas Hughes, who so recently had provided the inspiration for the *Manual for Co-operators*, was deeply and sadly entangled in the economic morass surrounding his failing community in Rugby, Tennessee; and George Jacob Holyoake had been enough offended, it seems, by the religious issues raised in the *Manual* to pull in his head for a time. There was, however, one important, long-standing ally, once described by Ernest Jones in a letter to Karl Marx as 'a very good, clever and honest young man, a good speaker, a good writer and a good democrat',[3] who had risen to prominence to take their place. That man was Edward Owen Greening who was becoming a veritable army on Neale's side. Neale could have rested content with the laurels of past combat and vicariously experienced the continuing fight through the efforts of this new, younger champion who entered the field with all of the 'right' colours flying. This temptation was resisted, but he did, however, allow Greening to become the spearhead of the offensive against the Wholesale directors and the main target of their inevitable counter-attack, thereby making more tenable his position as General Secretary, a technically neutral office.

It must not be supposed, however, that Neale and Greening represented a minority of two. According to the voting at the Annual Congress, there were many men in the ranks who were in essential agreement with them; potential supporters could even be found in the Co-operative Wholesale Society itself. But the majority were silent and indifferent, thus the main work had to be directed toward overcoming apathy and marshalling the more hesitant idealists into a united effort. The supporters of the federalist system always touted the Wholesale as a true democracy of consumers and, in theory, this was certainly the case. In practice, however, the apathy of the average store member and the ambition of the Wholesale's directors led by J.T.W. Mitchell had combined to produce a bureaucratic establishment which was conservative, inflexible, and self-perpetuating. As the Society's Quarterly Meetings illustrated, there was by no means unanimity of opinion behind all of Mitchell's policies – at times a majority stood in opposition to him – yet his adroit political manipulations as chairman usually enabled him to weather any crises and still win out. Being a surefooted parliamentary tactician he would often, when opposed to a particular policy, manoeuver the delegates into a deadlock, thus postponing the question, ostensibly for further investigation, until it lost its timeliness and died a natural death. Even as friendly a witness as Beatrice Webb (who wrote one of the most influential works of propaganda in praise of Consumers Co-operation) spoke of J.T.W. Mitchell in respectful, but less than flattering, terms.[4] Such was the system of management that Neale was wont to refer to as 'Caesarism', and its effects were most severely felt in the sphere of co-operative production.

In May 1880, the Congress assembled at Newcastle passed a Resolution to the effect that it was the positive duty of co-operators to give their preference to goods co-operatively produced. This was to be only one of many such injunctions to loyalty. The CWS, however, under J.T.W. Mitchell's leadership, refused to adhere to either the letter or the spirit of the Congress Resolution; indeed, it often went to the other extreme and turned business away from co-operative associations. While Mitchell, Watts and Nuttall constantly preached that the stores should show loyalty to the Wholesale Society, they adhered to a double standard when it came to production, preferring to buy on the open market in terms of a policy of 'self-interested competitive selection'.[5] One thing seems perfectly clear; they were determined to make the Wholesale Society and the chain of stores it represented completely self-sustaining, which meant, in practical terms, that wherever and whenever possible the Wholesale would manufacture the products it needed for itself. As might be expected, this policy ultimately resulted in the establishment of workshops in competition with already existing producers associations. Admittedly the total number of such 'individualist' producers co-operatives was small (some twenty societies in 1882, of which only five had a substantial volume of business, recording sales of over £10,000 each)[6] but that was all the more reason to support them. Moreover, Neale and Greening argued convincingly that the Wholesale's failure to aid such undertakings was partially responsible for the meagre number in the first place.

The behaviour of the Wholesale generated an unavoidable reaction: late in 1881, under the direction of Neale and Greening, a number of independent producers associations met at Bradford, at the Airdale Manufacturing Society, to determine how they could 'co-operate to mutually help each other, and stimulate the Wholesale societies and the stores to closer interchange of benefits with them'.[7] The directors of the CWS apparently considered this meeting a threat, and John Watts hinted ominously that they were considering a boycott of those productive societies that were involved in the venture; but nothing came of this rumour and the Bradford Session ultimately resulted in the launching of the Co-operative Productive Federation in 1882. The new body was designed primarily to act as an agency for its member societies, bypassing the Wholesale if necessary, to open new markets among the co-operative stores and elsewhere. Neale doubtlessly drafted the Rules for the Federation which were signed by him and Greening as well as by Joseph Greenwood, the very popular manager of the Hebden Bridge Fustian Society, George Newell of the Leicester Hosiery Society, John Lambert of the Airdale Manufacturing Society, and others less well known. The organisation exists to this day and in a recent pamphlet (1963) advertised 23 member societies, hardly much of an advance to show for 83 years of existence. Production of the sort envisioned by the Christian Socialists still remains on the periphery of the Co-operative Movement.

The CPF was the first organ for the promotion of Producers Co-operation to emerge in the 1880s; two more of even greater importance would follow shortly and further exacerbate controversy among co-operators. They were the Co-operative Aid Association and the Labour Association.

Hughes had little patience and less diplomacy where the Wholesale was concerned. In the 1870s he had worked tirelessly, but ineffectually, to reverse that body's decision against profit sharing and to bring about the establishment of a separate banking institution. By the early eighties, his nerves strained by the unanticipated difficulties of his venture in Tennessee, he wanted to knock the chip off Mitchell's shoulder and have done with it by moving the Congress to expel the CWS from the Co-operative Union. Neale and Greening, however, who knew the situation in the North country better than Hughes, disagreed, maintaining that co-operators, while willing to vote idealistically in Congress, would most certainly balk at splitting the Movement in two. Consequently, Hughes was deterred; and Greening later wrote about the aftermath to this difference of opinion as follows: 'I think Judge Hughes rather felt we had failed to back him up. At all events he took then the position of a "bystander" instead of a leader, and wrote to the *Co-operative News* under that title.'[8]

While Hughes' proposal appeared too drastic, there was a unity of feeling that something would have to be done, for those workmen in the factories managed by the consumers were being uniformly reduced to the same level as workmen in private concerns, and the Wholesale was discriminating against the independent co-operative workshops – in short, the principle of Producers Co-operation was losing by default. There was, moreover, a group of younger men rallying behind Neale, who like Thomas Hughes were impatient for decisive action. There was some outlet for their frustrations in the Co-operative Productive Federation, but this organisation was largely limited to marketing research and development for productive organisations already in existence. The Guild of Co-operators was also insufficient, being for the most part restricted to the South, and in any case its main function was the creation of new stores. What was needed was a lively organisation specifically dedicated to furthering the principles of profit sharing and co-partnership in industry.

Such was the background of the decision to form the Labour Association – the 'very short title' invented by Greening because (to use his own words) he had a 'love for brevity in names of public bodies'.[9] The founders of the Association included, in addition to Neale and Greening, such notables as Harold Cox, soon to gain prominence as an editor, journalist and politician, Bolton King, a pioneer of co-partnership farming, Edouard de Boyve of Nimes, an eminent French co-operator and Lloyd Jones. After Neale drew up the Rules and wrote the Association's first Declaration of Principles it was duly launched at a meeting held during the Derby Congress in June 1884. The legal title of the new co-operative body (not quite as brief as Greening intended) was 'The Labour Association for the Promotion of Co-operative Production'.[10] Its aim was, first of all, to persuade organisations within the Co-operative Movement to take labour into partnership; secondly, to persuade employers generally to do the same; and lastly, whenever possible to launch co-operative workshops on its own initiative. Hughes, recovering from the ill-humour that had occasioned his withdrawal from active co-operative work, soon joined, as did Ludlow. Indeed, the names of the old Christian Socialists appeared so prominent in the Labour Association that it was commonly referred to, praised and maligned, as their undertaking — which it most certainly was not. As Greening concluded:

> 'The Association can only be called the successor of the Christian Socialist movement in the sense in which a plant springing up from seed sown is the successor of the parent plant. I and others who formed the Association owed our inspiration to Judge Hughes and his colleagues, and took the only course which was open to us at the time to arrange for the continuance of their work.'[11]

Holyoake's name was conspicuously absent from the Labour Association's rolls at the start; even more than Neale he hesitated to take any action which might lead to an open division in the co-operative ranks, and so, distrusting the intentions of the new body, he waited until 1886 to join it, after which time he became a member of the Executive and one of its foremost spokesmen.

In January 1885, the Labour Association held its first congress at Hebden Bridge and it was reasonably well attended by both productive and distributive societies. Neale wrote a major paper for the occasion which formed, in a manner of speaking, the charter for the new association. As he delivered the paper it became clear to those assembled at Hebden Bridge that the General Secretary of the Co-operative Movement had lost nothing of his old fire. 'The deep source of our social evils,' he declaimed, 'I consider to be that the process of accumulation — the utilising the results of past labour — instead of being systematically carried on by reasonable concert for the common good of the whole body of workers, has been left to be effected by the natural instincts of that struggle, where — *"They may get who have the power, and they may keep who can"*.[12] Those listening were made aware that the new organisation they were honouring by their presence had become necessary through the default of the co-operative consumers — that its very existence served as an example of the fact that Neale's master plan was failing. He had always insisted that the Wholesale should serve as the centre for the establishment of co-operative workshops commanding as it did the great market provided by the stores. Neale used to argue that a major reason for the failure of the workshops established by the Christian Socialists was their lack of an assured market — precisely what an effective Co-operative Wholesale Society was meant to provide. He had constantly maintained that the steps toward the Co-operative Commonwealth began with stores and wholesales, after which, and only after which, co-operative workshops would logically follow. This was the sequence of steps which would ensure success. The Labour Association, then, appeared to represent a reversion back to Ludlow's panacea of beginning with co-operative production, the old policy of leaping in the dark.

Neale, however, had only shifted his tactics; he had not changed his views. It was the first and foremost intention of the Labour Association from its creation to continue trying to convince co-operators, *especially the Wholesale and the stores it represented*, to bring their policy of co-operative production back into line with the old ideals. It was with this objective in mind that in the autumn of 1885 the Association sent an impressive delegation, which included Neale and Greening, to meet with the CWS and point out to them 'in a fraternal spirit . . . the grave injury they . . . [were] doing the cause of co-operation by their failure to carry out co-operative principles in their productive works'.[13] Mitchell (he could be very accommodating) received them graciously, commenting that 'the Wholesale committee were as anxious as anyone that co-operative production should be carried out to its fullest extent; they only differed as to the method.'[14] The meeting had no influence whatsoever on the Wholesale's policy.

Conflict clogged the pathway of the Labour Association from the time of its creation. In the first place it did not have the field to itself, for a rival body existed, the Co-operative Aid Association, recently called into being by the Southern Section of the Central Board. From the outset the Aid Association had proven unattractive to the idealists because of its willingness to back the policies of the CWS. It was dominated by the federalists; indeed, its most important members,

Benjamin Jones and Henry Pumphrey, were officials of the Wholesale's London Branch. One might expect that because the Christian Socialist 'junta' had so long dominated the Southern Section all of its creations would surely follow their ideal of co-operative production. However, what Neale and his friends had been to the Southern Section of the Central Board in the 1870s, Benjamin Jones and his friends came to be in the 1880s, and it was the spirit of the latter which pervaded at the installation of the Aid Association. With Pumphrey's help, Jones formulated the Rules of the new body in such a way as to straddle the controversy over co-operative production without coming to grips with it. The prospectus of the Aid Association stated:

> 'The utmost freedom in the form of these productive societies will be encouraged. Whether they are federal or composed of individuals, the only desire will be to encourage co-operative effort in the direction of production, *feeling assured that if one form is better than another, it will, with freedom of choice, stand the best chance of being ultimately generally adopted.*'[15]

Such was Jones' formula for resolving the conflict between federalists and individualists, and he would cling contentiously to it in the years to come.

With the exception of this crucial concession to the policies of the Wholesale, the Aid Association pretty much followed the pattern Neale had suggested so often in the past, it being primarily an organisation designed to marshall the Movement's available capital for ventures into the promised land of co-operative production. However, as far as the idealists were concerned, Jones' compromise subtracted precisely the ingredient necessary to make the venture worthwhile. Indeed, Greening had a quarrel with Benjamin Jones as a result of it — the first of many such quarrels which would ultimately lead to a total breach between the two men. Greening condescendingly informed Jones that while he might become a member of the new organisation, it was still unsatisfactory, so he would at the same time press for the creation of another 'more advanced' association.[16] And as we have seen he was able to realise this objective the very next year when, at the Derby Congress, the Labour Association was brought into being.

The establishment of the Labour Association satisfied Greening — he was willing to let the matter rest — but Neale was pained by the situation. History seemed to be repeating itself. A decade ago there had been two competing banks within the Co-operative Movement and the ensuing struggle had occasioned the widespread use of the misleading terms 'individualist' and 'federalist', an unfortunate development to say the least. Now whenever Neale was confronted with disagreement and division he tried to sooth the pain by applying the balm of union. This had been his reaction to the banking question; it was again his answer to the rivalry between the Aid Association and the Labour Association. Over Greening's protests he busied himself in the preparation of a formal proposal that the two organisations unify their efforts, at least within the Southern Section. Doubtlessly Neale sincerely wished to promote harmony, but as an instrument of pacification his proposal was incredibly naïve. Greening was correct in believing that it would most surely have the opposite effect.[17]

Could there ever have been a union of action between these two bodies? The Labour Association was national in scope whereas the Aid Association was a creation of the Southern Section and therefore a local organisation: the former was basically opposed to the Co-operative Wholesale Society, the latter was dominated by men who owed their primary allegiance to it. Was it not implicit within Neale's proposal for harmony that the ultimate fate of the (local) Aid Association was to be absorbed by the (national) Labour Association, perhaps becoming one of its branches? Despite Neale's benign intent, this was the way Jones interpreted it; and in the spring of 1885 he launched a vicious attack against the Labour Association making it devastatingly clear that there could be no contact whatsoever between the two organisations.[18]

At first when Benjamin Jones spoke on behalf of the Co-operative Aid Association he referred to it as constituting, within the confines of the Southern Section, an ideal companion organisation to the Guild of Co-operators, the latter being primarily effective in the promotion of new stores while the former confined itself to production. However, just as Jones was beginning in the early 1880s to exercise a formidable power within the Southern Section, so the Co-operative Guild was coming to reflect more of the influence of the Christian Socialists with each passing year – their control over the Guild increasing even as they lost power within the Southern Sectional Board. It was inevitable under such leadership that the Guild would reach out further than Benjamin Jones intended and, bypassing the services of the Aid Association, enter the sphere of co-operative production on its own. Indeed by 1885 it had already made some beginnings in this direction, being deeply involved with three producers co-operatives: The Framemakers' and Gilders' Association, the Assington Agricultural Association, and the

Permanent Building Society.

The Co-operative Permanent Building Society proved to be the most durable of these productive works and Neale's son Henry, who had in the meantime become a Secretary in the Admiralty, figured very prominently in the making of this organisation as well as the others. Henry had presided over the Meeting of the Guild which founded the Building Society and Neale doubtlessly found it personally rewarding to see his son so deeply engrossed in the work; whereas the relationship between them had often been strained in the past, they were now effectively collaborating together. Moreover, Henry was not just an ordinary member of the Guild but had become one of its leaders.

The past few years had been sad ones for the family; it was therefore doubly comforting for Neale to have his son at his side. His daughter Henrietta had died in 1879, followed by his sister Charlotte in 1881 and his cousin Arthur Augustus in 1882 — the latter being the same cousin who had worked with him, and lost money, in the halcyon days of the Christian Socialist Movement. Three years later, on 3 November 1885, Arthur's brother, George Henry, died, adding further sadness. At the same time this death brought a complete change in the family's way of life, and a considerable fortune; for with the passing of George Henry Vansittart, the Neales acquired the old Abbey at Bisham.

The ever-present financial worries which had resulted from Neale's earlier extravagances were now forever laid to rest. Co-operation's 'Grand Old Man' (as co-operators imitatively dubbed him — borrowing from Gladstone's honours) had inherited an estate of nearly 2000 acres, and the manor house, Bisham Abbey, was an important historical monument. Neale had never expected to possess the Abbey. His cousins, George Henry and Arthur Augustus, preceded him in the inheritance, and as they were married (George twice) there was every indication that they would have heirs of their own upon whom to bestow the property. Even when it became clear that they would not have children, he had no reason to anticipate that the death of his cousins would precede his own. He was, after all, seventy-five years old in 1885 when he inherited the Abbey.

If Neale and his son had drawn together as a result of their mutual work in the Guild, the possession of Bisham brought them closer still. For in accordance with the will, while Neale received the manor, to his son Henry was bequeathed not only the furniture in the Abbey, but Apple House Farm and a number of cottages as well. Because of their dual ownership the father and son kept a joint household at Bisham which continued even after the latter's marriage in 1887. But there were drawbacks. The move to Bisham promised to make Neale's work as a co-operator more difficult. His family had always lived in and around the vicinity of London. Commuting between that city and Manchester had been inconvenient, it is true, but adding the extra jaunt to Bisham made it more so. Indeed, there were a few advantages to having a residence in London which compensated somewhat for its distance from Manchester, one of which was that Neale could remain an active member of the Southern Section of the Central Board. But Bisham, on the other hand, was relatively isolated and had the added disadvantage, characteristic of all large estates, that it would require considerable management.

Consequently, most co-operators felt that Neale was about to lay down his co-operative burden and retire. How could anyone wish to continue working when presented with the alternative avocation of managing his own country estate? The goal of retiring to the country did not die with the Industrial Revolution; its appeal became even greater. Neale had now acquired what most Englishmen sought as the social *summum bonum*. Even Thomas Hughes was unable to gauge correctly the intentions of his old comrade and warned co-operators to prepare themselves for Neale's inevitable disappearance.[19] Hughes' opinion was doubtless given extra weight because of his long-standing and well-known intimacy with Neale; but also lending credence to his prediction was the fact that at about the same time (4 December 1885), Neale resigned from his position as a member of the Southern Section of the Central Board. On that occasion he had stated simply that the added burden of managing a large estate made it impossible for him to continue both as General Secretary and as a member of the Board. In the spring of 1886, the apparent termination of his long career was emphasised when an etching of him was circulated, and the *Co-operative News* did a short biographical study;[20] the highlight came at the Congress at Plymouth which unanimously voted to raise funds for a 'Neale Scholarship' at Oxford 'as a small token . . . for the fifty years' service rendered to the co-operative cause by our general secretary'.[21] As Neale thanked the delegates for this honour, he himself referred directly to the possibility of his retirement by quoting from Horace: ' "Let the old horse go before he stumbles at last ridiculously to the ground." He might hope to remain a few years more, but the time was coming when he must be rather a spectator than an actor.'[22]

But by the end of 1886 co-operators took another look. Their 'G.O.M.' was more active than ever. As for old Bisham Abbey, he would spend his weekends working there, after travelling all night from

Manchester to arrive in time for breakfast. Often on Saturday nights he could be found at Greening's place in London, where the two of them planned their tactics for the war against the co-operative federalists — when this was the case he would go on to spend Sunday at Bisham, travelling back to Manchester on Monday to resume his duties as General Secretary.[23] It is probable that what might well be described as a co-operative awakening in France and Italy added weight to Neale's decision to continue his work; for in the 1880s he was actively involved as a key figure in the launching of Co-operative Unions in both of these countries. In any event it was the rumour of his retirement, not Neale himself, which disappeared from the co-operative scene in the middle of the 1880s.

Notes

The letter containing the opening quotation may be found in the Ely Papers, Wisconsin Historical Society, Madison.

1. As quoted by R. S. Sayers, *A History of Economic Change in England, 1880–1939* (Oxford, 1967), p.33.
2. He wrote articles in the *Co-operative News* such as, 'What has the Wholesale Done with the Profits of the Leicester Shoe Works?' Fifteen of the twenty-five per cent gross profits, he complained, were 'absorbed by the Wholesale in the process of getting the shoes from the producer to the consumer'. He calculated that at this rate the projected dividend to reach the consumer would amount to something a little in excess of 1/16d. on the pound. See *C.N.*, XII (1881), p.563.
3. Royden Harrison, *Before the Socialists; Studies in Labour and Politics, 1861–1881* (London, 1965), p.177.
4. Beatrice Webb, *My Apprenticeship* (London, 1926), pp.348, 372–373.
5. Phrase used by Edward Owen Greening; it appears to have been a common one. *C.N.*, XII (1881), 883.
6. G.D.H. Cole, *A Century of Co-operation, op.cit.*, p.204.
7. *C.N.*, XII (1881), 883.
8. Tom Crimes, *Edward Owen Greening; A Maker of Modern Co-operation* (London, 1924), p.52.
9. E. O. Greening, *A Pioneer Co-partnership; Being the History of the Leicester Co-operative Boot and Shoe Manufacturing Society Ltd. ('Equity' Brand).* (London, 1923), p. 33.
10. This was changed in 1902 to the Labour Co-partnership Association.
11. Crimes, *loc.cit.*
12. E. V. Neale, *The Principles, Objects, and Methods of the Labour Association (Now 'The Labour Co-partnership Association') By its*

First President and Hon. Legal Adviser, E. Vansittart Neale with which is included a Portrait of Mr. Neale and an Account of his Labours on Behalf of Co-operative Production. 3rd Ed. (London, 1913), p.7.

13. See *C.N.*, XVI (1885), 935.
14. *Ibid.*
15. *C.N.*, XV (1884), 541. Italics are my own.
16. E. O. Greening to Thomas Hughes, 10 August 1890.
17. E. O. Greening to Bolton King, 2 January 1885.
18. See *C.N.*, XVI (1885), 293–294.
19. *C.N.*, XVI (1885), 1122.
20. 'E. Vansittart Neale, Esq.', *C.N.*, XVII (1886), 325–326.
21. *C.N.*, XVII (1886), 622.
22. *Ibid.*, p.623.
23. E. O. Greening, 'Memories of Edward Vansittart Neale', *op.cit.*, p.72.

IX

THE ROAD TO DEWSBURY
1886—1888

> The nature of the conflict between the two ideals may
> roughly be explained in a very few words. One is profit-
> sharing, the other is profit-mongering.
>
> *Pall Mall Gazette*, 23 May 1888

Neale's boundless energy, his perennial youth, was the subject of
countless anecdotes. The Reverend Silas Farrington of the Upper Brook
Street Free Church in Manchester (a church which Neale served as
'Warden of the Chapel') told how he had known Neale to leave his
rooms shortly after nine in the morning, work at his office till eight in
the evening, attend a church committee meeting until ten and then lean
over to him and say, 'Would you mind taking the chair for the
remainder of this business? I begin to feel the need of something to eat,
as I have had nothing since breakfast.'[1]

Walter Houghton has written that 'except for "God", the most
popular word in the Victorian vocabulary must have been "work".'[2] If
this is true, and it certainly appears to be when one studies the lives of
the period's eminent men, then Neale was most typically Victorian.
Moreover, his work grew as he aged: he could not passively watch the
Co-operative Movement turn away from the old ideals, and consequently gave all of the energies of the evening of his life to turning it
back. The sobriquet 'old man in a hurry' was also true of Neale. Time
was precious and no amount of it was too little to be expeditiously
utilised. To an ordinary man, moving to Bisham would have been a
limitation, but Neale turned the commuting from a liability to an asset
as he spent his time on the train writing articles for the *Co-operative
News*. Even the night train presented no insurmountable obstacle, for he
supplemented the train's dim light with a candle, ingeniously hung from
the luggage rack by a piece of string. His caligraphy — unbearably bad
even under normal circumstances — was thereby rendered all but
inscrutable and had to be completely recopied at the *News* office
before going to the compositors.[3] But tricks like this enabled Neale to
write prodigiously despite the multifold demands of his regular job,
which, as the Co-operative Movement burgeoned out, were increasingly
burdensome. It was not uncommon for Victorians — for example,
Kingsley, Mill and Huxley, as well as the Arnolds — to write reams of

letters, periodicals and books, in addition to their regular jobs. And what Houghton has said of these men was also true of Neale:

> 'The explanation lies partly in their optimism – their confidence in the power of the mind to resolve every problem and of the individual to influence the course of events regardless of political or economic forces; and in their deep conviction that a critical age of transition and an uneducated democracy required immediate guidance in many areas. But there was also their frantic need to bury their doubts and anxieties under the distraction of objective and constant activity.'[4]

Neale could always be found at the centre of action. He attended as many meetings as he could, and there was an ever-growing number of them as more and more district conferences were being held within the regional jurisdictions of the Central Board. Co-operators grew accustomed to the old man and came to expect his presence. Even at the largest conferences he never went unrecognised; this would have been the case even had he not been the General Secretary, for with his deep-set, grave, piercing yet melancholy eyes, ponderous forehead accented by a receding hairline and hard jaw strengthened by a full beard, he was unforgettable. His sombre face curiously contrasted with his bright, quick, impatient and often impulsive personality. He had learned through the years to keep these sometimes problematic traits rigidly restrained, but occasionally, if he rose to speak when overly excited, he would race on so rapidly as to be scarcely understood – his thoughts far out-stripping his tongue. Fellow-workers at Manchester grew accustomed to his habits but most of them did not pretend to understand him. He lived in 'humble lodgings' on Portman Street, off Oxford Road, habitually bought a penny's worth of radishes for his tea and travelled third class when he returned on weekends to the magnificence of Bisham Abbey – an intriguing alternation between austerity and opulence later put to poetry by one of his admirers.

> All this his wealth had placed at his command,
> All this he put away with careless hand,
> Left unregarded even Bisham's shades,
> Its cool beech woods, wide lawns and fernclad glades,
> Its daisied meads, broad, softly flowing stream
> All rare, all lovely as a poet's dream,
> The old historic house, the cultured life,
> So rich in all things good, so free from strife.

All this he left for the grim, smoke-stained town
And in its dingy purlieus sat him down,
Heart-strong and wise, with tact and patience rare
To a great work which needed doing there.[5]

The desire to be in the best possible position to aid in the progress of the Co-operative Movements in France and Italy may have influenced Neale's decision to remain on as General Secretary after he had acquired Bisham Abbey in 1885. This, however, was certainly not the major reason since neither his influence among continental co-operators, nor the willingness of the English Co-operative Union to send him on foreign junkets, was in any way dependent upon his official status. Indeed, on the very day after his final retirement (12 September 1891), he was to be found leaving England as a delegate (along with J.T.W. Mitchell, a most unlikely travelling companion) to the French Co-operative Congress in Paris. While Neale could look to the slow, relatively calm advance of Co-operation abroad with a less than troubled mind, he felt that domestic events absolutely demanded his continuation as Chief Executive; and it was this that caused him to leave the 'cool beech woods' of Bisham for the 'grim, smoke-stained town' of Manchester. On 7 September 1887, Thomas Hughes wrote a letter to Richard T. Ely containing the following words: 'A long pending trial of strength is coming off between the Union and the Wholesale Society, the first representing the old (and eternal) principles of fellow work, the latter what they are pleased to call "*the business side*".'[6] This was the struggle which kept Neale at the helm, and the Dewsbury Congress (1888) was to be its ultimate climax.

The activities of the Wholesale and its supporters in the late 1880s made a major conflict inevitable; insensitive to the old ideals, those who represented the 'business side' of the Movement were on the march. Having long since severed his connection with the Guild of Co-operators, Benjamin Jones, for example, lost no opportunity to thwart the Christian Socialists – now the most important man in the Southern Section of the Central Board he went so far as to attempt to alter the Section's constitution in such a way as to disadvantage Neale and his friends.[7]

Independent co-operative workshops were facing extinction, not simply as a result of insufficient support, but because the Wholesale Society was deliberately opening new productive establishments in competition with them.[8] In addition there were signs that the

Wholesale was getting extremely careless with its reputation for fair labour practices; indeed, in the search for low price merchandise the evidence suggests that it patronised sweatshops.[9] Finally, if credence is given to the claims of the labourers, the directors of the Co-operative Wholesale Society were not only heedless of the origins of their products but in the Leicester Shoe Works bowed to the temptation to keep prices down by indulging in a little 'sweating' of their own, with the result that a serious strike ensued.[10] Neale and Greening called for the establishment of an independent tribunal to investigate the conditions which had lead to the strike, but Mitchell adamantly refused to entertain this idea. From the outset he had wished to keep the whole matter under cover insisting that there was no need for dialogue on the question: 'Was it possible,' he queried, 'to discuss their relations with their servants on all occasions when any difference arose?'[11]

Neale was the patient one, Holyoake and Greening somewhat less so, but Thomas Hughes could never contain himself for there was none of the compromiser in him. Hughes had maintained consistently that it was time to end the political game: the idealists must name their enemies and come to grips with them; the Wholesale must be fought openly as a major offender against co-operative principles. He had his chance to get things boiling at the Carlisle Congress in May 1887. Invited to speak on the topic of 'Co-operative Production' at the Exhibition which preceded and opened the Session, he directed his address against the Wholesale's policy of "centralisation". The speech by itself was astringent enough to have caused trouble, but Hughes was not content to smite his enemies with words alone and backed it, on the second day of Congress, with a double-barreled Resolution demanding that the CWS be reconstituted so as to be in harmony with the principle of co-partnership; that is to say, so that in its factories workmen should participate in both profits and management.[12] He must have taken his old co-operative allies by surprise, for Neale, Greening and Holyoake were not among the five names attached to the Resolution as initial supporters. However, if Holyoake was surprised, it did not take him long to recover, for he quickly seconded Hughes in a speech which rubbed even more salt in the Wholesale Society's wounds.

Unexpectedly, at this point Mr Hemm of Nottingham rose to cool the atmosphere with a counter-resolution designed to postpone the issue to the next Congress, and the surprise of the afternoon followed: Neale supported the amendment to postpone. He expressed the opinion in so doing, that Congress should not be asked to consider the question because there had been no advance notice and consequently no one was prepared for it. 'They ought not,' he felt, 'to endeavour to get a kind of snatch vote.'[13] Perhaps Neale thought that Hughes' motion might be defeated, thus cancelling, or at least blunting the impact of another such move in the future, or maybe he was irritated with Hughes for not having confided in him. Whatever his reasons, the effort brought success to Hemm's amendment. The question of co-partnership in the CWS workshops was to be saved for the Congress at Dewsbury. Hughes was astonished and chagrined but he got over it, as Neale spent the coming year arranging a major onslaught against the CWS.

To the detriment of the Movement as a whole, opinions had polarised. If Hughes had given voice to one extreme, then in similar fashion Mitchell bluntly took the other stating that 'there was no higher form of co-operative production upon the face of the earth than the Wholesale Society manifested in its co-operative works.'[14] Neale had come to agree with Hughes, the confrontation could no longer be postponed and he laid his plans accordingly. Indeed, he could not have avoided controversy over the issue even had he wanted to, for the Labour Association was strongly backing Hughes; its members were impatient for action and expected to be led by the older co-operative leaders. On 23 July 1887, Greening wrote to Hughes about it:

'The Executive of the Labour Association are somewhat puzzled by the want of a definite understanding of the policy to be pursued in their special work of agitating the rights of the worker in co-operation.

'They think yourself, Mr. Neale, Mr. Sedley Taylor, Mr. Holyoake, Mr. Joseph Greenwood and other recognised leaders on this question should meet and agree as to how our work is to be done. We understand now that Mr. Neale's proposal of coming to close quarters with the present committee of the Wholesale is desired by him to take effect after the Dewsbury Congress. The Executive are quite willing to follow this suggestion but want the policy for this year settled and the alternative course discussed:—

'What is to be done if Dewsbury refuses our motion? We have a good working Executive of this Labour Association mostly young working men, enthusiastic and self-denying, connected with Productive Associations and Stores in London. They are assisted by friends from the Working Men's College and Toynbee Hall but naturally look to the older co-operative leaders for advice.'

Tensions were building up on both sides of the controversy. Despite the fact that Benjamin Jones had been victorious in the struggle to control policy in the South, he deeply resented the idealists' continuing power to turn decisions against him. The Christian Socialists were particularly disconcerting, their calm assurance of always being right infuriating. Moreover, their past work for the Movement had gained them a place alongside the Equitable Pioneers in the minds of many co-operators, and it was difficult to attack a legend. But Jones was persistent. He determined to find a weak point in the armour of his opponents, and ultimately decided to storm Greening's Agricultural and Horticultural Association in the pages of the *Co-operative News*. Hughes, Neale and Greening, all three, were first subjected to scathing criticism, and then sarcastically, in the style of a running dialogue between several imaginary co-operators, called upon to 'give full opportunities for an inquiry into the progress, management, and results of the Agricultural Association'.[15] Jones implied that as a co-operative association it was a bad example, and that its managers should put their own house in order before attacking the Wholesale. The article was obviously more of an attempt to generate heat than to shed light, because the nature of the Association's operation was already well known. In the first place it was an unusual undertaking in that it had not been formed to raise the condition of workingmen per se, but rather to stop the adulteration of agricultural products — its chief customers were, of necessity, farmers and landowners, men not numbered among the socially or culturally deprived classes. Secondly, because of the nature of the product it supplied, the Association did not fit, exclusively, into either the producers or the consumers category; it was as much involved with retailing and wholesaling as with producing. Jones well knew that the standards applying to the ordinary co-operative society were of little use to the Agricultural Association, yet he insisted on making an issue of the latter's co-operative imperfections.

It was Edward Owen Greening who came to the Association's defense, at the outset writing to Hughes that the time had come 'to let Mr. Jones and co-operators generally understand that we quite appreciate his position and his attitude as one who tries to ride on two horses at once'.[16] After several articles had been exchanged in the *News*, with escalating bitterness, Jones terminated the episode with an unusually offensive personal tirade in which even Neale was singled out as having 'attacked co-operators and co-operative institutions, in the Congress report, where there is no opportunity of making a reply'. At the end he had a word of advice for his antagonists: 'The best thing they can now do is to throw off the pharisaical habit of "thanking God that they are not as other men," then repair to the pool of Siloam and to the river Jordan, so that they may receive their sight, and wash and be cleansed of their leprosy.'[17] Jones directed the really explosive sections of the article at Greening – the title itself reading, 'Mr. Greening Pleads Guilty' – and it brought about a complete and public breach between the two men. The time would come when Greening would refuse even an invitation to Bisham Abbey if he knew that Benjamin Jones was likely to be there.

Actually, Jones was too politically adept and generally imperturbable a man to have raised such a hot issue for purely personal reasons. While he had no aversion to removing the Christian Socialists from their pedestal and immensely enjoyed the business of testing the trigger-like tempers of Hughes and Greening, his primary motive for attacking the business practices of the Agricultural Association lay in a more objective sphere. The move was well timed. Jones knew of Neale's decision to open a decisive campaign against the CWS at the coming Congress at Dewsbury, and he determined to steal the march with a counter-offensive. In any case, with the Wholesale under the suspicious scrutiny of co-operators as a result of their manufacturing and purchasing practices, it was politically opportune to divert attention by casting aspersions on organisations with which the idealists were affiliated.

While this was going on in the summer and autumn of 1887, Jones' opponents were busy marshalling support and plotting strategy. At a garden party held at Bisham Abbey Neale was able to do some friendly canvassing among co-operative leaders in general; and later, a festive gathering at the Hebden Bridge Fustian Manufacturing Society served as an informal party caucus for the profit sharers. Neale had arranged for Lord Ripon to chair the celebration at Hebden Bridge, which included a conference, a luncheon, a public meeting and the official christening of a new steam engine, to which was affixed a brass plate inscribed with the following words:

'Started by E. V. Neale, Esq., M.A., July 30th, 1887; named "Thomas Hughes" by the Most Noble the Marquis of Ripon, K.G., October 15th, 1887.'[18]

The speeches for the occasion, especially those by Neale and Ripon, all pointed in the direction of the impending Congress.

After these festivities Neale could easily have been lulled into a false sense of security. He knew, however, that those co-operators who got together annually to celebrate the successes at Hebden Bridge were hardly representative of the Movement at large; indeed, with a few prominent exceptions, those who opposed the principle of profit sharing did not trouble themselves to attend. Greening's fear (expressed in his letter to Hughes, 23 July 1887) that the vote at Dewsbury might be adverse was not without foundation. Although the enthusiasts for profit sharing were at their strongest because of the unpopularity of the Wholesale's recent activities, it would have been a mistake to assume that they were not at least evenly matched by those activists who stood on the right wing of the Movement. As was the case with most political controversy, the struggle would be for the support of the broad, indifferent, relatively ideal-less mass in the middle – the 'silent majority' – and in this effort the right wing had the advantage of a popular, simple argument in line with the common prejudice of the day. William Henderson, President of the Kilbirnie Society stated it bluntly: 'The policy I wish pursued with all co-operative servants is to pay them a fair day's wage for an honest day's work. I think it is a bad idea to pander to, pet, and spoil servants.'[19] The popularity of this attitude not only among the committeemen but in the rank and file, indicates how little remained of Co-operation's socialist origins. Indeed, if words have any meaning, it is difficult to speak consistently about working men, or to use the term 'working class', when referring to the Co-operative Movement. Beatrice Webb called J.T.W. Mitchell and his Board of Directors working-class capitalists, but even this is inadequate. Co-operators were, for the most part, the children of labouring men, but in an industrialised economy, this did not preclude a change of status. Indeed Alfred Marshall, the Victorian economist, believed that 'perhaps nearly half' of the older industrialists in 1850 had worked their way up from a cottage.[20] If people had been classified socially by birth alone, it would almost be possible to refer to the Industrial Revolution itself as a 'working-class movement'.

When Neale had written to Holyoake congratulating him on being chosen President of the Congress at Carlisle, he had speculated about the timing of his own assumption of that office. 'For myself,' he musingly confided to his friend, 'I want to hold back, till the time comes, when I propose to retire, and can sing the song of the dying swan.'[21] Then, quite unexpectedly, he was nominated as the next President; fate seemed to have abandoned its customary impartiality in order to favour the profit sharers, as this meant that he would preside at Dewsbury. The timing could not have been better. There was no question of Neale's retirement in 1888, and when he sat down to write his Presidential Address, he forgot the words he had written to Holyoake and contemplated no swan's song. As the year got underway, and the annual event loomed large in the minds of all of those who had taken sides in the controversy over co-operative production, debate on the question arose constantly. On January 17th Benjamin Jones delivered a paper on the 'Progress, Organisation, and Aims of Working Class Co-operators', before the Royal Statistical Society. Although he still strenuously protested neutrality, his words poured forth in a torrent of support for the Wholesale's view of federalism – and he deliberately set out to prove the impracticality of the doctrines of 'the individual productive or autonomist school'.[22] As may well be imagined, the discussion afterwards was most exhilarating with Neale and Holyoake both present to make an affirmation of their faith in the strongest possible terms. The younger members of the Executive of the Labour Association were now getting strong leadership from the older co-operators, and the latter were not merely reacting to the propaganda efforts of the federalists, but were taking the offensive.

The Movement's idealists, young and old alike, were heralding the forthcoming get together as a critical turning point. Sedley Taylor, from Trinity College, Cambridge, a new defender of profit sharing, lectured the Leicester Society on 'The Present Crisis in Productive Co-operation'; and Neale, along with Ripon, Hughes and Holyoake, wrote an open letter to the *News* (31 March 1888) under the title 'Extension of the Co-operative Principle, an Address to the Members of all Co-operative Societies', which detailed the impending Congress decision on profit sharing in the Wholesale workshops and solicited support. Neale took great pains to keep Lord Ripon actively involved in the controversy, exploiting to the fullest extent the Marquis' willingness to work for the cause of co-operative production. This was no great task. The latter had agreed to sign the above address without having taken any part whatsoever in its drafting, and readily accepted an invitation to preside at Dewsbury on the second day. The habit of deference being what it was, even among co-operators, it was useful to have a peer of the realm on one's side. But had not all this happened before? Was it not reminiscent of the old tournament with the CWS over profit sharing and the banking question of a decade ago? At that time Neale had won Congressional decisions, but it had not been sufficient. Why would the result be any different this time? The *Co-operative News* sounded an introductory note that was both sad and true: it prophesied that 'Congress cannot, as we are satisfied it will not, dictate to the membership of the Wholesale how it should conduct its business . . . The discussion at Dewsbury, in a word, will be more academic than practical.'[23]

Finally, on Whit Monday morning, 21 May 1888, the twentieth Annual Congress of delegates from the co-operative societies of Great Britain and Ireland met in the Industrial Hall at Dewsbury under Neale's presidency. Despite the ring of truth to the solemn prophesy in the *Co-operative News*, this was the high point of Neale's career. There would never be another Congress like it. It was at once the apogee and the ending of the power of the profit sharers, for a precipitous decline in their fortunes immediately followed which reached its low point in 1892 when Neale died.

The theme of his Inaugural Presidential Address came as no surprise to the delegates; it turned about the problem of poverty amidst plenty and told of the great benefits which Co-operation '*has yet to realize* through the application of equity to production'.[24] Although inconsistent in quality, the speech had its sublime moments. Despite his age Neale had considerable sensitivity to the needs of his times. Extreme poverty and labour unrest were widespread, grimly contrasting with the great increase in resources and wealth brought about by the Industrial Revolution. Many educated Englishmen had fallen under the influence of Henry George's *Progress and Poverty*, not a few attending his very popular lectures, and by the late 1880s they were trying to explain the enigmatic connection between the two themes in his title.[25]

Neale referred to *Progress and Poverty* in his Address; he appears to have had no doubt that Henry George had described the symptoms correctly but he differed in the diagnosis. Refusing to follow George in ascribing all social ills to the private appropriation and exploitation of land, Neale concluded that poverty and labour discontent came primarily from the fact that the process of industrialisation had alienated the individual producer both from the materials of his work and the direct enjoyment of the fruits of his labour. It was necessary to restore the labourer to his former position of command over these resources; therefore Co-operation, not the single tax on land, was the proper prescription. Co-operation alone would remove the artificial barriers that had arisen between capital, labour, distribution and consumption. At the present, he told the delegates, the store has answered half of the question by removing the opposition between consumer and distributor, it must go on to reduce that existing between capital and labour.

Neale repeated again, even more strongly this time, that he would ultimately have the Movement progress beyond mere profit sharing to the settlement of communities where industrial and agricultural interests would be harmonised, cultural opportunities of the city combined with the peace, cleanliness and beauty of the country, and manual work freed from repetitive and meaningless drudgery. Neale's goals were radical enough to disturb the conservative instincts of not a few of the assembled co-operative delegates. He described the public ownership of land as the 'keystone of the completed arch that will bridge over the waters of misery'. He refuted the consumers' claim that labour was entitled only to a fair wage by retorting that 'the whole wage system is a direct outcome of competitive struggle, whose evils it is the express object of co-operative production to correct. You cannot correct the evils by maintaining the system.' And finally, he asserted his belief that the time would come 'when the law makers of this country will represent co-operative societies'.[26]

Neale's Communitarianism was archaic. It was infused with nostalgia for a way of life which industrialisation had made almost impossible, at least for that large part of the population which he desired to emancipate. Yet his critique of capitalistic society was timely as well as prescient as he berated those of his fellow co-operators who had come to terms with it. Neale tried to isolate the root causes of poverty and labour unrest and eliminate them, and he found these causes inherent in the industrial system itself. Capitalism expropriated the wealth produced by the many only to splurge it in the service of the few: Co-operation must seek to restore its usefulness to the many. Competition subordinated men to things: Co-operation must subordinate things to men. It is very interesting to read in Neale's address that his contemporaries attributed discontent among the working classes to the influence of agitators. A perennial nostrum to say the least! Neale, however, on the other hand, correctly blamed discontent on the inequity between rich and poor and would replace the system which had caused the inequity. But this would never be accomplished, he feared, by any mechanism which merely divided profits among consumers. Therefore, he declared, 'let the combat be engaged', the only adversary to be feared was 'Compromise'. Though growingly bedevilled by doubts, Neale retained his belief 'that "progress" shall cease to be wedded with "poverty".' And he rested his case in this faith: 'Rather do I augur that some Holyoake of the future will be able to record of the co-operators of Great Britain, "They had moralised distribution and exchange; they went on to moralise production".'[27]

Lord Ripon, who spoke as President on the second day of the Congress was less sanguine about the future. He too had little or no confidence in the ability of Co-operation to emancipate labouring men through the distribution of dividends to consumers, and he too, having heard 'the bitter cry of outcast London', was deeply concerned about poverty. But he was not so willing to accommodate himself to gradual change as was Neale; he warned his listeners that there were many men who were unwilling to wait for the promise of better things in the future – 'men stirred to anger by the condition of the poorest class in our large towns . . . ' – co-operators must move quickly.[28]

Beatrice Potter was one of the visitors to the Dewsbury Congress. At that time she was a youthful social investigator – a liberal cum socialist – and was doubtlessly personally responsible for much of the immediate interest in the question of the poor because of her recent article in the *Nineteenth Century* on the subject of 'Dock Life in East London'. She had investigated poverty with Charles Booth and her piece on the dockers became one of the more important sections of his deservedly famous work on the *Life and Labour of the People in London*. The thousands of families she had seen living in the horrifying conditions of the East London slums had left her completely disillusioned with the system of capitalism, and it was while she sought for a 'practicable alternative to the dictatorship of the capitalist in industry', that she decided upon a study of Co-operation. This quest had brought her to Dewsbury.[29] In subsequent Congresses she met and became engaged to her future husband; and her research resulted in the publication of *The Co-operative Movement in Great Britain*, which overwhelmingly supported the CWS position on co-operative production. This haphazard and opinionated work has had an influence far out of proportion to its value as history. Perhaps more than any other volume on Co-operation, it has been responsible for permanently branding Neale and his co-workers as impractical and assigning many of their most valuable contributions to historical oblivion.

Her later career as a Fabian was also greatly instrumental in gaining converts to the dogmas of J.T.W. Mitchell; indeed, her husband was the first. Nearly two months before the Dewsbury Congress Sidney Webb had opened a debate at University Hall, London, on the subject 'Is Co-operation a Failure?' On that occasion he had condemned the Movement for having 'sunk into a mere shopkeeping affair', and at least partially agreed with Neale's views about the consumers' panacea.[30] After his marriage, however, Sidney Webb's ideas underwent some transformation, so that by 1893 he could describe combinations of consumers as manifestations of collectivism, and suggest that they have been one of the 'great factors in whatever progress has been made since

1842'[31] in elevating the condition of the labouring classes. As is now well known, Consumers Co-operation figured very prominently in the works that Sidney Webb later wrote jointly with his wife.

From the publication in 1891 of Beatrice Potter's history of Co-operation until the time of Guild Socialism less and less attention was devoted to the 'impractical' idea of the co-operative workshop, and even during the latter movement, with its resurgence of interest, Neale's contributions to the fund of knowledge on the subject were all but totally forgotten. He could never have imagined that this energetic young woman who visited the Congress at Dewsbury would cast such a dark shadow to obscure his scores of years of work on behalf of Producers Co-operation.

But setting aside the future, Dewsbury was the time of Neale's success, for interest in co-operative production was at its peak. His Presidential Address as well as Ripon's turned about this subject and prize papers were read on it. The reward came after much discussion, debate and irresolution when Congress again put its authority behind the principle of profit sharing.

Notes

1. Pitman, *op. cit.*, p.75.
2. Houghton, *op. cit.*, p.242.
3. Bamford, *Our Fifty Years, op. cit.*, p.33.
4. Houghton, *op. cit.*, p.261.
5. W.H.R., *Edward Vansittart Neale and the Christian Socialists* (London, n.d.), p.11.
6. Ely Papers.
7. See E. O. Greening to Holyoake, 21 November 1885; Greening to Holyoake, 24 December 1885; and Greening to Holyoake, 14 March 1886.
8. See e.g., the controversy over the production of cocoa, *C.N.*, XVII (1886), 877–878, 1105, 1192–1193, 1198–1199; *C.N.*, XVIII (1887), 1138–1139.
9. *C.N.*, XVII (1886), 881–882, 1120, 1194, 1242; *C.N.*, XVIII (1887), 956–957.
10. See *C.N.*, XVII (1886), 1194–1195, 1214–1216; *C.N.*, XVIII (1887), 227, 231, 246–247, 280–281. E. O. Greening, *A Pioneer Co-partnership: being the History of the Leicester Co-operative Boot and Shoe Manufacturing Society Ltd. ('Equity Brand')* (London, 1923), passim.
11. *C.N.*, XVIII (1887), 246.
12. *Ibid.*, p.577.
13. *Ibid.*, p.579.

14. *Ibid.*, p.598.
15. *Ibid.*, p.743.
16. Greening to Hughes, 23 July 1887.
17. *C.N.*, XVIII (1887), 1006.
18. *Ibid.*, p.1044.
19. *Ibid.*, p.960.
20. See W.H.B. Court, *A Concise Economic History of Britain* (Cambridge, 1964), p.175.
21. Neale to Holyoake, 1 April 1887. Holyoake Papers.
22. Benjamin Jones, *Progress, Organisation, and Aims of Working Class Co-operators* (London, 1888), p.9. For a comment on the statistics Jones used see *Eighth Annual Report of the Labour Association* (1892–93), p.16.
23. 'The Dewsbury Congress', *C.N.*, XIX (1888), 300.
24. *C.N.*, XIX (1888), 486.
25. 'Where the conditions,' George wrote, 'to which material progress everywhere tends are most fully realised – that is to say, where population is densest, wealth greatest, and the machinery of production and exchange most highly developed – we find the deepest poverty, the sharpest struggle for existence, and the most of enforced idleness.' Quotation from Jerome Hamilton Buckley, *The Triumph of Time* (Cambridge, 1966), p.55.
26. *C.N.*, XIX (1888), 489, 491.
27. *Ibid.*, p.491.
28. *Ibid.*, p.505.
29. Beatrice Webb, *My Apprenticeship, op.cit.*, p.336.
30. *C.N.*, XIX (1888), 299.
31. *C.W.S. Annual, 1893,* (Manchester, 1893), p.554.

X

"HANDS UP AND HEADS DOWN,"
1888—1892

Blessed are they who expect nothing for they shall not
be disappointed.
Thomas Hughes to George Holyoake, 19 December 1892

On 1 November 1890, Neale and Holyoake brought a motion in favour
of profit sharing before the General Board and Shareholders Meeting of
the Co-operative Newspaper Society; they were voted down 24 – 16.
Newspaper Society employees would have to be content with their
wages. Holyoake gave an account of the occasion in which he found, by
stretching a point, one 'hopeful sign' in the way the men had voted,
'namely, those who held up their hands against the motion held their
heads down'. He concluded from this that 'Manchester co-operators
have at least this merit, that though other workmen would do as they
did, they were ashamed of doing it.'[1] Surely shame was the very last
emotion felt by the Newspaper Society's directors as they voted the
motion down; perhaps they wished only to avoid the stern glances of
disfavour emanating from Co-operation's oldest active veterans. But
heads up or heads down, the measure was lost, and such negative votes
typify this period. While it was awkward for co-operators to oppose the
moral injunctions of Neale and his friends, especially in their presence,
oppose they did, and with a growing impatience at being constantly
forced to make decisions they considered to be both irritating and
irrelevant.

In concluding his Presidential Address at Dewsbury Neale had
paraphrased two famous lines from Tennyson's *In Memorium*, expressing the hope that some historian of the future would look back and say
that it was co-operators who

'Rang out the darkness of the land,
Rang in the Christ who is to be.'

He was fond of quoting Tennyson, as what Englishman of Neale's
generation was not? The great poet laureate was the spokesman for the
mid-century, putting its hopes and aspirations into verse. There were
curious parallels between Neale and Tennyson: both lived over eight
decades, their births and deaths came within a year; both, because of
the force of religion in their lives, danced emotionally to the music of

millennialism and what the one expressed in poetry the other attempted to realise through the practical medium of Co-operation; and finally both by the late 1880s, being the masters of a generation gone by, were unable to continue effectually to communicate. Englishmen were growing deaf to the poetry of progress – what J. H. Buckley calls 'The Recession of Progress' had already begun. Buckley used Tennyson as a prime example by contrasting *Locksley Hall*, written with the fervent optimism and faith which introduced the Victorian era, with *Locksley Hall Sixty Years After* (1886) which strikes an entirely different note in its disillusioned utterance, 'Let us hush this cry of "Forward" till ten thousand years have gone.'[2] If this was the voice of the new era it would suit co-operators well, only to them it would not be an utterance of disillusion but a sigh of contentment as they settled comfortably for things as they were.

The responses to the changes in late-century were varied. The Fabians, for example, blamed the failure of progress on capitalism and would resuscitate England with their own variety of Democratic Socialism; yet they were children of the new era in too easily accepting the 'necessity' of centralisation and bureaucratic control. Though Neale's utopianism drew its inspiration from a different generation, the renewed fervency with which he advocated it was his particular response. His life-long dissatisfaction with the status quo became extreme in the evening of his life, as like so many of his thoughtful contemporaries he failed to adjust to changes that appeared to him retrogressive. He bewailed the obtuse behaviour of modern co-operators: the few who had cynically accommodated themselves to the ugly realities of late-century England while feathering their own nests, and the many who knew no other way of being and consequently aspired to nothing greater. It was a puzzle to Neale how some co-operative societies could allow their surplus capital, collectively raised, to be squandered on objects completely unrelated to social progress such as individual homes for their wealthier members. The investment was sound enough, but what a waste it was to build 'private cells in the large prison-houses called towns, where competition immures a yearly increasing proportion of our population',[3] when one could as easily build associated dwellings and, ultimately, home colonies.

The signs were many that the sand was running out on the old idealism. Even while the Dewsbury Congress was bestowing its laurels on Neale, the voting papers for members of the CWS Board were opened, and when the counting was completed, it was found that the societies had backed Mitchell with the largest number of votes ever recorded. Neale's theories were hopelessly out of phase with the majority of co-operators. This is not to say that they were always against him; when confronted with an idealistic resolution at Congress the majority, expressing itself through the elected delegates, usually responded favourably, but outside of this periodic Congressional catharsis, they were simply not interested. Both in the Co-operative Union and in the Wholesale it was collective indifference which led the way to bureaucratic control, despite the outward democratic trappings. Neale did not have to tell co-operators that Mitchell sat at the head of a dedicated few who authoritatively ruled an indifferent mass; it was plain enough for all of those who cared to see, for an analysis of the May 1888, vote for the Wholesale Committee showed that out of 826 societies eligible, only 338 had voted, and judged by past elections this was an unusually good turnout.[4]

If the Congress at Dewsbury represented the high point for Neale, then the Ipswich Congress, 10 June 1889, indicated the beginning of his decline. Benjamin Jones was chosen President for the second day and in his address he made a conscious effort to demythologise the Christian Socialists, for the first time casting aspersions on their contribution to the Co-operative Movement. The delegates were treated to just under sixty minutes carefully calculated to downgrade Neale and his friends. Jones protested against the worship of heroes, especially when their excellences were imaginary, and he made it clear that even Holyoake was included in this category. He minced no words:

> 'The real fact is that the Christian Socialists were only a graft on the tree of co-operation that was already growing vigorously and bearing fruit abundantly. The graft was after a French model, and it quickly died away. A little of the sap has mingled with the sap of the main trunk, and produced a few mixed blooms; and several of the gardeners who tended the graft, have, at different times, more or less intermittently, helped in the cultivation of the rapidly growing co-operative tree.'[5]

Beatrice Potter, who held Jones to be one of the three most intimate of her working-class friends, described him as 'a combination of a high-minded grocer, a public-spirited administrator and a wire puller'.[6] It was unfortunate that although she was dubious about his cynical tendency to confuse ends and means, she was already falling prey to his pragmatic views on Co-operation.

Yet if the contentious Jones was representative of the new spirit that had come to pervade the Co-operative Movement, the old as represented by Neale was not to be discounted entirely. The latter was determined to make the Congress at Ipswich declare itself in favour of profit sharing, and again he was successful.

Neale waited until the proper moment in the debate on the issue, then rose to speak passionately in favour of the working man's claims. Even he must have been surprised by the reaction. 'Never in any previous Congress,' the *Co-operative News* editorially reported, 'do we remember such an expression of appreciation as that which followed Mr. Neale's appeal. The applause was both hearty and unanimous, and cheers again and again were given for our "G.O.M.". '[7] He thus was capable of turning a decision his own way, but what actually had Congress voted for? At this stage it is certain that the enthusiasm of the delegates was more for Neale himself than for the words he spoke in favour of Producers Co-operation. He had already become an institution: at the Exhibition of Co-operative Products associated with the Congress at Carlisle, a customer could buy Neale's picture for sixpence, woven in silk on a jacquard loom before his very eyes; and the Exhibition at Dewsbury featured watch dials, by the Coventry Watch Makers, bearing Neale's hand-painted likeness. Co-operators looked at him much as Parliamentarians looked at Gladstone. But the ideas of old men never seem to matter. When in 1889 Beatrice Potter spoke of J. C. Gray as the Working Secretary of the Co-operative Union because Neale was too aged to be a living force, there appeared, on the surface, to be some truth to her statement. But in reality she was quite wide of the mark, for her description took no cognizance whatsoever of the young and loyal aides-de-camp who moved to Neale's commands. Neale's power had seldom been visible, and this was even more the case in his old age. In any event Neale and his friends had won the vote for profit sharing at Ipswich; what they could do with it once again remained to be seen.

In the meantime Neale and Greening were making preparations to hold the Second National Co-operative Festival at the Crystal Palace in August, the greatest spectacular ever to be sponsored by co-operators. It had become a common practice in the 1880s to hold exhibitions of co-operative products in conjunction with the Annual Congress; however, in 1888 it had occurred to Greening that such an event could be separated from the Congress and made an important institution in its own right, and that by the full use of its potential to attract customers, it could greatly stimulate co-operative production of the co-partnership variety. The first Festival, held at the Crystal Palace, had turned out so successfully that it was determined to maintain it on an annual basis. Greening was a promoter beyond rival: with a year to plan and the special aid of Neale, Holyoake and Mrs Mary Laurenson (who became Chairman of the Women's Committee of the Festival), he turned the next celebration in 1889 into an unparalleled co-operative extravaganza.

Squeezed together into a schedule that meshed like clockwork the following events competed for attention: a flower, fruit and vegetable show; a home industries exhibition; a productive exhibition; a balloon ascent by the celebrated aeronaut, Capt. Dale, accompanied by the Crystal Palace Band; athletic competitions for prizes, featuring running and walking matches and a tug-of-war to the music of the Anchor Band of the CWS employees; a two-hour concert by a choir in excess of 5,000 voices singing the 'Village Blacksmith' and 'The Triumph of Labour'; dancing; performances of Mr Lockhart's trained elephant; a fountain display; music by Her Majesty's Scots Guards, a rendition of Mr Robertson's play, 'Caste', by the Dramatic Club of the Civil Service Stores; a Presidential Address by Neale followed by speeches from Holyoake and Greening; a floral ballet called 'A Golden Dream' ('Out of caves and rocks came countless fairies, dressed as owls and bats, hopping and circling before our eyes'); and last but not least the Crystal Palace fireworks designed by C. T. Brock and Co.[8] There must hardly have been time left in the day, between festivities, to view the products on display. But those who knew the Movement's inner workings understood that all the ballyhoo counted for little – what was really significant about the Second Festival was the absence of the Co-operative Wholesale Society.

Mitchell had strongly resented the treatment received by the CWS at the initial Festival in August, 1888 (where it had found itself in the position of the unnoticed if not unwanted stepchild) and had consequently determined to boycott the next one. His behaviour was not unjustified: the origin of the idea for the Festival was clearly related to the offensive against the Wholesale's manufacturing policies which Neale had timed to follow the Dewsbury Congress; its most prominent promoters were Neale, Holyoake and Greening, all Mitchell's enemies; and it was clear from the list of subscribers that this fete was the special interest of the Labour Association. Indeed, the Festival gave precedence only to those associations which practiced profit sharing.[9]

Moreover, not a few co-operators resented the fact that it was called a National Festival when its support was drawn chiefly from the

Southern Section. In an attempt to rectify this, Neale and Greening arranged to have the organisation reconstituted so that it would meet annually in different cities throughout England; however, due to lack of support from the northern consumers societies, it continued to meet in London. Mitchell adamantly maintained his intransigent opposition to the new body, and when the topic was brought up, he angrily protested that it was a 'private interest', which had 'started without proper authority, and without any real constitutional basis', and was 'unco-operative'. When the Newspaper Society was requested to supply some money from its reserve fund to guarantee the new undertaking, he stoutly insisted that this would be 'supporting a policy which if carried out would lead to a breaking up of the Co-operative Movement',[10] thus convincing the Society to refuse its support. At the shareholders meeting where this decision was ratified, one man could not see how 'singing, etc.' could help spread co-operative production, another declared the whole thing to be a 'gigantic advertisement for the Agricultural and Horticultural Association', and a third spoke of the Festival as a fad.[11] Neale could at least take assurance from the fact that the Festival, as a part of his new offensive, was attracting attention.

But the Festival remained only one facet of the primary task of convincing apathetic and unwilling co-operators to carry out the commands of both the Dewsbury and Ipswich Congresses as they related to the all important question of co-operative production. In December, Neale mailed a questionnaire/circular to the societies requesting information and asking them to state whether or not they were willing to carry out a system of profit sharing. The response was disappointing to say the least; despite the fact that Neale had included stamped envelopes for replies, there were only 487 returns from the 1503 circulars sent out. The Committee on Production which had sponsored the circular concluded (on 22 February 1890) that

'. . . any further action would be futile. Judging from the paucity of replies it is evident that amongst the general body of our members very little interest is taken in this question, and we must trust to more active educational work in the future to prepare the ground for a fuller and fairer discussion of these weighty questions.'[12]

Almost two years had now elapsed since Dewsbury. The report of the Committee on Production called for 'more active educational work' when during this period Neale had been doing his utmost. If the official

resolutions of two Congresses, a great Festival, countless personal
visitations at society, district and sectional meetings, as well as a myriad
of articles and addresses, were not enough, then perhaps it was not
going to be possible to turn the tide.

Neale was doubtlessly at his lowest ebb at the end of February
1890: he was an old man, the winter and his depressed mental state had
affected his physical condition. Less than a month later on 21 March,
near the end of his customary walk home from the office at City
Buildings, Manchester, Neale slipped on a curbstone in crossing the
street and fell heavily, seriously bruising his thigh. It was fortunate that
he had fallen almost opposite his apartments, for no one was around to
help and he could not have gone very far alone. The injury was so
serious that he was forced to remain indoors under doctor's care for
almost two weeks before he was well enough to leave for Bisham
Abbey, on the morning of his eightieth birthday, to recuperate in a
more congenial atmosphere. Greening was most alarmed when he heard
of the accident, for he was one of the few who was aware that Neale's
physical condition made such a fall especially dangerous. Several years
earlier while Neale was staying at Greening's house in Camden Square,
the latter noticed that he walked painfully and on inquiry further
learned that he had a hernia in a condition so advanced as to prevent
effective relief by the use of a truss.[13] Greening was justified in his
fears for a little over two years later this hernia was to prove the cause
of his friend's death.

The most remarkable thing about the accident and its aftermath was
Neale's ability to work while convalescing. His life had been for some
time merely a history of the Co-operative Movement: it would remain
so even as he hobbled about on crutches indoors. He continued to move
within a mass of papers, letters and reports, carrying out the commands
of past Congresses and preparing for the new one soon to be held in
Glasgow. Before he had left Manchester he was already busy at work on
the Central Board's Report, and at Bisham he kept a mountain of
administrative detail moving while yet finding time to worry about his
friends. Greening had written an angry letter to J. C. Gray (the
Assistant Secretary of the Co-operative Union) declining to place his
name in nomination for election to the Southern Section of the Central
Board.[14] Surely this was a rash move, and Neale wished he had been
able to prevent it. Yet his customary cheerfulness was returning – a few
nagging anxieties notwithstanding. In a letter to Holyoake on the 8th of
April he expressed hope for a profit-sharing plan which he and Greening
had submitted to the Wholesale, and also made optimistic references to

his injury: 'I continue to mend physically,' he wrote, 'and hope in a few days to be allowed to use the peccant limb, and get back to work at Manchester.'[15]

The Earl of Rosebery served as President of the Congress at Glasgow and in his speech he noted with humour that he had been 'hooked' by Neale and 'gaffed' by Maxwell (Chairman of the Scottish CWS).[16] Hooking the busy Earl had proved no mean feat especially for a convalescent; and despite their personal friendship Neale found it difficult to keep him hooked. The Congress was scheduled for 26 May. As late as 19 May Rosebery had written to him, 'I am afraid there will be no manuscript of my address — there is certainly none at present',[17] but despite procrastination the Earl delivered the Presidential Address as scheduled. It was neither outstanding nor unusual: the delegates were treated to the common interest-begotten prejudices of the Liberal party as Rosebery praised Co-operation because it was a voluntary means of uplifting labour, which did not ask for 'the support or the assistance, but only the benevolent neutrality of the state'.[18] When he called upon the delegates to make greater efforts in the respective spheres of homebuilding, social insurance, and agriculture, he obviously hoped that this would enable the government to avoid increasing its own responsibilities in these areas — an increase in responsibility which was then being insistently preached by many socialists.

Neale himself, having recovered by this time from his injury, was very active at Glasgow as were his supporters in the profit-sharing conflict. He loved the work and knew that his services were indeed valuable, however, he now realised that there must soon come an end. On June 23, he wrote to a co-operator and friend in St Louis, John Samuel, 'Thanks for your kind enquiries after myself. I have got over my accident better, and sooner than I was justified in expecting, but I cannot get over my 80 years, and feel that I must not look for much more prolongation of an activity, which has already exceeded the usual bounds of human life.'[19] Not long afterwards Neale finally made up his mind to retire as General Secretary and announced this decision at the meeting of the United Board on 5 September; he was then reappointed for one last year, giving the Board time to choose his successor, and a testimonial on his behalf was planned for the Congress at Lincoln in 1891. Yet he continued to be unusually busy. In the months that followed he became more and more apprehensive about the progress, or lack of it, of his last efforts to advance the principle of profit sharing. It was at this juncture, in the autumn of 1890, that the question was brought before the Co-operative Newspaper Society, and with 'hands up and heads down' voted out.

Neale could not quietly accept misfortune and thus began the year 1891 without lessening the pace of his activities, once more refusing, against his own better judgement, to pay any heed to advanced age or physical weaknesses. While home for a weekend he had so much pain and discomfort that his physician warned him against travelling back to Manchester, and disregarding this warning he precipitated a recurrence of his hernia; consequently early spring found him again confined to his room. But his recuperative powers were still extraordinary; within only a few weeks he was on a train heading for the Lincoln Congress, where he would make only a passing and indirect reference to his recent illness: 'I am about to retire,' he said, 'not because I am weary of the cause, but because nature begins to give me unmistakable hints that she is growing weary of me.'[20]

The Congress was held in May and even the weather seemed to be conspiring against men over sixty; there were jokes about calling it the 'Cold Congress' or the 'Winter Congress' as the mild days of spring suddenly turned bitter with rain, hail, sleet and snow, just as the delegates started to arrive. Any dampness of spirit this may have occasioned, however, was soon dispelled at a pleasant dinner given by the Lincoln Society for the benefit of co-operative officials at the Saracen's Head Hotel; Neale and Holyoake found the occasion a fitting one to gain a little extra warmth by splitting a 'modest bottle of Barsac' between them.[21] The session opened for business on Monday, the 18th, with the usual Presidential Address (delivered by A.H.D. Acland) after which Abraham Greenwood rose with a short anecdotal comment-ary, to make a presentation of gifts to Neale for his many years of service. Greenwood, the old Rochdale veteran and founder of the CWS, was in fact one of the oldest witnesses to Neale's long career. He told the delegates the story of how they had first met some forty years before, when Neale and the other Christian Socialists had journeyed North to attend the opening of the Rochdale Society's new corn mill, 'and in order not to soil their coats they turned them inside out'.[22] Finishing with humourous reminiscences, Greenwood presented him with a gold watch and chain, an album filled with the pictures of the present members of the Central Board, and, most important, a fully subscribed scholarship at Oriel College founded in his name. At the same time a fine oil painting of Neale — the one which still hangs in Bisham Abbey — was given to his wife, but as she was unable to be present, it was gratefully accepted by his daughter Edith. Then, in rapid succession, George Hines with the delegates joining in the chorus, sang

'Our Own Old English Gentleman'; three cheers were given at the bidding of J.T.W. Mitchell; and Neale himself arose to make the belated swan song of which he had written to Holyoake early in 1887. The latter took the form of another brief but eloquent exposition of his life's great dream 'of a world of industrial institutions systematically directed to the attainment of general well-being' and of 'an earth where . . . town and country life, no longer antagonistic, will unite their attractions for the continual delight of the fortunate population.'[23] That morning's session concluded after M. DeBoyve read a short adulatory address to Neale on behalf of the co-operators of France.

The Lincoln Congress, despite the weather, was another high point in Neale's last years but now he received honour and respect only – he could no longer conjure up waves of enthusiasm in favour of his ideas. The magic was gone. Acland's Inaugural Address set the mode as he made the 'good-humoured hint' that had the Wholesale not been so strenuously criticised it might have behaved ' "more adventurously, and perhaps more equitably," in the very direction which its critics desired'.[24] Indeed, there were developments at the Congress which must have soured Neale's outlook despite all of the honours that were heaped upon him and the hurrahs he heard sounded in his behalf; on the second day, for example, when the question of aid to co-operative production in Ireland was raised, the views of J.T.W. Mitchell could hardly have left him optimistic about future prospects.

Horace C. Plunkett had been the philanthropic founder of the Co-operative Movement in Ireland and, thanks largely to his efforts and those of J. C. Gray, that country had recently been designated as a separate Section of the Central Board. It was apparent almost from the start that due to the extreme poverty of the Irish people, the conditions there were absolutely minimal for the success of the co-operative store; the situation was, in fact, almost the exact opposite of that which existed in England: to be successful, the Consumers Movement demanded a well-fed and self-conscious aristocracy of labour, the product of a mature, industrial economy, whereas predominantly agricultural Ireland constituted what one might today call an 'under-developed country', its labour force consisting in a hoard of religiously divided and economically indigent peasants. At the Congress of Glasgow (1890) Plunkett had referred gravely to the failure of stores but pointed out that the business of co-operative dairying, on the other hand, lined the Irish co-operative cloud with silver.[25]

By the time of the Lincoln Congress, good news about Irish

co-operative production was spreading fast and Plunkett requested English support. Little was now heard about the poor consumer; the creameries were successful and in Plunkett's mind promised to bring to the Irish peasant, in addition to economic emancipation, a spirit of unity transcending the deep religious and political differences which had heretofore been so destructive. He was now asking the British consumers, as Neale had so often in the past, to aid new, struggling, but hopeful producers associations. This would surely put the Wholesale Society's directors to the test: Mitchell and his supporters had often maintained that they opposed such independent co-operative enterprises chiefly because they were the impractical brain children of the Movement's theorists; but Plunkett had been won over by practical necessity not co-operative theory. How would the Wholesale respond?

Recognising his own views clothed with new life, Neale recommended that the United Board be authorised to grant £200 to help pay for some of the propaganda that would be necessary to promote co-operative production as it applied to Irish dairy farming. Neale's effort was rewarded with success — Congress voted the money — but Mitchell proclaimed himself opposed, expressing the opinion that the Movement must go forward in Ireland in the sphere of distribution as well as production.[26] Benjamin Jones, as was his wont, appeared on both sides: while supporting Neale's plea for a grant, he declared that ' . . . the present creameries were an imperfect form of co-operation, and to get more British sympathy they would have to share profits with the consumer'.[27] As the Wholesale planned to purchase large amounts of Irish dairy products, Jones' idea was naturally appealing to most British co-operators. But it was equally naturally repugnant to Neale, to say nothing of the poor Irish peasant farmer who would see his hard-earned profits dribbled away among Englishmen much wealthier than himself. Such a policy would be exploitative. However, in the long run the Wholesale's insistence on a dividend was the least of Ireland's co-operative problems.

The Wholesale had initially been a great help to Irish Co-operation, but it soon became a hindrance as it refused to countenance any enterprises apart from its immediate ownership and supervision. Although it served a democratic (one might even use the term collectivist) clientele, the CWS, like private capitalist organisations, pursued a policy of monopoly at home and, whenever possible, economic imperialism abroad. They had begun with depots in India for the purchase of tea and ended by growing it on their own plantations: Ireland, although part of the United Kingdom, would be treated no differently. Had Neale lived to 1895 he would have seen the English CWS establishing its own creameries in Ireland in competition with indigenous Irish co-operatives; watched the Irish Section of the Co-operative Board wound up and the annual grant discontinued; and finally been disappointed by the complete separation of the Irish Agricultural Co-operative Movement from the Co-operative Union in an atmosphere of mutual recrimination.

Edward Vansittart Neale officially retired at the meeting of the United Board held on 11 September 1891, but there was not even a hesitation in the continuity of his efforts. Neale's was not a typical retirement: he did not withdraw into an ineffectual limbo of reminiscences to die gradually with the slowing down of mind characteristic of old age; but rather, like a fine old clock recently wound for the last time, kept going punctually, not losing a minute, until at the end he ran out all at once. As he grew older Neale liked to counsel people that it was better to wear out than to rust out, and as September slipped into October he was especially active, tying up all the loose ends of his work as General Secretary, and attending those pleasant but sad, nerve-taxing farewell meetings which always accompany retirement. At the same time there was no lessening of his duties as legal consultant for the Labour Association and the Guild of Co-operators, which made the usual demands upon his leisure time.

During the Midland Sectional Conference in Birmingham, Neale received a farewell gift of luggage and delivered a paper entitled, 'The True Objects of Co-operative Production'. It was his signal that, despite retirement, there would be no change in the order of his priorities and that all the good will in the world would not suffice to silence his insistent pen. Only death could stop him from writing propaganda on behalf of Producers Co-operation. The paper at Birmingham, however, was unusual in its emphasis: while it contained the expected words of admonition to the consumers societies, Neale had turned to meet a threat from a different quarter. 'Socialism' was on the march, and he once again moved forward to do battle with it.

Bernard Shaw predicted a revolution for 1889 – the year Sir William Harcourt cynically declared 'we are all Socialists now'. Shaw was wrong, yet while there was no revolution, marked changes had taken place in the decade since the publication of *Progress and Poverty*. The belief that the government must sometimes intervene to insure the welfare of the masses had become widespread, and the doctrine of State Socialism had correspondingly gained in popularity. In Neale's youth and middle age the word 'socialism' was synonymous with Co-operation: its soldiers followed an army of independent generals who derived their authority from such divergent sources as Charles Fourier and Karl Marx. Indeed, the word could be used very loosely – even John Stuart Mill had laid claim to it. But by the late 1880s all had changed; political or state socialism had come so to dominate the field that it fell heir to the whole tradition. What Neale was prone to call 'social socialism', that is collective self-help, was no longer commonly referred to as socialism at all.

Since Chartist times he had opposed himself to political socialism but never with greater urgency than in this the Indian Summer of his life. Indeed the theories of George Julian Harney and Ernest Jones seemed everywhere revived; the cry was for the 'rights of labour', and the TUC several years running declared itself for the nationalisation of land. From 1888 Neale had deluged the *News* with letters of controversy (carried on with such notables as William Jameson, Honorary Secretary of the Land Nationalization Society, and Sidney Webb of the Fabians) as well as articles and comments all designed to denude state socialism of its extravagant claims. This potpourri of hastily written propaganda, when collected together, constitutes one of the clearest expressions of Neale's social thought at its most mature.

He still took pains to indicate that his goals were revolutionary – that he remained an apostle of thoroughgoing social change – but to him the methodology of such change was as important as the goal, the ends and means must be consistent with one another.

> 'I am very desirous of seeing a thorough alteration . . . a social revolution as great as the revolution which the introduction of railways has wrought in the system of travelling existing when I was a boy: only one brought about by similar means, i.e., not by the violent destruction of the former system, but by the peaceful growth of another more perfect mode of conveyance, which has gradually replaced that system because it is more perfect.'[28]

He saw history as a logical process in which the accumulation of private wealth in an atmosphere free from violence was a necessary stage on the way towards a higher social order. In the earlier period of man's development, he argued, the meagre bounties of nature's harvest went to the strongest, the struggle for survival being the final arbiter of change. Labour was then sterile; it was not productive of wealth as its results could not be stored up. Civilization had developed as man applied his reason – not his brute strength – to introduce law and order in place of struggle, by 'repressing violence and fraud, securing the possession and transmission of property, and enforcing the performance of contracts'.[29] Law secured man's liberty so that he could safely accumulate property and improve upon it through invention and the direction or management of labour. Thus labour under law was productive of wealth, as it was possible to store up its results. Neale defined the term labour very broadly, rejecting the traditional socialist tendency to emphasise only its purely physical aspects: he would not have agreed with Feargus O'Connor's old nostrum that men with 'fustian jackets and unshorn chins' were the sole producers of wealth:

> 'What, then, does create wealth, if physical labour does not ...? I reply, the intellectual and moral qualities by which physical labour is guided and aided. Observation, discovery, invention, perseverance in overcoming difficulties, acquired skill, forethought, economy — these and similar qualities are the parents of wealth.'[30]

These intellectual and moral qualities guiding physical labour and upon which wealth was based, he reasoned, could only survive in an atmosphere of order.

Neale explained that socialists became a retrogressive force when they advocated the destruction — either by legislation or violent revolution — of the very rights and liberties under law that had made civilization in its present stage of development possible. For one segment of the population to deprive another segment of its property by violence was to revert back blatantly to the old animal law of the survival of the fittest. But even if it were accomplished democratically, in the name of the 'rights of labour', it would still be wrong to confiscate property without compensation; although under a subtle guise, brute strength would still have been the reversionary arbiter. Any method involving the assertion of the rights of one group, however large, at the expense of another, only served to weaken the legal ground upon which the rights of all men were founded without advancing that higher social order of fraternity that both Neale and the socialists claimed as their goal.

Actually there was little threat from the more volatile varieties of socialism and anarchism, the advocates of which preached violent overthrow or practised 'propaganda by the deed', for their influence in England was small (at least as compared with the Continent), and in any case they were not likely to be very successful at converting co-operators. However, that variety of 'middle class' socialism falling

under the denomination Fabian (which had published its doctrines in a
series of tracts between 1887 and 1891) was quite another matter. Its
antecedents were uniquely English and it could, as indeed it did, prove
an attractive doctrine for co-operators. Outside of the fact that he
would tend to agree about 'the inevitability of gradualness', Neale had
very little else in common with the Fabians. They saw the implementation of democracy as an immediate objective, while he described such
a course of action as trying to build the point of a pyramid first. Neale
continued to insist, as he had for so many years past, that at this stage
of man's development, democracy was irrelevant — having faith in its
efficacy would lead only to disillusion and despair. He was not far from
being right. George Bernard Shaw, although providing the most
exaggerated example, was not altogether untypical. He had lost much
of his faith in democracy by 1897, not so very long after having written
the classic Fabian tract in its defense. In an essay on 'The Illusions of
Socialism', he proclaimed 'that the main hindrance to Socialism was the
"stupidity of the working-class".'[31] Neale, having spent a fortune in
attempting to establish labourers as their own employers, had been long
aware that turning them into idealistic socialists was not a feat to be
accomplished overnight. But he would not, however, like the Fabians,
bypass the problem by premeditating a high degree of bureaucratic
control. He was also sceptical of, though not actually opposed to, the
Fabian penchant for piecemeal economic and social reform, feeling that
in the long run this would be productive of no really essential change in
the present system.

   In the address which Neale read at the Midland Sectional Conference
at Birmingham, he indicated that co-operators were being distracted
from the right course of action by the enormous development of
consumers societies on the one hand and the spread of modern
socialistic fallacies on the other. Both distractions had in the meantime
been menacingly combined into one by Beatrice Potter's deft but
distorted history of Co-operation. A pithy statement that Beatrice
made at Tynemouth in August 1892, shortly after her marriage to
Sidney, explains with revelatory succinctness the essence of the book's
thesis: 'The ideal of the associations of consumers is that of the
co-operative or socialist state — the management of industry by salaried
officials for the profit of the whole community.'[32]

   Anyone familiar with Benjamin Jones would have had little
difficulty in tracing most of Beatrice Potter's co-operative notions to
him. The ideas which he had extemporaneously sown at Ipswich in his
Presidential Address were carefully harvested by Miss Potter: in her

book the Christian Socialists were again censured for being *individual-istic* and of *foreign* derivation as contrasted to the consumers' 'democratic form of co-operation which sprang out of the Owenite ideal'.[33] In comparing the two schools of co-operative thought she resembled Benjamin Jones even in her tendency to over-indulge sarcasm.

> 'The term *Individualist* has been used within the Co-operative movement for the last twenty years to denote that school of Co-operators who insist that each separate manufacturing establish-ment shall be governed (and if possible owned) by those who work therein; the profits being divided among these working proprietors. Hence the cry "the mine for the miners," "the land for the labourers" (I do not know whether they would add the school for the school masters, or the sewers for the sewer-cleaners). Those Co-operators who, on the other hand, advocate the democratic administration of industry (after the model of political democracy) are usually styled *Federalists*.'[34]

Even she recognised, however, that there was a potential for exploit-ation in the consumers system, there being a natural conflict of interest between consumers and workers. It was not difficult to find the worker labouring long hours for low wages in co-operative workshops — indeed there were occasions when co-operators engaged in practices that approached sweating. This she proposed to remedy by the maintenance of strong trade unions. To summarise briefly, the socialist state as she envisioned it would involve, in the political sphere, an omnicompetent, democratic government protecting the welfare of all its citizens and functioning smoothly thanks to the work of dedicated and disinterested civil servants appointed in terms of ability. The economic system would operate in the same fashion; great democracies of consumers and trade unionists (guided by benevolent bureaucrats) would rationally reconcile conflicting interests.

In her views on Co-operation she was neither more nor less than the ideological successor to John Watts, 'Billy' Nuttall, Mitchell and Jones; it was only 'in her anxiety to capture the co-operative machinery for the service of socialism' (to borrow a phrase from the editor of the *Co-operative News*) that she added a new dimension to the consumers' theory.[35] Actually Beatrice Potter's penchant for Consumers Co-operation was, in view of her background, easy to forecast; her apprenticeship with Charles Booth made her suspicious of the abstract methodology of the well-established economists to say nothing of castle builders like Neale and the other producers theoreticians. She had sprung into the investigation of Co-operation fresh from her new birth as a social scientist, sceptical of *a priori* assumptions about how things ought to be and determined to study the history of institutions as they existed. She, therefore, readily gave her attention and loyalty to the consumers' side of Co-operation; on what she thought to be the realistic hard rock of things as they were, she built the foundation of her socialist theory. But Beatrice Potter was no more able 'to capture the co-operative machinery for the service of socialism' than Neale had been. The 'realism' she so very much admired in organizations like the CWS was actually indicative of a lack of vision as well as a loss of imagination. The ideal of complete Co-operation — of Communitarianism — had been destroyed by this kind of realism; so also would be the ideological concoctions of the Fabian socialist. The ambition of the average co-operator reached little beyond the dividend, his interest in Co-operation was individualistic. This was a fact of life that no socialist, utopian or realist, was destined to change.

Where Beatrice Webb had begun to build her theories, Neale left off to grope for a new footing. 'I have given up all hope of directly obtaining our objects through the present union,' Neale wrote to Thomas Hughes in the spring of 1892.[36] In the last year of his life he abandoned the Consumers Movement which he had supported for more than forty years and turned his attention toward the creation of an entirely new union of co-operators centering its activities about co-operative production.

It had not been easy for him to decide upon such a course of action; he was a founder of the Union and to abandon it was to face the stark reality of years of wasted effort. Was it not too late in life for him to contemplate a new beginning? He reached 82 years of age on 2 April. Looking back he recalled the old colleagues who, one by one, had severed their connections with the Co-operative Movement: old Owenites like Henry Travis had been the first, others like Walter Morrison had followed, and most recently Thomas Hughes had stepped out of the co-operative limelight to become a 'Bystander', albeit a very active one. For over a decade Hughes had been demanding a major battle in the Movement to expel the materialistic leaders of the CWS, while, to the contrary, Neale had staunchly maintained that such an internal conflict would do irreparable harm to the cause of Co-operation, and Greening had supported him in this opinion. But finally by the spring of 1891 even Greening had had enough and was ready to take up the firebrand when on 9 May he wrote to Thomas Hughes:

'I have a letter from Joseph Greenwood in which he speaks of your discouragement at the present aspect of things inside our Co-operative movement.

'I have the same feeling myself because I can see that Mitchell and Co. now realize that our Labour Association Workshops no longer fail of themselves but have in fact learned how to succeed. And realising this Messrs. Mitchell and Company mean first to shut out all our new Workshops from affiliation to the trading federal centre – the Wholesale – and next to fight our Workshops by establishing dependent Workshops of their own to manufacture the same class of goods. So we have only outgrown the era of inexperience and failure to enter an era of battle for life with all the concentrated capital, custom and organisation of the movement in the hands of our enemies.

'It is a serious position. We have already five businesses in which Workshops started by the two Wholesales are competing against our self-governing Workshops for the support of the Stores. I confess I can see no way out but a fair fight for the control and government of the movement. That is to run men willing and wishful to carry out the original principles of the movement, for all the offices now held by our opponents including the Chairmanship of the Wholesale.

'Is it possible to carry out such a struggle and would you be willing to sanction and help it. For myself I find it so hopeless to continue a mere bickering contest inside the Central Board and the Co-operative Newspaper Committee that I have resigned my seat in both the bodies. But I would willingly fight in a determined movement to obtain a majority on those bodies and on the Wholesale Board. Nothing less than a majority can effect anything important now.'

For still another year Neale had stood alone in trying to maintain the old policy of conciliation, but then he too gave in, and the spring of 1892 found him in council with E. O. Greening to establish entirely new guidelines for the future.

Neale now agreed that because of the Wholesale's diehard opposition to any productive workshop not under its own management, some drastic counteraction would have to be taken. Persuasion had been tried at Congress after Congress, and no effort had been spared to get the message across to the rank and file co-operative consumers, but all without success. He was forced to admit to Greening that there were only two courses of possible action remaining: an electoral struggle to regain control of the Central Board as well as to take over the Wholesale and the *Co-operative News*; or the creation of some new organ or organs pledged to the old ideals. Ostensibly he opposed the former alternative (which Greening favoured) because of its divisive character, the introduction of 'the spirit of party' into the Movement; but Neale was also aware, as Greening should have been, that such an electoral struggle would doubtless have resulted in an overwhelming defeat.[37] In any case, at Neale's insistence they decided to take the second course of action, their ideas finally crystallising into a plan to form a great alliance of all organisations and individuals favourable to the workers' side of Co-operation. Neale had in mind a resuscitation of the old Christian Socialist Society for Promoting Working Men's Associations 'on enlarged lines', he wrote to Hughes to explain:

'What I wish to form, or see formed, is an alliance of all those who wish to see production carried on upon the lines you and I have advocated, in order to give support to existing or newly formed societies, and to prevent them from drifting on the rocks of simple joint-stockism. I propose to register this Union under the Industrial Societies Act.'[38]

John Ludlow, recalling how during Christian Socialist days Neale had championed the consumers' cause, wrote in his manuscript autobiography, 'If he could only have anticipated such conclusions by forty years!'[39]

As their plans matured, the projected alliance took on greater dimensions. Neale decided that it should have an international character; this was a logical development for he had helped to found Co-operative Unions in France and Italy, had been regular in his attendance at foreign Congresses, had continued to contribute articles to *La Co-operazione Italiana* and *L'Emancipation* (in their respective countries the propaganda equivalent of the *Co-operative News*), and his involvement in International Co-operation had grown even as his faith in the British consumers movement had dwindled. The participation of foreigners, particularly Frenchmen, would be very advantageous. Two of the major leaders of the French Co-operative Movement were dedicated profit sharers: Edouard DeBoyve, editor of *L'Emancipation* and founder of the French Congress; and Charles Robert, President of the Society for the Participation in Profit as well as of the House of Leclaire's Society for Mutual Aid. That the French were thus far tracking an idealistic path towards Productive Co-operation was

indicated by the fact that M. Robert had been recently chosen as
General Secretary of their Co-operative Union. It was a lucky
development for Neale that both DeBoyve and Charles Robert were in
attendance as delegates at the Rochdale Congress, where they took part
in an informal discussion on the proposed new alliance, and gave Neale
their full support.

After Rochdale, Neale went ahead with plans for holding a
preliminary Conference of all interested parties, scheduling it to meet at
the forthcoming Co-operative Festival. He sent off letters to his many
friends in Europe inviting them to participate, and with Greening's
collaboration drew up a 'Proposal for an International Alliance of the
Friends of Co-operative Production'. It constituted a simple but
effective call to action:

> ' ... the authors of the present proposal invite all societies, firms,
> and individuals, who desire to see the present antagonism between
> capital and labour removed, and the way prepared for that higher
> social order which we hope to arise from co-operative work, to join
> in an International Alliance for the purpose of supplying to
> Co-operative Productive Societies, and to all the friends of Industrial
> Co-partnership, that important element of success, a central point of
> unity, which the Wholesale Societies ought to, but do not at present,
> furnish.'[40]

The proposal was widely circulated. It was Neale's hope that they could
count on the active support of the Labour Association, the Productive
Federation, the Guild of Co-operators, and perhaps a few of the
Sections of the Central Board and some consumers societies as well. It
had been his specific intention to design the alliance as a body
complementary to, not in conflict with, the consumers societies — an
exemplary model by which consumers could be made to see 'that the
spheres of production and consumption, though they should be closely
allied, must be kept distinct, if the permanent welfare of the working
population is to be secured by co-operation'.[41] Encouragingly, on 22
July Greening wrote to Neale, 'I am getting British adhesions very
freely.' Neale was having similarly good luck with foreign co-operators.

To look a little way into the future, the preliminary Conference met on
schedule (22 August 1892) in the Council Room of the Crystal Palace
in conjunction with the Festival. With a great deal of enthusiasm the
meeting planned to establish a Provisional Council of the International
Alliance and Neale, Holyoake, Greening and Mrs Laurenson were

among those selected to appoint its membership. Most important of all it was resolved that the Alliance should hold its first Congress in Great Britain in conjunction with the next National Co-operative Festival in August 1893.

Some of the oldest and most well-known friends of Co-operation, such as the indestructible E. T. Craig, and Hodgson Pratt, had attended the Conference at the Crystal Palace, but Neale himself was not there to take part in its proceedings. He had less than a month to live and his final illness had recently confined him to his bed. Unfortunately without his influence, plans for the coming International Congress faltered, then foundered on the rocks of personal disagreements — largely over who was to be included in, or excluded from, the new Alliance — and as a result it was not held until 1895, at which time the circumstances were quite different.

Notes

1. *C.N.*, XXII (1891), 1025.
2. Buckley, *op.cit.*, p.53ff.
3. From Neale's address at Dewsbury. *C.N.*, XIX (1888), 489.
4. *Ibid.*, p.587.
5. *C.N.*, XX (1889), 643.
6. See Beatrice Webb, *My Apprenticeship*, *op.cit.*, pp.356–357, 359–360.
7. *C.N.*, XX (1889), 702.
8. *Ibid.*, pp.878–879.
9. See *C.N.*, XIX (1888), 803; also *C.N.*, XX (1889), 918.
10. *C.N.*, XX (1889), 646, 872.
11. *Ibid.*, p.873.
12. *C.N.*, XXI (1890), 248.
13. *C.N.*, XXIII (1892), 1121. See also Greening to Neale, 30 March 1890.
14. Greening to Gray, 2 April 1890.
15. Letter available in Holyoake Papers.
16. *C.N.*, XXI (1890), 513.
17. Letter available in Neale Papers.
18. *C.N.*, *loc. cit.*
19. Letter available in Samuel Papers.
20. *C.N.*, XXII (1891), 496.
21. *Ibid.*, p.510.
22. *Ibid.*, p.495.
23. *Ibid.*, p.496.
24. *Ibid.*, p.509.
25. *C.N.*, XXI (1890), 571.

26. *C.N.*, XXII (1891), 544. See also *C.N.*, XXI (1890), 573.

27. *C.N.*, XXII (1891), 544. The italics are my own.

28. E. V. Neale, 'Capital, Labour, and Land', *C.N.*, XX (1889), 38. Neale wrote several letters to the editor under this caption beginning late in 1888.

29. *Ibid.*, p.39.

30. E. V. Neale, 'Capital, Interest, and Labour', *C.N.*, XXII (1891), 736. See also E. V. Neale, 'True and False Socialism', *C.N.*, XXIII (1892), 43.

31. A. M. McBriar, *Fabian Socialism and English Politics, 1884–1918* (Cambridge, 1966), p.84.

32. Beatrice Webb, 'Co-operation and Trade Unionism', *C.N.*, XXIII (1892), 973.

33. Beatrice Webb, *The Co-operative Movement in Great Britain* (London, 1899), p.118.

34. *Ibid.*, pp.75–76.

35. *C.N.*, XXII (1891), 708–709. At the Co-operative Festival in August (1891) Holyoake charged that this new dimension would destroy Co-operation in the interest of Fabian Socialism and labelled the doctrine preached by the new book 'Potterism'. Holyoake had intended the term in good humour – it was received in quite a different spirit by Benjamin Jones, who perhaps perceived his own brain child to be under attack: 'To hope to conquer by the use of a phrase,' he wrote, 'and to think that the coining of a word will defeat an opponent, is to imagine ourselves Frenchmen in the days of the Second Empire, instead of sober-minded British citizens . . . . I wondered at Mr. Holyoake's bad taste, and at the impertinence of this method of treating a lady.' See *Ibid.*, p.905.

36. Hughes, 'Neale', *op.cit.*, p.188.

37. Greening to Greenwood, 27 March 1892. See also Greening to Neale, 27 May 1892; Greening to Greenwood, 2 June 1892.

38. Hughes, 'Neale', *loc.cit.*

39. Ludlow, Autobiography, Ch.XXX, p.546.

40. *Proposal for an International Alliance of the Friends of Co-operative Production* (n.p., n.d.), p.5. See also Greening to Neale, 27 July 1892; Greening to James Hole, 27 July 1892; Greening to Hughes, 31 July 1892.

41. Hughes, 'Neale', *loc. cit.*

XI
BISHAM ABBEY
1891—1892

I was ever a fighter, so — one fight more,
The best and the last!

Browning, *Prospice*

Greening did most of the leg work for the new International Alliance
while Neale participated largely by mail; for although the latter would
frequently sally out to meetings and conferences to give counsel and
generate enthusiasm among his supporters, most of his last year was
spent at Bisham Abbey. He finally found time to devote to being a
country gentleman.

In the account which Florence Vansittart Neale gave of her
father-in-law's dealings with the old feudal estate, there was one
example of bad judgment which appears to shed further light on his
character. She noted that he had sold a piece of property between
Marlow and the Bisham Church (later to be called 'Stonyware') for a
good deal less than its value, it being afterward resold at more than
double the price he had received.[1] Neale's faith in the basic goodness of
men was the cause of his error in this instance as it had been so many
times in the past; for despite the loss of thousands of pounds — not
infrequently because this faith was betrayed — he consistently refused
to impute anything less than the best of motives to those with whom he
had dealings. Among the family papers is a note that Henry made
concerning another similar problem arising out of his father's resolute
determination to look only for the good in people:

'The disposition to trust everyone was on some occasions a
misfortune, as he would insist on trusting persons quite unworthy of
trust, and was deceived & cheated accordingly. Quite at the end of
his life he let the house here called Bisham Grange to a swindler in
spite of the efforts made by his family to prevent it. We wished for
further inquiry, which could easily have been made, as to character,
etc., but he only rebuked us for being so uncharitable and let the
house with the result that the man ran up debts to the amount of
£700 or 800 in the neighborhood and then bolted leaving some rent
unpaid and taking a quantity of furniture he had obtained on credit
& had not paid for.'

Herein lay the source of Neale's strength of character, but it was also the cause of his failure to wield the kind of power necessary to realise his ideals. Most of the world's great men have used others as means to their own ends; but he had faith in people, saw them as rational ends in themselves, and depended solely upon voluntary good will for the realisation of his ambitions. Man's heritage is ennobled by men like E. V. Neale; it is unfortunate that they are stamped with the label 'unrealistic' by the worldly wise, and that their beneficent injunctions for the most part go unheeded.

Neale spent his last months of life in a countryside full of historical interest as well as breathtaking beauty.[2] But even among these varied and pleasant surroundings he resisted the temptation to change his order of priorities and chiefly devoted himself to writing co-operative propaganda. In addition to directing the preparations for the International Alliance, much of his latter day polemic against the state socialists issued forth from Bisham, and there is certainly irony if not easily caricatured pathos in the scene: an old man residing amidst the scenic splendour of a medieval abbey, the owner of more acreage than the naked eye could assimilate, writing tirades against state socialism which numbered among its dogmas the nationalisation of land. It would seem, unless one knew the writer well, to be a self-serving occupation indeed. There were two works written by Neale at Bisham which above all others occupied his heart as well as his mind: they were the 'Co-operative Faith and Practice', (which appeared under Thomas Hughes' name as well as his own) and 'Thoughts on Social Problems and Their Solution'.

The 'Co-operative Faith and Practice' was a thumbnail version of the *Manual for Co-operators*, containing a restatement of Christian Socialism, as well as another exposition of the method by which co-operators could ultimately reach the Promised Land envisioned by the Movement's pioneers. It was the old refrain that Neale had endlessly repeated; but it seemed as though it was worth one more effort if for no other reason than to refute Beatrice Potter's charge that he and Hughes advocated the creation of isolated, competing, petty-capitalistic, unco-operative, individualistic workshops. Neale's scheme was and had always been essentially 'federalist'. He had never desired to see productive societies standing entirely by themselves and again emphasised the significant and necessary role that he hoped the Wholesale Society would play in bringing about their unification.[3] The general tone of the address was militant without being uncompromising; indeed Hughes was by no means satisfied that it went far enough and on 12 January he wrote to George Jacob Holyoake:

' . . . I am glad you like it, which proves that Neale is a wiser soldier than I in the Co-operative host, or at any rate goes a good way towards proof. If I had my way it would have been a much keener attack on that stronghold which the devil has managed to plump down in our midst & which may yet set the good time back for a generation. I had written this time last year to decline the usual gift of the Wholesale Annual, but didn't send it and the book back on Neale's urgent protest. Still I am not sure that the time has not come for taking off the gloves with Mitchell & his tail, who have no faith in co-operation (or anything else) that "goes down deeper than their dinner".'[4]

Perhaps Hughes was right. On the eve of spring, 1892, the CWS suffered through another strike at the Leicester Shoe Works. As on previous occasions Greening jumped to the workmen's defense while the CWS Committee showed no sympathy whatsoever for their point of view. Even Sidney and Beatrice Webb, inclined as they were to foster the consumers' cause, always insisted that it would be necessary to maintain trade unionism in the Movement's factories because otherwise co-operators tended to deal with labourers in the same antagonistic fashion as their counterparts in private industry.

On 6 June Neale was present at Rochdale to attend the Twenty-fourth Co-operative Congress, this time as a delegate; it was the first one to be held since his retirement. J.T.W. Mitchell delivered the Presidential Address and Neale was taken aback by what he heard. The address was a punning incoherency abounding in the first person pronoun. In reference to the annual proclamations in support of profit sharing, he declared that it was 'time that namby-pambyism was crushed in these Congresses'. Robert Owen, he said, so far as he could gather, 'did not believe so much in co-operation; he thought the tribe of merchants could do business for them as well as they could do it for themselves.'[5] That was Mitchell's attitude toward Co-operation's past, he was equally positive about the future: 'So far as I am concerned all my labour and my efforts and the power of my voice will be in favour of making consumption the basis of the growth of all co-operative organisation.'[6] His statements on labour – and presumably the idea of bonus – ran in the same vein:

'I want as much as anyone to see the elevation of labour. I think labour ought to be elevated. But how? That is the question. How? Simply by making the interests of our common humanity equal all round. I don't believe in the selection of a few to receive the contributions of the many, and watch them enjoy the luxuries I ought to have a share of.'[7]

The most coherent statement to come out of Mitchell's manifesto was the pronunciation that Religion, Temperance and Co-operation were the three great forces for the improvement of mankind, and that Co-operation 'as a commercial force, supported and sustained by the other two . . . is the grandest, the noblest, and the most likely to be successful in the redemption of the industrious classes.'[8] Religion, Temperance, Co-operation – this could well be a description of the basis for Neale's creed. But Mitchell gave entirely different meanings to these terms:he did not accept the broad all-comprehensive religion of brotherhood and unity which Neale preached, nor a Co-operation with its roots imbedded in the old ideals; and when Mitchell spoke of temperance, he really meant total abstinence. Neale's belief in temperance was more in line with the true meaning of the word; he hated the 'confusion of use with abuse which has been the fruitful parent of all ascetic or semi-ascetic absurdities'.[9] It was a common practice for temperance advocates within and without the Labour Movement to criticise workingmen's clubs for serving alcoholic beverages. Neale had always in the past leapt to their defense.

'This is really the position always cropping up. Gambling is a bad thing, therefore there shall be no games at cards or backgammon. Betting is mischievous, therefore away with races. Plays have often been immoral, therefore there shall be no theatres. That men should "put an enemy into their mouths to take away their brains" is a great evil, therefore no alcoholic drinks shall be sold. Carry out this principle to its legitimate conclusion, as is done by the thorough-going ascetic, and you have to "unpeople earth that you may people heaven," banishing families as the nurses of selfishness, and reducing food to what is just enough to prevent starvation.'[10]

The lives of Mitchell and Neale make a fascinating study in contrasting Victorian virtues. Mitchell was the image of John Bull even in his physical appearance. His humble origins did not allow him the graceful luxury of self-abnegation: he was conscious of position, resolutely prejudiced, commercially-minded as well as ascetic, attributing his personal success to a combination of morality and practicality.

In most ways he reflected the attitudes of the bourgeoisie. Neale, on the other hand, manifested those attributes of the aristocratic tradition which were in the Victorian mind frequently associated with the word 'nobility', having that unconscious belief in the superiority of his class which made personal humility possible and predisposed him to consider democracy an absurdity. Unfortunately, Neale's background was a liability in that it hindered his understanding of the psychology of self-made men. His high-flown, Oxford-bred moral intellectualising in itself tended progressively to antagonise co-operators like Mitchell and the younger generation that followed as well.[11]

Mitchell's strongly worded address at Rochdale was the cue: the Wholesale Society would no longer sit inoffensively still under criticism, the time had come to take the initiative, it was 'Mitchell and his tail' who took their gloves off, not Thomas Hughes. Even Benjamin Jones no longer attempted in any way to hide his bias behind the cloak of impartiality as he submitted the following Congress Resolution:

> 'That in the opinion of this Congress the best method of consolidating co-operative production, is to organise and work it as an adjunct to retail and wholesale distributive societies, leaving the individual shareholding productive societies the, at present, wide field of supplying the outside market.'[12]

Although the Resolution did not pass on to become a statement of Congressional policy (Jones withdrew it himself in favour of referring the matter to the Sections for further consideration), it had become clear by the end of the summer of 1892 that, ratified or not, it represented the opinion of most consumers societies. In any case, this was the policy that the Wholesale Society had successfully preached and was not about to abandon. No productive society, however revered in the history of the Co-operative Movement, was safe from its inroads: in the last months of his life Neale was chagrined to hear that the CWS planned to do all of its own printing, thereby running direct competition with the old, thriving and well-established Co-operative Printing Society.[13]

Neale was seriously discouraged by these developments, and particularly by the spirit manifested at the Rochdale Congress. Both Thomas Hughes and Edouard DeBoyve testified to the fact that it was during this Congress, after Mitchell's abusive speech and the essential lack of response to it, that Neale confirmed his intention to promote an International Alliance, indeed that he came to consider it an absolute necessity. But it would be a mistake to place too much emphasis on the

Rochdale Congress as a turning point, for as we have seen, the events which took place there only confirmed what was already impending.

In the spring of 1892 Benjamin Jones gave official notification that the Southern Section of the Central Board would no longer continue to sanction and support the Guild of Co-operators, which favoured profit sharing and had come to be dominated by the idealists. The Section voted a last subsidy of £10 for the Guild, then severed relations. Jones (whose ambitions at this time were leading him to seek a new career as a Liberal-Radical member of Parliament for Woolwich) went even further by suggesting 'that the Guild should consider the advisability of winding up, as we cannot recognise it as an auxiliary body for the future'.[14] Holyoake, a member of both organisations, was the first to take umbrage:

> ' . . . it was as though we were a board of poor-law guardians telling a pauper he would get no more assistance . . . The Guild is not a puppet whose strings are pulled by the Southern Board or any board . . . To tell gentlemen like Mr Hodgson Pratt, Mr Henry Neale, or his distinguished father, Mr Vansittart Neale, Mr Thomas Hughes, Mr Minet, its treasurer, and Lord Ripon, the President of the Guild, that now we have withdrawn £10 from them, and they had therefore better "consider the advisability of winding up" – is, in my opinion, the strangest thing a co-operative propagandist board ever did.'[15]

Finally the whole sad issue was taken under consideration by the Guild itself at its Annual Meeting in Essex Hall, Strand, on Saturday, 13 August. Vansittart Neale was present – it proved to be the last meeting he attended before he died.

In most ways it was an ordinary Session of the Guild, Neale being surrounded by some of his oldest and dearest friends: the Marquis of Ripon was presiding, supported by Holyoake, Greening, Hodgson Pratt, and Neale's own son, Henry, who was still an officer and leading member. The meeting expressed its regret at the attitude of the Board but none of those present felt, in view of the much work yet to be done, that there was any reason for winding up the Guild's efforts. They also recorded their desire to be represented at the coming Conference of those interested in the International Alliance to be held at the Crystal Palace. Neale's last public act at this meeting must have hurt him more deeply than anyone realised: the apostle of union, the compulsive federalist, made the motion which officially severed the work of the Co-operative Guild from that of the Central Board.[16] He had long and faithfully served both organisations; they were now parted asunder, victims to the spirit of party which he had fought all of his life.

Within a fortnight Neale was supposed to preside over the Flower, Fruit and Vegetable Show, as well as the Conference to inaugurate the International Alliance (both to be held during the Co-operative Festival) but due to a serious recurrence of his hernia, he was unable to be present for either event. Neale's last letters reflected only cheerfulness: he wrote to express his pleasure at the success of the Festival and to wish similar good fortune to those who would inaugurate the International Alliance. Meanwhile his physical condition was steadily deteriorating, but no hint of this could be found in his correspondence with co-operators; indeed, on 27 August the Newspaper Society received word from Neale to the effect that 'a slight attack of an old complaint would prevent him from attending the Newspaper Society's meetings on that day'.[17] When it became certain that he could only be saved by surgery, the family decided to move him to a nursing home in London for the purpose. This procedure was obviously a final resort for a man of his age, yet when Neale wrote to his friends, he made it seem as though the trip was for pleasure, an indication of recovery; he told them only that 'his physician thought he might be able to come up to London in a week or two'. Neale then wrote from London still giving no hint of his actual condition. Everyone assumed that he would shortly be back directing affairs again. Therefore the next communication came as a shock; it was a notification from Henry that his father had passed away:

> 'It was hoped an operation could be performed, and he was removed to London, but his strength never permitted its being undertaken, and he sank this morning (September 16th). I fear his sufferings were considerable, but they were much alleviated by medical care, and he bore them and the approach of the change with great patience and fortitude.[18]

A few days later (19 September) Henry also notified George Holyoake, commenting that the family had reason to believe that Neale had known for some time that he was unlikely to recover, 'But from his brightness,' wrote Henry, 'and apparent enjoyment of everything it seemed to us he might live for many years.'[19] Thus Neale died as he had lived; thinking first of others rather than himself, he was unwilling to share his pain with friends and relatives.

Although he remained physically active during the last months, manifesting all of the attributes of the 'old man in a hurry', this was not reflected in his writings where he seems to have given himself over to the consolations of utopian speculation. Shortly before he died he delivered a paper on Robert Owen (at a meeting of a small private club called the 'F.D.M.' in memory of Frederick Denison Maurice); and his final article, 'Thoughts on Social Problems and Their Solution', ran in a similarly utopian vein. The latter work, which was going through the process of publication as he died, was not one of his best. His tendency to be complicated and overly elaborate was more than ever in evidence; yet there is power, even elegance, in the fervency of his hope which makes an impact despite the angularities of his mode of expressing it, especially as the article constitutes a last testament. He sums up his thoughts on the past, and with a Marxist-like confidence expresses his faith in the future. The history of human progress, he asserts, can be seen as having moved through two great stages of development and is about to enter the third: they were, 'the Individualist, the Legal, and the Social, embodying respectively the principles of Liberty, of Order, and of Mutuality'.[20] Society had moved forward in the past by superimposing Order on Liberty and thus providing the security to persons and property necessary for the accumulation of wealth. The permanent welfare of mankind now required that men progress to the Social stage where by the triumph of the principle of Mutuality an equitable distribution of this wealth would be assured. This triumph would be attained by the practice of Association, Love providing the motivating power. Most men conclude their lives looking backwards; Neale concluded his looking ahead.[21]

Edward Vansittart Neale's funeral was held on the afternoon of 21 September 1892. For five days the flags over the principal buildings of the CWS in Manchester, Newcastle and London were flown at half-mast. Amidst intermittently driving rain and the rumble of thunder, the funeral procession, led by Neale's children, Constance, Edith and Henry, and with his dear friends George Jacob Holyoake and Edward Owen Greening bringing up the rear, moved slowly from Bisham Abbey to a silent grave by Bisham's ancient church — the same church which years before as a youth he had dreamed of serving as a clergyman. John Ludlow wrote a fitting epitaph:

> 'The ancients held that "he whom the gods love dies young." The truth of the saying is deeper than they understood it to be, for they meant it only of youth as measured by years. He whom God loves dies young, whatever may be his age. And Vansittart Neale died young at eighty-two.'[22]

Notes

1. Florence Vansittart Neale, MSS on Bisham Abbey.
2. See, e.g., the description in G. J. Holyoake, 'The Garden Party at Bisham Abbey', *C.N.*, XXII (1891), 854–855.
3. Thomas Hughes and E. Vansittart Neale, 'Co-operative Faith and Practice', *Supplement to the Co-operative News* (2 January 1892), 26.
4. Holyoake Papers.
5. *C.N.*, XXIII (1892), 609.
6. *Ibid.*, p.610.
7. *Ibid.*
8. *Ibid.*
9. E. V. Neale, 'Free and Easy', *C.N.*, IX (1878), 337.
10. *Ibid.*
11. See e.g., Percy Redfern, *John T. W. Mitchell; Pioneer of Consumer's Co-operation* (Manchester, 1923), passim.
12. *C.N.*, XXIII (1892), 616.
13. One of the delegates at the half-yearly Shareholders Meeting of the CPS (13 August 1892), asked a pertinent question: 'Was it too much to ask the Wholesale on its part to exercise loyalty to co-operative institutions that had been called into existence side by side with itself, and that when one of these societies had become a great success, the Wholesale should not seek to start in competition with it?' *Ibid.*, p.922.
14. *Ibid.*, p.517.
15. *Ibid.*
16. *Ibid.*, p.929.
17. Pitman, *op.cit.*, p.31.
18. G. J. Holyoake, 'The Late Mr. Vansittart Neale', *C.N.*, XXIII (1892), 1066.
19. H. J. Vansittart Neale to G. J. Holyoake, 19 September 1892. Holyoake Papers.
20. E. V. Neale, 'Thoughts on Social Problems and Their Solution', *Economic Review*, II (1892), 518–537. The quotation is from p.518.
21. See esp. *Ibid.*, p.536.
22. J. M. Ludlow, 'Some of the Christian Socialists of 1848 and the Following Years', *Economic Review*, IV (1894), 33.

POSTSCRIPT

> Men fight and lose the battle, and the thing that they
> fought for comes about in spite of their defeat, and
> when it comes turns out not to be what they meant, and
> other men have to fight for what they meant under
> another name.
>
> *Dream of John Ball*, William Morris

All differences were resolved by death as the co-operators, enemies as
well as friends, stood by the side of Neale's grave on that rainy
afternoon. The family was surprised at the great number of visitors who
came to pay their last respects, and when the funeral was over the
eulogizing began: letters poured in from England, Scotland and Ireland,
from Europe and the rest of the world; sent by individuals as well as
societies, they took up page after page of the *Co-operative News*.
Several poems were received, one of them by E. T. Craig, doubtlessly
the oldest living co-operator, then nearly blind and deaf. Among the
letters from abroad was one addressed to John Ludlow from Professor
Brentano of the University of Munich (23 September 1892) which read,
'Of the names of the men who have done most to bring the social
evolution in England into a peaceful way, his name will stand
foremost.'[1] It seemed almost as though those who had formerly
opposed him were making special expiation for having done so.
Benjamin Jones was a case in point as he wrote of his 'infinite sadness
for the loss of as near an approach to the perfect man as we can hope to
see in this imperfect world'.[2] Indeed Jones was one of those
co-operators who seemed the most anxious to turn Vansittart Neale
into a legend: a committee arranged for a large photograph of Neale (a
life-sized head and bust) to be placed in the Union's central office, and
he sponsored the making of smaller reproductions of it available for
co-operative board rooms throughout England.

Meanwhile several attempts had been made to persuade England's
political and religious leaders to honour Neale. Some months before his
death, without his knowledge, his friends had sought a Peerage for him,
but to no avail. As Ludlow caustically phrased it, 'a Conservative
Government on the eve of a General Election, would do nothing for the
most popular Conservative in England.'[3] And after Neale was gone,

application was made to the Dean of Westminster to have a memorial of some sort placed in the Abbey. Jones was also involved in this effort, having been chosen as one of a co-operative deputation (which included J. C. Gray, the new General Secretary) to consult with the Dean. But as was the case with the application for the Peerage, they were unsuccessful; the Dean of Westminster, with some justification, explained that the walls of the cathedral were already too overcrowded with plaques.

Undaunted, the Central Board turned to the Reverend Dr Gregory, the Dean of St. Paul's, and this time their efforts were rewarded, the final result being that a marble tablet was unveiled at a memorial service in the church's crypt on Saturday, 3 March 1894. It bore a carved likeness of Neale and the inscription read:

> Labour and Wait
> Edward Vansittart Neale
> Born April 2, 1810
> Died September 16, 1892
> He neither power nor riches sought,
> For others, not himself, he fought.
> Union is strength.[4]

'I am greatly concerned,' Greening wrote to Hughes a week before the Memorial Service, 'to see the downward course the Union appears to be taking since Mr. Neale's death. I don't know where our movement will be . . . now that Mitchell and Co. . . . dominate both the Wholesale and the Union. We appear to be hurrying towards destruction.'[5] A verse from E. T. Craig's poem eulogizing Neale read:

> 'He taught the rule of profit-sharing to
> The sons of toil whose labour made the wealth
> Of all the world.'[6]

But the 'rule of profit-sharing' had not fared so well even while Neale was alive, and after his death it soon had no status at all. He was the dyke which had prevented the last remnants of the old idealism carried over from his younger days from being inundated by the 'practical' capitalistic nostrums popular during his old age. There was no one with either the necessary temperament or ability to take his place to prevent such an inundation. Hughes, who was showing his age, was too much the fire-eater and as Neale's influence upon him wore thin month by month he became more reckless in his desire to bring issues to a boil. Greening was too temperamental and had an unfortunate tendency to antagonise; he found his level, below the necessary mark, as a first rate promoter; he was a man of no little capability but he remained a leader without much of a following.

The Southern Section where the Christian Socialists so long prevailed, if used as a sort of litmus paper to test for the presence of co-operative idealism, would have given a purely negative reaction. Benjamin Jones had quickly fallen heir to London. 'It is now a straight, square fight between us in the South,' Greening wrote to Hughes (8 May 1893):

> 'Mr. Jones has abandoned his "Aid" Association; left the Guild of Co-operators; openly attacked the Festival; joined hands with the Fabians and does his best, to stop the work of the Labour Association, the Federation of Productive Societies and the profit sharing workshops composing our side of the movement.'[7]

In the same letter he expressed the hope that in the coming Congress at Bristol (1893) they could once again weld together those individuals and associations who were true to the old teachings, to offset 'the ring which holds the purse-power of the Wholesale'. But Neale was the amalgamator and he was gone; no great union of idealists rose at Bristol to foil the CWS nor, as we will see, was Greening even able to activate the International Alliance, at least not as planned. Symptomatically, the next few Congresses finally saw an end to the annual profit-sharing Resolutions; the whole troublesome issue moved from front and centre to the periphery.

The harmony that Neale had sought was gradually lost as Greening became irresolute and ever more compromising while Hughes, up to his death in the spring of 1896, maintained a rigid, intransigent stand.[8] Holyoake remained pretty much as always while his close friends seemed to pull in different directions, but he did not have enough strength to harness them together as Neale had done. Both men wrote to him in the spring of 1895: Hughes queried, 'Do you agree with me that this Congress will be probably our last chance of getting the Union back on to the original and only safe lines, and teaching the Wholesale that they must conform or depart?' — while Greening counselled to the contrary, 'I don't like to read . . . that Judge Hughes regards this as his and your last chance . . . We must shape our proposals so as to make it possible for our opponents to accept them without wounding their *amour propre*.'[9] As recently as 1893 Greening had talked about 'welding together' all the profit sharers, but by 1895 his resolve had so far weakened that when Holyoake made a similar suggestion, he responded by protesting that this involved too great a risk. Many societies were not 'advanced' enough on the idea, he insisted, and might be lost if an amalgamation were insisted upon.[10]

The CWS retained the monopolistic flavour of its past, running competition with and conquering one independent productive society after another as its empire expanded to meet the needs of a new century. By 1904 it was making offers to buy the Leicester Hosiery Society, promising to pay 37s.6d. for each £1 share. This was enticing ·enough from a pecuniary standpoint. However, if the Society consented to sell, it would lose its independence and in the process abandon the principle of Co-partnership. Thus the determination was made to resist the offer, but when the retail stores, at the advice of the Wholesale, began to withdraw both their custom and capital from the society, it finally had to capitulate. The CWS made a similar but unsuccessful attempt to take over the Wigston Hosiers (which is still in existence).[11] 'All power to the consumer', the credo of the CWS, which Hughes was wont to call the 'guts gospel', made one of its greatest triumphs in 1912 when the Wholesale Society took over control of the Co-operative Insurance Society. There were bitter complaints, but by that time such behaviour was expected as a matter of course. Who then thought of the CWS as an organisation dedicated to the progress of the producing classes?

One more question remains to be answered. What was the fate of Neale's last great effort – the International Alliance of the Friends of Co-operative Production? The answer may be briefly stated: it emerged as an international co-operative alliance which ultimately eliminated those of its members who were 'friends of co-operative production'. Things had gone badly from the start. On 6 January 1893, Greening had written to Holyoake in reference to the Alliance, 'I am trying hard now to organise the work in order to make up for Mr. Neale's absence. It is not easy.' This was an understatement. With Neale gone, Greening got absolutely no co-operation from the Union; in fact, the Union began to conspire against him. The General Secretary, J. C. Gray, with the very willing collaboration of Benjamin Jones, worked to defeat him by journeying to France, Italy and Germany to make contacts for an international alliance which would be completely under the control of the Co-operative Union, and consequently unfettered by any narrow idealistic views about co-operative production.[12] As was to be expected this caused considerable consternation, and those foreign co-operators who were interested grew suspicious: when Gray declared that Greening and his friends did not have the sanction of the Central Board, a few Italian co-operators actually withdrew their support.[13] Everything remained in a state of confusion until the spring of 1895, by which time it was evident that there could be no alliance at all apart from the collaboration, and financial support, of the Co-operative Union; consequently Greening commenced to negotiate with Gray. The support of the Union came at a high price to Greening's principles, for the ultimate result was that the International Alliance was forced to abandon its original intention to make profit sharing a condition of membership.[14]

Some kind of compromise had been clearly necessary, but equally clearly Greening had gone too far. Completely open membership in the new alliance would lead, almost automatically, to its being dominated by that most overwhelmingly preponderant kind of co-operative organisation – the consumers society. And as consumers societies were in turn dominated by the CWS, it might be said, in short, that that body had won another clearcut victory. By agreeing to open membership, Greening had condemned himself and his profit-sharing friends to political oblivion: ironically they would again become a helplessly small minority in an organisation which they themselves had done the most to create. The alarming aspect of the whole episode was that Greening apparently had taken it upon himself to compromise with Gray without any assurance that he would be supported by his old friends. When the First International Congress met in London (August 1895) at the time of the Crystal Palace Festival, the principle of open membership was carried by the delegates, but not before G. J. Holyoake had registered his strenuous opposition, jumping to his feet and demanding to know 'whether profit-sharing was to be eliminated altogether'.[15] Greening later explained to him that the intention was to 'bring the CWS and the profit-sharing societies to a common understanding. For this reason, membership . . . must be made possible for the Wholesale Society'.[16]

Complaining bitterly about Greening's behaviour, DeBoyve had written to Holyoake and the latter responded in a similarly negative vein: 'The moment Mr Greening brought in the Co-operative Union he brought in the enemy which neutralised the Congress and turned it into nothingness.'[17] Evidence that Greening had been mistaken in compromising with the Union was not long in making its appearance; when Gray gave his report on the International Alliance to the Co-operative Congress at Woolwich (1896), for all intents and purposes it appeared as though the new organ had been the special creation of the Co-operative Union alone. 'By the way,' Greening queried Gray, 'why did you suppress ... all account of the steps taken by Mr Neale and myself to found the present Alliance?'[18] Gray's neglect was diagnostic – in the future their work in launching the Alliance as an organ in aid of co-operative production would be largely forgotten.

The Second International Congress met in Paris in 1896 where its development could be seen as curiously parallel to that of the English Co-operative Union: individual delegates, in this case venerable old co-operators like DeBoyve, Charles Robert, G. J. Holyoake, and E. O. Greening, were able to push through a Resolution favouring the sharing of profits with labour – a dictum in no way binding on the members of the Alliance (now predominantly consumers societies). It had been, for the most part, merely a question of tactics which had divided the efforts of Holyoake and Greening at the outset of the new international work; they had soon again joined hands to fight the battle for profit sharing within that body. However, by the time of the century's turning, Co-operation's younger leaders had grown tired of the nagging voices of the old stalwarts. Consequently Gray attempted to transform the International Alliance into a carbon copy of the English Co-operative Union, by proposing that its membership be restricted to societies exclusive of individuals; this would have had the effect of eliminating, thus altogether stifling, the profit-sharing idealists. Recognising the danger of Gray's resolution, Greening and his friends moved to counteract it: 'We have established grocery and provision stores in such numbers,' they warned the delegates assembled at the Fourth Meeting of the International Congress at Paris (July 1900), 'that they constitute 1400 out of 1700 societies and ... would be absolutely all-powerful. The producing societies which seek primarily to en-franchise labour would be swamped. Societies of credit, of propa-gandism, of house building, of recreation, etc., would scarcely have a chance of being recognised.'[19] Heretofore the small numbers of these latter co-operative organisations had been somewhat balanced by the fact that individual members of the Alliance frequently made it a point to champion their rights. Would Co-operation have survived at all if in the earlier years a move had been made to exclude the many individuals, such as Neale, who had devoted themselves selflessly to its advancement? To restrict the Alliance to societies and their repre-sentatives exclusively was to deprive the international movement of its foremost champions. John Ludlow, too, stood with his old colleagues on this question.[20]

The idealists temporarily won their point at Paris in 1900, but the ultimate result was never in doubt: by 1902 the further admission of individual members to the ranks of the International Co-operative Alliance was suspended – and in 1921 individual membership was entirely eliminated, but by that time few except Greening remained to care.

Notes

1. *C.N.*, XXIII (1892), 1098.
2. *Ibid.*, p.1099.
3. Ludlow, 'Obituary, Edward Vansittart Neale', the *Economic Journal*, II (1892), 754.
4. Pitman, *op.cit.*, pp.52, 60. To the chagrin of Neale's friends, J. T. W. Mitchell presided over the Memorial Service and unveiled the tablet. See E. O. Greening to Hughes, 25 February 1894; and esp. Mack and Armytage, *Thomas Hughes, op.cit.*, p.262.
5. Greening to Hughes, 25 February 1894.
6. *C.N.*, XXIII (1892), 1080.
7. Greening to Hughes, 8 May 1893.
8. See e.g., Hughes to Holyoake, 9 May 1893. Holyoake Papers.
9. Hughes to Holyoake, 7 May 1895; Greening to Holyoake, 8 May 1895. Holyoake Papers.
10. Greening to Holyoake, 1 May 1895.
11. E. O. Greening, *A Democratic Co-partnership; Successfully Established by the Wigston Hosiers Ltd., Leicester* (Leicester, 1921), pp.33–34, 62.
12. Greening to Hughes, 13 November 1894.
13. Greening to Holyoake, 9 January 1895.
14. Greening's letter books for 1895 abound with material about the oncoming International Congress. References to the negotiations with Gray are too numerous to cite individually.
15. Crimes, *Greening, op.cit.*, p.81.
16. *Ibid.* See also *Report of the First International Co-operative Congress, August, 1895* (London, 1895).
17. M. DeBoyve to G. J. Holyoake, 13 July 1896; Holyoake to DeBoyve, 17 July 1896. Holyoake Papers.
18. Greening to Gray, 1 June 1896.
19. See George J. Holyoake and Edward Owen Greening, *To the Delegates Assembled at the 4th Congress of the International Co-operative Congress at Paris, July, 1900*. This was a printed flyer distributed at the Congress. Available at Library of the Co-operative Union, Manchester.
20. Ludlow to Greening, 4 September 1898. See envelope entitled 'E.O.G., I.C.A. (International Co-operative Alliance) Papers', Library, Co-operative Union.

BIBLIOGRAPHY

I. BOOKS, PAMPHLETS AND DOCUMENTS
BY EDWARD VANSITTART NEALE
CHRONOLOGICALLY ARRANGED

[The most important of Neale's myriad articles and addresses, not separately published as pamphlets, have been discussed in the text and references appear in the footnotes.]

Feasts and Fasts: An Essay on the Rise, Progress, and Present State of the Laws Relating to Sundays and Other Holidays, and Days of Fasting; with notices of the origin of those days, and of the sittings and vacations of the courts. London, 1845.

The Real Property Acts of 1845, Being the Acts to Render the Assignment of Satisfied Terms Unnecessary; To Amend the Law of Real Property; To Facilitate the Conveyance of Real Property; and to Facilitate the Granting of Certain Leases. With Introductory Observations and Notes. London, 1845.

Thoughts on the Registration of the Title to Land: Its Advantages and the Means of Effecting it with Observations upon the Bill to Facilitate the Transfer of Real Property Brought in by Mr. Henry Drummond and Mr. Wood. London, 1849.

Memoir Relating to the Position and Prospects of the Associations. London, 1850. 11 pp.

The Characteristic Features of Some of the Principal Systems of Socialism: A Lecture Delivered at the Rooms of the Society for Promoting Working Men's Associations, 76 Charlotte Street, Fitzroy Square. London, 1851. 44 pp.

Laws for the Government of the Society for the Formation of Co-operative Stores. London, 1851. 11 pp.

Prospectus of the Central Co-operative Agency. [n.p., 1851?, Available at Goldsmiths Library] 4 pp.

Report of a Meeting for the Establishment of the Central Co-operative Agency . . . May 30, 1851. London, 1851. 24 pp.

Scheme for Formation of the Working Associations into a General Union. London, [1851?]. 15 pp.

Sketch of a General Establishment for the Realisation of Industrial Reform to be Called the Co-operative Agency. London, [1851?]. 8 pp.

Labour and Capital. A Lecture Delivered by Request of the Society for Promoting Working Men's Associations, at the Marylebone Literary and Scientific Institution, on the 29th of March. London, 1852. 34 pp.

May I Not Do What I Will With My Own? Considerations on the Present Contest Between the Operative Engineers and Their Employers. London, 1852. 70 pp.

Suggestions to Aid in the Formation of a Legal Constitution for Working Men's Associations. London, 1852. 34 pp.

Prize Essay on the Best Means of Employing the Surplus Funds of the Amalgamated Society of Engineers, etc., in Associative or Other Productive Objects. London, 1855. 32 pp.

The Co-operators Handbook, Containing the Laws Relating to a Company of Limited Liability with Model Articles of Association Suitable for Co-operative Purposes. London, 1860. 32 pp.

Letters on Associated Homes, between Colonel Henry Clinton and Edward Vansittart Neale, Esq. London, 1861. 18 pp.

On Typical Selection, as a Means of Removing the Difficulties Attending the Doctrine of the Origin of Species by Natural Selection. London, 1861. 10 pp. [Reprint of an article appearing in the *Proceedings of the Zoological Society of London* (January, 1861), 1–11. Available at the New York Public Library.]

'Co-operative Wants', [a poem written by Neale in 1862], *Songs and Readings for Co-operators.* Manchester, 1895, pp.30–31.

The Analogy of Thought and Nature. London, 1863.

The Doctrine of the Logos. n.p., 1867. 28 pp. [A reprint of an article which appeared in the *Theological Review* (October, 1867). Available at the British Museum.]

Genesis Critically Analysed and Continuously Arranged. With Introductory Remarks by Edward Vansittart Neale. Ramsgate, 1869.

Does Morality Depend on Longevity? London, 1871. 17 pp.

The Mythical Element in Christianity. London, 1872. 60 pp.

The New Bible Commentary and the Ten Commandments. London, 1872. 15 pp.

The Central Co-operative Board: Its History, Constitution and Use. Manchester, 1874. 8 pp.

The Distinction Between Joint Stockism and Co-operation. Manchester, 1874. 8 pp.

The Principle of Unity; the Life of Co-operation. Manchester 1875. 8 pp.

Reason, Religion, and Revelation. London, 1875. 31 pp.

The Industrial and Provident Societies Act, 1876, Published by Direction of the Central Co-operative Board. With an Introduction by E. V. Neale. Manchester, 1876.

The Economics of Co-operation; Being Papers Read at Conferences at Wigan, Shipley, and Runcorn, on July 14th, August 4th, and September 1st, 1877, Respectively, by E. V. Neale. Manchester, 1885. 30 pp.

True Refinement: Being a Paper Read at a Meeting of the Rochdale Working Men's Club (Winter Session, 1876–77). Manchester, [1877?]. 15 pp.

What is Co-operation? A Conference Paper, Reprinted from the Co-operative News, for General Circulation. Manchester, 1877. 8 pp.

Why Should the Rich Interest Themselves in Co-operation? and How Can They Promote It? Manchester, 1877. 15 pp.

The "Co-operative News" and Why Co-operators Should Support It. Manchester, 1878. 12 pp.

Land, Labour, and Machinery. Manchester, [1879?]. 22 pp.

Associated Homes: A Lecture ... with Three Engravings of the Familistère at Guise, and a Biographical Notice of M. Godin, Its Founder. London, 1880. 29 pp.

(With Thomas Hughes) *A Manual for Co-operators.* Manchester, 1881. [In the biography I have made use of the Revised Edition published by the Central Board in 1888.]

Association and Education; What They May do for the People: An Address Delivered at the Third Anniversary of the Beccles Co-operative Society, September 27, 1882. Manchester, 1882. 16 pp.

The Economic Aspect of Co-operation; A Paper Read at the Derby Congress, Whitsuntide, 1884. Manchester, 1884. 11 pp.

Economy and Trade Departments. Special Question. What is the Social Condition of the Working Classes in 1884 as Compared with 1857, when the First Meeting of the National Association for the Promotion of Social Science was held in Birmingham; and In What Way Can the Working Classes Best Utilize Their Saving? A Paper Read at the Birmingham Congress of the National Association for the Promotion of Social Science, September, 1884. London, [1844?]. 30 pp.

(With J. Woodcock) *Copyhold Tenure, and Copyhold Enfranchisement. Papers Read at a Lancashire Conference held at Rochdale, October 31, 1885.* Manchester, 1885. 16 pp.

The Principles, Objects, and Methods of the Labour Association (Now "The Labour Co-partnership Association".) By its First President and Hon. Legal Adviser, E. Vansittart Neale with which is included a Portrait of Mr. Neale and an Account of his Labours on Behalf of Co-operative Production. 3rd Ed., London, 1913. 16 pp. [First published in London, 1885, under the title, *The Labour Association for Promoting Co-operative Production Based on the Co-partnership of the Workers: Its Principles, Objects, and Methods.* 12 pp.]

The Common Sense of Co-operation; a Paper Read ... at the Congress held at Plymouth; Whitsuntide, 1886. Manchester, 1886. 8 pp.

The Social Aspects of Co-operation. London, 1887. 16 pp.

(With Thomas Hughes) *Co-operative Faith and Practice.* Manchester, [1892? First published as an article in the *C.N.*, January, 1892.] 15 pp.

(With E. O. Greening) *Proposal for an International Alliance of the Friends of Co-operative Production.* [n.p., 1892? A MSS list of those associated with the scheme is appended to this document. Available at the Co-operative Union Library, Manchester, Lancs.]

Five Reasons Why I Am a Co-operator. Manchester, n.d. 2 pp.

The Principles of Rating Applied to Co-operative Stores. Manchester, n.d. 12 pp.

The Right of Nomination. Manchester, n.d. 8 pp.

II. Writings about Neale

Craig, Edward Thomas, 'In Memorium, E. Vansittart Neale', *Co-operative News*, XXIII (1892), p.1080.
Dictionary of Labour Biography, vol.I, pp.252–255.
Dictionary of National Biography, vol.XIV, pp.138–141.
Greening, Edward Owen, 'Memories of Edward Vansittart Neale'. *Co-operative Official*, IV (January–December, 1923), pp.71–72.
Hughes, Thomas, 'Edward Vansittart Neale as Christian Socialist', *Economic Review*, III (January, 1893), pp.38–49, 174–189.
Lee, H. W., *Edward Vansittart Neale: His Co-operative Life and Work*, Manchester, 1908.
Ludlow, John Malcolm Forbes, 'Obituary, Edward Vansittart Neale', *Economic Journal*, II (December, 1892), pp.752–754.
Ludlow, John Malcolm Forbes, 'Some of the Christian Socialists of 1848 and the Following Years', *Economic Review*, III (1893), pp.486–500; IV (1894), pp.24–42.
Pitman, Henry, *Memorial of Edward Vansittart Neale, General Secretary of the Co-operative Union, 1873–1891. Including a Description of the Memorial Service in Saint Paul's Cathedral*, Manchester, 1894.
W. H. R., *Edward Vansittart Neale and the Christian Socialists*. London, n.d. This short pamphlet contains an interesting poem about Neale. I have been unable to determine the name of the author.

III. Manuscript Collections, in order of Importance

Edward Vansittart Neale's Personal Papers: in the possession of the family, Bisham Grange, Marlow, Bucks.
Miscellaneous Neale Letters and Papers: Co-operative Union Library, Manchester, Lancs.
Mississippi Valley Trading Company Papers: Co-operative Union Library.
Edward Owen Greening Papers: Co-operative Union Library.
George Jacob Holyoake Papers: Co-operative Union Library.
John M. F. Ludlow Manuscripts: Cambridge University Library.
Robert Owen Collection: Co-operative Union Library.
Richard T. Ely Papers: Wisconsin Historical Society, Madison, Wisconsin.
John Samuel Papers: Wisconsin Historical Society.
E. R. A. Seligman Collection: Columbia University, N.Y.C.
J. M. F. Ludlow Tracts: Goldsmiths Library, University of London.

IV. Selected Source Materials

[For the most part the following is limited to published works generally useful in studying the origin and development of conflicting ideals within the Co-operative Movement. Although serials are omitted, it should be noted that the *Co-operative News* is the most important single source of information for the period after 1871; specific references to this and other periodicals may be found in the text and footnotes.]

Acland, Arthur Dyke and Jones, Benjamin, *Working Men Co-operators: What They Have Done, and What They Are Doing. An Account of the Artisans Co-operative Movement in Great Britain, With Information How to Promote It,* London, 1884.

Baernreither, Joseph Maria, *English Associations of Workingmen.* English ed. . . . with a preface by J. M. Ludlow, London, 1889.

Bailey, Jack, *The British Co-operative Movement,* London, 1955.

Bamford, W. M. *Our Fifty Years (1871—1921) A Jubilee Souvenir of the 'Co-operative News' the First Number of which was Published on September 2nd, 1871,* Manchester, 1921.

Brabrook, Edward William, *Provident Societies and Industrial Welfare,* London, 1898.

Brown, W. Henry, *A Century of London Co-operation,* London, 1928.

Brown, William Henry, *The Rochdale Pioneers: A Century of Co-operation,* Manchester, n.d.

Brown, William Henry, *Rochdale Pioneers; the Story of the Toad Lane Store, 1844, and the Origin of the Co-operative Union, 1869,* Manchester, 1931.

Carr-Saunders, A. M.; Florence, P. Sargant; and Peers, Robert, *Consumers' Co-operation In Great Britain,* New York, 1938.

Christensen, Torben, *Origin and History of Christian Socialism, 1848—54.* Aarhus, 1962.

Cole, G.D.H, *A Century of Co-operation,* London, 1944.

Crimes, Tom, *Edward Owen Greening; A Maker of Modern Co-operation,* London, 1924.

Davies, Margaret Llewelyn, *The Women's Co-operative Guild, 1883—1904,* Kirkby Lonsdale, Westmoreland, 1904.

Digby, Margaret and Gorst, Sheila, *Agricultural Co-operation in the United Kingdom,* 2nd Ed. Oxford, 1957.

Garnett, Ronald George, *A Century of Co-operative Insurance; The Co-operative Insurance Society, 1867—1967: A Business History,* London, 1968.

Greening, Edward Owen, *A Democratic Co-partnership; Successfully Established by the Wigston Hosiers Ltd. Leicester,* Leicester, 1921.

Greening, Edward Owen, *A Pioneer Co-partnership: Being the History of the Leicester Co-operative Boot and Shoe Manufacturing Society Ltd.,* London, 1923.

Greenwood, Joseph, *The Story of the Formation of the Hebden Bridge Fustian Manufacturing Society Ltd.,* Manchester, 1888.

Gurney, Sybella, *Sixty Years of Co-operation, with Portraits of Robert Owen, E. Vansittart Neale, J.T.W. Mitchell, George Jacob Holyoake,* 3rd Edition. London, n.d.

Hall, Fred, *The History of the Co-operative Printing Society, 1869—1919,* Manchester, n.d.

Harrison, J.F.C., *A History of the Working Men's College, 1854–1954*, London, 1954.

Harrison, J.F.C., *Robert Owen and the Owenites in Britain and America; The Quest for the New Moral World*, London, 1969.

Harrison, J.F.C., *Social Reform in Victorian Leeds: the Work of James Hole, 1820–1895*, Leeds, 1954.

Harrison, Royden, *Before the Socialists; Studies in Labour and Politics, 1861–1881*, London, 1965.

Holyoake, George Jacob, *Bygones Worth Remembering*, 2 Vols. New York, 1905.

Holyoake, George Jacob, *The Co-operative Movement Today*, London, 1891.

Holyoake, George Jacob, *The History of Co-operation*, 2 Vols. Revised and Completed. New York, 1906.

Holyoake, George Jacob, *The History of the Rochdale Pioneers*, 10th Edition. London, 1893.

Holyoake, George Jacob, *The Logic of Co-operation*, London, 1873.

Holyoake, George Jacob, *The Policy of Commercial Co-operation as Respects Including the Consumer, Partly in Reply to Mr. Ludlow*, London, n.d., [1873?].

Holyoake, George Jacob, *Self-Help a Hundred Years Ago*, London, 1890.

Holyoake, George Jacob, *Sixty Years of an Agitator's Life*, Sixth Impression. London, 1906.

Jefferys, James B., *The Story of the Engineers, 1850–1945*, London, 1945.

Jones, Benjamin, *Co-operative Production*, Oxford, 1894.

Lechevalier St. André, Jules, *Five Years in the Land of Refuge*, London 1854.

Mack, Edward C. and Armytage, W.H.G., *Thomas Hughes; the Life of the Author of Tom Brown's Schooldays*, London, 1952.

Masterman, Neville, *John Malcolm Ludlow; the Builder of Christian Socialism*, Cambridge, 1963.

Maxwell, William, *The History of Co-operation in Scotland; Its Inception and Its Leaders*, Glasgow, 1910.

McCabe, Joseph, *Life and Letters of George Jacob Holyoake*, 2 Vols., London, 1908.

Pollard, Sidney, 'Nineteenth-Century Co-operation: from Community Building to Shopkeeping', *Essays in Labour History*, ed. by Asa Briggs and John Saville, London, 1967.

Raven, Charles Earle, *Christian Socialism, 1848–1854*, London, 1920.

Redfern, Percy, *John T. W. Mitchell: Pioneer of Consumers' Co-operation*, Manchester, 1923.

Redfern, Percy, *The New History of the CWS*, London, Manchester, 1938.

Redfern, Percy, *The Story of the CWS; The Jubilee History of the Co-operative Wholesale Society, Limited. 1863–1913*, Manchester, 1913.

Saville, John, 'The Christian Socialists of 1848', *Democracy and the*

Labour Movement, ed. by John Saville, London, 1954.

Saville, John, *Ernest Jones, Chartist; Selections from the Writings and Speeches of Ernest Jones. With introduction and notes by J. Saville*, London, 1952.

Webb, Beatrice, *The Co-operative Movement in Great Britain*, London, 1891.

Webb, Beatrice, *My Apprenticeship*, London, 1926.

Webb, Catherine, *The Women with the Basket; The History of the Women's Co-operative Guild, 1883–1927*, Manchester, 1927.

Webb, Sidney and Beatrice, *The History of Trade Unionism*, Rev. Ed., London, 1920.

Yearley, Clifton K., *Britons in American Labor: A History of the Influence of the United Kingdom Immigrants on American Labor, 1820–1914*, Baltimore, 1957.

INDEX

Trade Union Congress, 121, 199
trade union movement, 35, 42, 43, 50n,
    72, 86, 92, 119, 137, 202, 211
*The Transactions of the Co-operative
    League*, 40, 41, 50n
Travis, Henry, 40, 89, 203

Union of Working Smiths, 35
United Board, 108, 128, 194
United Educational Home Company,
    141
University Hall, London, 184
Upper Brook Street Free Church, 173
Utopian Socialism (see Socialism,
    utopian)

van Sittart, Peter, 12
Vansittart, Arthur A., 54, 169
Vansittart, George, 11, 12, 169
Vansittart, Nicholas, 11, 16
Valeroux, Hubert, 90
Vignano, Francesco, 90

Ward, Mrs. Humphrey, 147
Watts, John, 4, 79, 96, 104, 106, 108,

110, 112, 114, 120–121, 123–126,
    161, 162–163, 202
Webb, Beatrice, 2, 4, 8, 89–90, 147–
    148, 162, 180, 184–185, 189, 190,
    201–203, 208n, 210, 211
Webb, Sidney, 89–90, 91, 184–185,
    199, 211
Wesley, John, 12, 24
Whiley, Henry, 108
Wigston Hosiers, 221
Wilberforce, Henry, 27n
Wilberforce, Robert, 15
Wilberforce, Samuel (Bishop of
    Oxford), 54
Wilberforce, William, 5, 11, 12, 13, 16,
    20, 21, 26n, 32, 54
Woodin, Joseph, 34
Working Class Housing, London, 143
Working Men's Clubs and Institutes,
    135, 136, 137, 212
Working Men's College, 44, 177
Working Tailors Association, 30, 32,
    44, 54

Young, G.M., 12